# Writing as
# Learning

## Second Edition

# Writing as
# Learning

## A Content-Based Approach
## Second Edition

Andrew Rothstein
Evelyn Rothstein
Gerald Lauber

**CORWIN PRESS**
A SAGE Publications Company
Thousand Oaks, CA 91320

*For information:*

Corwin Press
A Sage Publications Company
2455 Teller Road
Thousand Oaks, California 91320
www.corwinpress.com

Sage Publications Ltd.
1 Oliver's Yard
55 City Road
London EC1Y 1SP
United Kingdom

Sage Publications India Pvt. Ltd.
B-42, Panchsheel Enclave
Post Box 4109
New Delhi 110 017  India

Printed in the United States of America

*Library of Congress Cataloging-in-Publication Data*

Rothstein, Andrew.
Writing as learning: A content-based approach/Andrew Rothstein,
Evelyn Rothstein, and Gerald Lauber.-2nd ed.
     p. cm.
Includes bibliographical references and index.
ISBN 1-4129-4960-2 or 978-1-4129-4960-6 (cloth)
ISBN 1-4129-4961-0 or 978-1-4129-4961-3 (pbk.)
   1.  English language—Composition and exercises—Study and teaching. 2.  Creative writing.
I.  Rothstein, Evelyn. II.  Lauber, Gerald. III.  Title.
LB1576.R756 2007
372.62′3—dc22                                                      2006020225

This book is printed on acid-free paper.

06  07  08  09  10  10 9 8 7 6 5 4 3 2 1

| | |
|---|---|
| *Acquisitions Editor:* | Cathy Hernandez |
| *Editorial Assistant:* | Charline Wu |
| *Production Editor:* | Beth A. Bernstein |
| *Copy Editor:* | Cate Huisman |
| *Typesetter:* | C&M Digitals (P) Ltd. |
| *Proofreader:* | Word Wise Webb |
| *Indexer:* | Ellen Slavitz |
| *Cover Designer:* | Lisa Miller |

# Contents

**Preface to the Second Edition**                                          xi
    Acknowledgments                                     xii

**About the Authors**                                                      xiii

**Introduction**                                                           1
    The Rationale of Writing as Learning                1
    The Distinction of Writing as Learning              2
    What Is Teaching Writing?                           2
    How to Use This Book                                3

1. **The Elements of Writing as Learning:**
   **Strategies, Genres, Topics, and Tools**                              9
    The Writing Teacher and the Writing Classroom       9
    Strategies for Writing                              10
    Setting Up the Notebook                             11
    The Genres of Writing                               12
    Tools and Materials for Writing                     15
    What Should I Write About?                          17
    The Student as Writer                               19
    Guidelines for Revising and Editing                 20
    Writing and the Computer                            21

2. **Building Vocabulary With Taxonomies: Words Are Free!**               23
    The Gift of Words—Creating Taxonomies               23
    The Power of Words (aka Vocabulary)                 23
    Organizing Student Vocabulary                       24
        The Building of the Personal Thesaurus   25
    Advance Organizing and Assessment of Prior Knowledge   26
        Continuous Note taking      28
        Vocabulary Development       29
    Development and Assessment of New Knowledge          30
        Taxonomy Especially for Kindergarten and First Grade   30
        Building a Personal Identity Taxonomy   31

Two Related Taxonomies 32

Taxonomies in the Upper Grades Through High School 33

Internet Links 34

**3. Composing With Keywords: Have Words, Can Write** 35

Have Words, Can Write 35

What Is Composing With Keywords? 35

Introducing Composing With Keywords 36

Procedure for Sharing Sentences 38

Composing With Keywords
for Both Factual and Fictional Writing 39

Composing With Keywords as a Response to New Learning 41

Composing With Keywords in the Content Areas 41

Additional Student Writing Using Composing With Keywords
at Different Grade Levels 43

Composing With Keywords for Specific Vocabulary Building 43

Internet Links 44

**4. Metacognition: Writing Is Thinking** 45

What Is Metacognition? 45

Metacognition for Writing or Writing for Metacognition 46

Getting Started With Prior Knowledge 46

Writing Metacognition Statements 47

Using Pre- and Postmetacognitive Writing 50

Starting Sentences for Metacognitive Writing 50

Combining Taxonomies,
Composing With Keywords, and Metacognition 51

Using Metacognitive Writing to Consolidate
Writing With Subject Areas 53

Internet Links 55

**5. Defining Format: Write to a Martian** 57

Defining Our Words and Constructing Meaning 57

What Is Defining Format? 58

Using Defining Format in All Grades and Subjects 60

Teaching Categories 61

Using Defining Format for More Complex Terms 62

Defining Format Application 63

Note taking and Outlining 63

Paragraph Development 64

Comparing and Contrasting 66

Expanded Explanations 66

Combining and Reviewing 68

Internet Links 68

**6. Morphology, Etymology, and Grammar: Every Word Has a Story** 69

Morphology, Etymology, and
Grammar—A Triplex in the Scheme of Writing 69

The Role of Grammar in Teaching Writing 70

Categories of Nouns 72
Categories of Verbs 75
Categories of Adjectives 77
Sentence Stretchers 81
Understanding Parts of Speech by Using Defining Format 83
Morphology—The Study of the Formation of Words 85
Notes on Verbs 86
The "Be" Verb 86
Etymology 89
Words and Their Stories 89
Borrowings and Lendings 90
British English and American English 91
Internet Links 92

7. **Profiles and Frames: Organize Your Writing** 93
Writing and Organization 93
What Is a Profile? 93
How to Use Profiles 94
Art Profile 94
Career Profile 97
Sports and Games Profile 99
What Is a Frame? 100
Frames for Primary Grades 100
Frames for the Intermediate Grades
and for Middle and High School 102
ABC Stories—Framework for Innovating on Literary Structure 106
Internet Links 109

8. **Who's Who: Know Who You Know and Know Who You Are!** 111
Who's Who: The Humanity in Writing 111
Focus for Writing Biographies 112
Setting Up Taxonomies for Biographical Writing 112
Using Frames for Biographical Writing 113
Expanding the Taxonomy for Elaboration and Details 115
Using Who's Who to Write Autobiographies and Memoirs 118
Frames for Autobiographies and Memoirs 120
Additional Who's Who Profiles 124
Internet Links 128

9. **Reasons, Causes, Results—The Basis of the Essay:**
**Think in Threes** 129
Think in Threes 131
The Basic Essay Frame 132
Personal Essays 132
Persuasive Essays 134
Explanatory Essays 136
Summaries of Three Different Essay Genres 137
Expanding the Essay 137
Internet Links 139

| 10. | **Where in the World: Everybody Has to Be Someplace** | **141** |
| | Geography as Knowledge and Vocabulary | 141 |
| | Where in the World: A Strategy for Location and Setting | 142 |
| | Where in the World and Teaching Writing | 142 |
| | Morphology, Etymology, and Where in the World | 147 |
| | Profiles and Frames for Where in the World | 147 |
| | Reasons, Causes, Results for Where in the World | 151 |
| | Combining Who's Who and Where in the World | 157 |
| | Integrating Where in the World Across the Curriculum | 157 |
| | The English Language and Where in the World | 160 |
| | Internet Links | 162 |
| | | |
| 11. | **Premises, Premises: Let's Make a Movie!** | **163** |
| | From Book to Film | 163 |
| | Steps in Premises, Premises | 164 |
| |    Developing the Criteria for Book-to-Film | 164 |
| |    Creating a Filmmaking Taxonomy | 165 |
| |    Teaching the Premise Statement | 165 |
| |    Writing the Character Profiles | 166 |
| |    Writing the Treatment | 169 |
| |    Preparing the Storyboard | 169 |
| |    Writing the Script | 169 |
| |    Set Design | 171 |
| |    Costume Design | 171 |
| |    The Program and the Credits | 172 |
| | Premises, Premises in the Intermediate and Middle Grades | 173 |
| |    Historical Fiction | 173 |
| |    The Fairy Tale—A Book-to-Movie | |
| |       Activity for Intermediate and Middle School Students | 174 |
| |    Writing a Treatment for Fairy Tales | 176 |
| | Innovating on Fairy Tales for | |
| |    Dramatic or Filmed Performances: *Plaintiff v. Defendant* | 177 |
| |    Using a Profile Template | 179 |
| | Book-to-Movie in the High School | 181 |
| | Internet Links | 182 |
| | | |
| 12. | **Quotable Quotes: Words Inspire** | **183** |
| | Quotable Quotes for Remembrance, Inspiration, and Response | 183 |
| | Using Quotable Quotes | 183 |
| | Quotable Quotes From the World of | |
| |    Mother Goose and Other Children's Rhymes | 184 |
| |    Kindness to Animals | 184 |
| |    Quotable Quotes From Children's Literature | 187 |
| |    Quotable Quotes From Aesop | 188 |
| | Historical Quotable Quotes | 189 |
| |    Quotable Quotes of American Presidents | 189 |
| |    Quotable Quotes in the Fight for Freedom and Equal Rights | 189 |
| |    Quotable Quotes From Women in History | 191 |

Other Quotable Quotes 191
Internet Links 193

**13. Personifications and Interactions: Know Thyself** **195**
Personifications and Interactions: Another Point of View 195
Personifications and Interactions Across the Curriculum 196
Personifications and Interactions in the Primary Grades 196
 Deepening Word Knowledge 198
 Keeping a Journal 199
 Animal Job Application—An Anthropomorphic Point of View 201
 Comparing Concepts and Terms 201
Understanding Behaviors of Literary Characters 205
Understanding Historic Figures 206
Using Personification and Interactions in Content Areas 207
Internet Links 208

**14. Writing as Editing: Writers Are Editors** **209**
The Red Pen 209
Writers Are Editors 209
Teaching Editing 210
 The Draft Copy 210
 The Editing Taxonomy 210
 The Four Improvers of Writing 211
 Using Transitions 212
Peer Editing by Reading Aloud 214
Peer Review 214
Teacher Editing 215
Rubrics 216
Internet Links 219

**15. Writing—A Curriculum Unifier: A Goal for Every Student** **221**
Integrating Writing Across the Curriculum 221

**References** **231**

**Index** **235**

# *P*reface to the Second Edition

**W**riting continues to be "in." Students are being *asked* to write in science, in mathematics, in social studies, in health and physical education, and, of course, in language arts. The SAT—the Scholastic Aptitude Test—now requires students to write. Taking the writing test is no longer an option.

What we're not sure is "in," however, is the *teaching* of writing. Yes, there's some teaching. Students know about draft copies and the green and red underlining on the computer. They know that spelling and punctuation and length all count in getting a grade. They know they must stick to the topic and follow the rubrics. There are students who know about a thesis statement and about certain genres, such as persuasive essays or narratives. This is all good, because we know that good writers are good readers, and often good writers are good thinkers. Plus, we admire and honor good writers and think well of them.

What concerns us and many of the teachers we have worked with are the students who need instruction in how to write—and not how to write just for tests or to pass a course. They need (and often want) help and strategies for writing letters, stories, journals, opinions, humor, and whatever else can be written. Most students we have met (and once were ourselves) would like to get back positive comments, which we call *VG*—very good. Because, when the first draft of a piece of writing is *very good*, revision and polishing can only make it *excellent*.

Our goal in *Writing as Learning*, which follows from our goal in teaching writing, is to provide teachers and their students with as many instructional steps as possible, so that all students begin with VG. We believe we can accomplish this goal by showing students how to gather and use the ingredients that good writers use, which include

- Having words
- Composing using those words

- Writing about what we know
- Knowing that there are many writing genres each with its own style or template
- Always knowing who we are writing to
- Knowing that the first piece of writing is just the starting place

Writing well is not easy—neither for good writers nor for not-so-good writers. It takes lots of energy and kind, gentle editors. We offer this book, humbly, but also with confidence that carefully guided instruction based on well-researched strategies and lots of patience and understanding can bring students the pleasure that comes from hearing someone say, "Wow this is great! Did you write this? I just loved reading it."

We suggest that you start from the beginning and move with your students at a rate that works for them. Make writing the center or unifier of your curriculum, so that your students have a record of their learning and the memories of learning to write while actually enjoying it. A simple way to keep a record of writing is in a notebook, which we call the Notebook. We have provided detailed information on setting up the Notebook and its continuous use throughout the school year.

We offer this book with confidence knowing that students who are taught to write do write better and even get to enjoy writing. We also know that when your students enjoy writing, you will definitely enjoy reading what they have written.

## ACKNOWLEDGMENTS

Corwin Press gratefully acknowledges the contributions of the following reviewers:

Robert L. Bangert-Drowns
Associate Dean for Academic Affairs
University at Albany School of
    Education
Albany, NY

Cliff B. Barrineau
AP Statistics, Trigonometry,
    and Algebra Teacher
Dreher High School
Columbia, SC

Terry Bordo
Fourth Grade Teacher
Cunninghan Elementary School
Vineland, NJ

Susan D'Angelo
Fifth Grade Gifted Education Teacher
Pineview School for the Gifted
Osprey, FL

Renee Drewicke
Fourth, Fifth, and Sixth Grade Teacher
Herman Elementary School
Herman, MN

Kimberley Gomez
Assistant Professor of
    Curriculum and Instruction
University of Illinois at Chicago
Chicago, IL

Faith Washburn
Curriculum Coordinator
Wailupe Valley Elementary School
Honolulu, HI

# About the Authors

**Evelyn Rothstein** has been an educational consultant specializing in teaching writing across the curriculum for the past 20 years. With a background in classroom teaching and a specialization in linguistics and language development, she has trained teachers and implemented her strategy-based Writing as Learning and Write for Mathematics programs in hundreds of schools and school districts throughout the United States. In addition, she is a consultant for the National Education Alliance focusing on writing, language, and cognition. Dr. Rothstein is a graduate of the City University of New York and Teachers College, Columbia University; she holds degrees in education, speech, reading, and psycholinguistics. She is the author of numerous books and articles, including *Teaching Writing, Staying at the Top, Creative Writes,* and *Easy Writer.* She is currently working on her next book, *Grammar That Works,* as coauthor with her son, Andrew Rothstein, as well as a series of children's books and memoirs.

**Andrew Rothstein** has had a distinguished career as teacher, administrator, and researcher. His diverse and enriching experiences in international schools, special education, public schools, and consulting have given him a broad perspective on the contexts in which children learn. As an author and presenter, he has achieved wide acclaim for his work in improving school performance by focusing on improving instruction and its supervision. His work in integrating many subject areas through writing has been highly effective in improving test scores in districts across the country. Dr. Rothstein earned a master's degree in special education from the University of North Carolina at Chapel Hill and a doctorate in educational administration from New York University. As a school principal, Dr. Rothstein led site-based improvements that resulted in strong increases in student academic performance. While superintendent of a regional school serving children with severe physical disabilities and health impairments, Dr. Rothstein reorganized staff development, created new curricula, and integrated technology into the instructional program for children from prekindergarten through high school. Dr. Rothstein has taught and lectured at several major universities and has been a senior consultant with the National Urban Alliance. Currently he is curriculum manager for the National Academy Foundation. He is a coauthor of *Write for Mathematics, Second Edition,* which is also published by Corwin Press.

**Gerald Lauber**, currently chief operating officer of the National Urban Alliance, previously served as superintendent in three New York state school districts, where he initiated programs to meet the needs of diverse student populations while stabilizing long-range fiscal plans. Under his administration, state-of-the-art computer-assisted instructional programs as well as innovative writing and mathematics programs were put into place. As president and CEO of Purewater Sciences and Metric Technologies, he developed a corporate perspective on what schools must provide to prepare children for success in the workplace and the world in which they live. Dr. Lauber's writings have appeared in *Electronic School, THE Journal, American School Boards Journal, New York State Education, Viewpoints, Newsday,* and other publications. Dr. Lauber coauthored *Writing as Learning* and *Write for Mathematics.* He has MA and MEd degrees in school administration from Teachers College and an EdD in systems administration from New York University.

# Introduction

*The most important method of education always has consisted of that in which the pupil was urged to actual performance.*

~Albert Einstein (1954, p. 60)

## THE RATIONALE OF WRITING AS LEARNING

A major premise of this book is that by learning to write in their subject areas, students learn (more) about their subject areas. Here's a simple example of this premise, taken from *Write for Mathematics* (Rothstein, Rothstein, & Lauber, 2006). Early in the teaching of mathematics, the student learns that 4 + 4 = 8. Yet behind this basic addition fact lies a world of mathematical concepts that emerges as a student is taught to write an explanation of what this algorithm means. The example below, composed by a third grade student, shows the steps of awareness of accumulated knowledge. (The mathematical vocabulary that this student has had to learn to write this piece is shown in boldface.)

> I now know that I know a lot about **mathematics** when I had 4 + 4. **First**, the **sum** is 8. But that's not all. I have **added two even numbers**, so I must get an even number as a sum. When I **add** two of the same numbers, the **amount** is **doubled**. My teacher told me that if I add **three** of the same numbers, the sum is **tripled**. I can write this problem in a **horizontal** way like 4 + 4 or in a **vertical** way like
>
> $$\begin{array}{r} 4 \\ + 4 \\ \hline \end{array}$$
>
> **Both** ways give me the same answer because if I have 4 and **count** 4 more, my sum is 8. I also know that the two numbers I have added are called **addends**.

You may be thinking that asking a student to write out such a lengthy explanation may take up too much time when you have to get on with mathematics (or social studies or science). The benefit, however, of writing is the improvement in student performance in "every academic area" (Reeves, 2002, p. 5). Additional research shows that learning how to write in all the content areas enhances thinking, creating, and communicating and increases the learning of the content itself (Langer & Applebee, 1987; Maxwell, 1996; Scarborough, 2001).

## THE DISTINCTION OF WRITING AS LEARNING

In this book, we make a distinction between asking students to write and teaching them to write, so that writing truly becomes a way to learn. Many teachers assign writing as a means of assessing their students' knowledge of a subject or topic. Students are often asked to demonstrate their learning by writing an essay or summarizing a chapter or analyzing a character. Many state tests require students to demonstrate their knowledge in writing, especially in the content areas. Students may have to explain how they solved a mathematics problem, explain an historical event, or write a persuasive essay. Therefore, it is incumbent on teachers of all content to prepare students for the expectation that they will need to demonstrate their knowledge in written form.

*Writing as Learning* is designed to support teachers in developing systematic instruction that incorporates writing strategies into teaching a wide range of content. Therefore, it makes learning more efficient, builds mastery, and prepares students for assessments. It expands a teacher's repertoire of instructional strategies beyond demands for form and substance by giving students the means to organize their thinking and writing. This moves teaching beyond "inert knowledge" (Perkins, 1992) to active knowledge.

*Writing as Learning* helps students overcome obstacles to successful writing. Students are often challenged because they are unsure about such questions as, how do I start? What should I say? Who am I writing to? Is this what the teacher wants? How long should it be? How will it be graded?

## WHAT IS TEACHING WRITING?

A writer must be fluent and organized. *Fluency* imparts the idea of an accomplished speaker and is used in a complimentary way. It implies a way with words and certainly a knowledge of words related to a specific topic or subject. Students who are learning English as a second language often struggle with fluency—not enough words or the right words or the best words.

*Organization* (in writing) means having progression, relatedness, and complete ideas. But there is an additional factor in the meaning of organized when it comes to writing. It means knowing the typical format or pattern of the genre in which one is writing—a letter, a poem, a biography, an essay, or something else. In fact, everyone who writes must know that all writing is genre-based and cannot be a haphazard collection of words or sentences. To achieve this essential fluency and organization, students need writing instruction.

The case for teaching writing is strengthened by the work of Gardner (1983, 1993) who defines intelligence as "the ability to solve problems or fashion products" (1983, p. x). Writing, specifically, draws upon and nurtures linguistic intelligence. Gardner cites writing as a means of building rhetorical ability that teaches students to persuade or convince others. Writing enhances linguistic knowledge through the "mnemonic capacity" or the mind's ability to remember information (1993, p. 92). Students who are taught to develop and maintain organized lists on specific topics (which we call taxonomies) get an essential tool for learning how to store and retrieve vast amounts of data lodged in their brains (Jensen, 1998).

By using writing as an expression of linguistic knowledge, students become aware of the writing of others—their style, vocabulary, humor, and information. Linguistic knowledge is essential to producing clear, lively, in-depth writing that is audience-friendly and that gives the writer confidence and a desire to write more.

When students are taught writing strategies, they build fluency and organization. Students in our Writing as Learning program receive frequent, guided opportunities to apply and practice these strategies in every curriculum area throughout their school years. Teaching writing should not be a haphazard activity but rather a continuous process for learning. To enable you to create a writing program that teaches students to learn deeply, meaningfully, intelligently, and actively, we offer the following recommendations, detailed in the chapters of this book.

Make writing a curriculum unifier. Writing draws together multiple subjects and helps students understand the unity or interrelatedness of subject matter. For example, in the mathematics class, students write about problems related to economics, geography, or history. In the English or language arts class, students may need to use the vocabulary of mathematics, geography, or sports. Implement a systematic approach to teaching every student to use writing as a tool for learning by all teachers in every grade and subject. Build and extend from what students write best. When you work from the students' comfort zone, they acquire the confidence to write in many other genres.

So now, imagine students who have been taught to write systematically and developmentally from kindergarten through twelfth grade. Each year, they have created their own personal thesauruses; written biographies and autobiographies; expressed a wealth of knowledge; created fables, myths, and folk tales; and developed opinions in personal, persuasive, and explanatory essays and articles. Furthermore, as they created all of this writing, they understood and applied the appropriate conventions of written grammar and spelling. This vision can be achieved for almost all students.

# HOW TO USE THIS BOOK

This book presents 12 specific strategies for students of all ages. They learn how to gather the words they need to write and how to use the appropriate organizing formats for saying what they need to say. To visualize this approach to teaching writing, refer to the Planning Wheel in Figure 0.1. It illustrates the relation of a subject or topic to the writing strategies and shows the concept of an integrated approach to teaching any subject or topic.

For example, the rectangle in the center might represent the 13 colonies or animals of the African jungle. Each spoke of the wheel represents a different writing

**Figure 0.1** The Planning Wheel

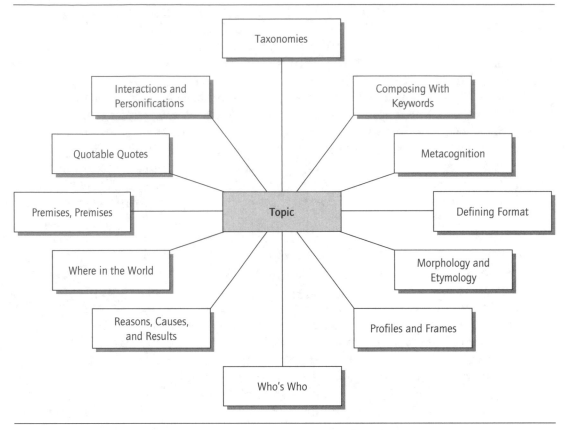

strategy that may stand alone or be used in combination with other strategies to write about the topic. Table 0.1 shows the learning extensions and writing genres associated with each spoke of the wheel.

The book is arranged in a sequence we recommend for teaching the strategies. Each strategy must eventually become part of an integrated approach so that within a school year, the students have been introduced to all or most of the strategies and have made them part of their writing repertoire. Once students know all of the strategies, they can select strategies appropriate to the task. By following this arrangement, you will guide your students in developing a powerful vocabulary (fluency) and introduce them to the appropriate genres or formats (organization).

There are two categories of strategies in the Writing as Learning program, those that build fluency through student vocabulary and those that build fluency through organization. Vocabulary and organization must be fully integrated; otherwise, students will not develop fluency. Chapters 8–13 demonstrate how to integrate the initial strategies in a variety of curriculum areas and genres.

Go slowly in introducing the strategies, making sure the students have extensive modeling and practice.

The list below shows how this book is organized. Every strategy has a chapter and a slogan. There are suggested Internet links for each strategy. The bibliography provides excellent information on writing and teaching, and there are several templates in each of the different chapters to get your students started.

**Table 0.1**    Definitions, Extensions, and Genres for the Strategies in the Planning Wheel

| Strategy and Definition | Learning Extensions | Genre Focus |
|---|---|---|
| **Taxonomies**—Alphabetical lists of terms related to the subject or topic (e.g., *algebra, borrow, calculate, divide* is the beginning of a Taxonomy for mathematics) | • Fluency and organization<br>• Vocabulary building<br>• Advance organizing<br>• Note taking<br>• Pre- and postassessment | • ABC books<br>• Personal thesauruses<br>• Personal dictionaries |
| **Composing With Keywords**—Using the words from the Taxonomies to compose sentences and paragraphs | • Sentence composing<br>• Paragraphing<br>• Focusing on topic | • Response logs<br>• Journals<br>• Poetry and acronyms |
| **Metacognition**—Thinking about thinking by building self-awareness of knowledge and writing with starters such as "I know that I know" | • Questioning<br>• Research<br>• Response to learning<br>• Higher order thinking | • Explanation of factual knowledge<br>• Inquiry into new knowledge<br>• Note taking and reflection |
| **Defining Format**—A three-part template to define a term (e.g., *triangle*) that consists of the question (e.g., what is a triangle?), the category, and the characteristics | • Questioning<br>• Categorizing<br>• Detailing<br>• Vocabulary building<br>• Paragraph development | • Explanation of factual knowledge<br>• Descriptive writing<br>• Research writing<br>• Compare and contrast |
| **Morphology and Etymology**—The study of the formation and history of selected words related to the subject or topic (e.g. *add, additional, addend*, etc.) | • Grammatical accuracy<br>• Spelling patterns<br>• Expanded vocabulary<br>• Language history | • Word stories<br>• Alliteration<br>• Myths and legends<br>• Poetic forms |
| **Profiles and Frames**—Templates for outlining information in a broad spectrum of topics and subjects | • Biographic research<br>• Subject area research<br>• Paraphrasing<br>• Outlining and recreating | • Report writing<br>• Oral presentations<br>• Research writing |

*(Continued)*

**Table 0.1** (Continued)

| Strategy and Definition | Learning Extensions | Genre Focus |
|---|---|---|
| **Who's Who**—Formats for writing about a person's accomplishments: biographies, autobiographies, and memoirs | • Biographic research<br>• Literary interpretation<br>• Character development<br>• Personal writing | • Autobiography and memoir<br>• Biography<br>• Literary analysis<br>• Book review |
| **Reasons, Causes, Results**—An organizational format for essays in various genres; it includes reasons, causes, results, and procedures | • Outlining<br>• Detailing<br>• Paragraphing<br>• Focusing on topic | • Personal expression<br>• Persuasion<br>• Explanation<br>• Information |
| **Where in the World**—Organizers for writing about geography, settings, places, maps and charts, and other aspects of the world and universe | • Geographic and historic research<br>• Map and globe interpretation<br>• Use of charts and graphs | • Geographic and historical issues<br>• Social issues<br>• Explanatory and factual writing |
| **Premises, Premises**—Organizational templates for making books into films, plays, and other dramatic material | • Innovating on literary structure<br>• Writing dialogues<br>• Interpreting characters<br>• Detailing | • Play and film writing<br>• Monologues and dialogues<br>• Fiction and nonfiction formats<br>• Character development |
| **Quotable Quotes**—Using notable quotations to include in writing or as responses to ideas and beliefs | • Response to ideas of others<br>• Making inferences<br>• Writing succinctly<br>• Making literary connections | • Social and moral issues<br>• Research<br>• Opinions and beliefs |
| **Personifications and Interactions**—Strategies for writing assuming the persona of a person, animal, or object in order to write from a different perspective | • Research<br>• Audience and voice<br>• Imagination and creativity<br>• Insight and empathy | • Letters in different formats<br>• Humor<br>• Reality and fantasy<br>• Research |

- Chapter 1: "The Elements of Writing as Learning" provides an overview of the book and defines the purposes of teaching specific strategies.

- Chapter 2: "Building Vocabulary With Taxonomies" provides students with the means for collecting vocabulary words so that each can build a personal thesaurus for writing.

- Chapter 3: "Composing With Keywords" gives students practice with their Taxonomies and other sources to develop sentence-building skills in a variety of genres.

- Chapter 4: "Metacognition" provides students with an organized format for thinking and writing about what they know, need to know, or want to know to build reflection and the ability to share their knowledge.

- Chapter 5: "Defining Format" guides students to define terms by asking a question, stating the category to which the term belongs, and adding the characteristics that distinguish it.

- Chapter 6: "Morphology, Etymology, and Grammar" focuses on analyzing the structural components of the words and learning the history of words. Students learn not only the meaning of the words but also the depth of the word meanings. The purpose of the chapter is to teach expansion of word meanings and the application of grammar for clarity and accuracy.

- Chapter 7: "Profiles and Frames" builds on the strategies introduced in the previous chapters by concentrating on organizational templates that can be used across subject areas. These templates help students structure and organize their writing, while still allowing student originality and creativity.

- Chapter 8: "Who's Who" provides integrated strategies for writing about people, including the genres of biography, autobiography, and memoir.

- Chapter 9: "Reasons, Causes, Results—The Basis for the Essay" teaches students the structure and format for writing personal, persuasive, and explanatory essays.

- Chapter 10: "Where in the World" gives the students templates and other organizers for writing about places of geographical significance. Geography receives special focus in this book because it is part of many genres and serves as a curriculum unifier.

- Chapter 11: "Premises, Premises" shows students how to transform a book or story into a "movie" to dramatically present events. This strategy offers the student a creative process for writing Premise Statements, a story treatment, scripts, and dialogue.

- Chapter 12: "Quotable Quotes" helps students connect their own writing with the words of literary characters and famous (or infamous) people. Through this connection, students gain a fuller understanding of significant statements to enrich and support their own writings.

- Chapter 13: "Personifications and Interactions" provides a strategy that teaches students to assume a persona and write from that persona's point of view. This is a creative form of writing that is vivid and exciting, requiring in-depth knowledge.

- Chapter 14: "Writing as Editing" recognizes that writing and editing are essential to each other. Procedures for revising and editing are included as well as a variety of rubrics for different purposes and different grade levels.

- Chapter 15: "Writing—A Curriculum Unifier" is an illustration of a lesson plan for applying all of the strategies to one topic.

We believe that *Writing as Learning* will provide you with concrete and practical ways of helping your students learn how to write and learn from their writing. We also expect students will learn to love what they have written.

*Words Are Free!*

*Have Words,
Can Write*

*Writing Is Thinking*

*Write to a Martian*

*Every Word
Has a Story*

*Organize
Your Writing*

*Know Who You
Know and Know
Who You Are!*

*Think in Threes*

*Everybody Has
to Be Someplace*

*Let's Make
a Movie!*

*Words Inspire*

*Know Thyself*

*Writers Are Editors*

*A Goal for
Every Student*

**CHAPTER ONE**

# The Elements of Writing as Learning

## Strategies, Genres, Topics, and Tools

*Student writers need a whole array of organizational strategies from which to choose in order to make their idea shine.*

~Ruth Culham (2003, p. 73)

## THE WRITING TEACHER AND THE WRITING CLASSROOM

In the introduction, we pointed out that writing is strongly linked to improved academic performance in all subjects. The implication of this linkage is that all teachers in all subjects need to include writing in their teaching. By extension, we believe that all teachers need a repertoire of effective writing strategies that can be applied across the curriculum. Finally, we advise that all teachers in a school (or school system) share a set of common strategies that students recognize and learn to use flexibly. Essentially, according to VanTassel-Baska (1996), the teacher teaches writing so that writing becomes "a part of an integrated comprehensive set of activities used to enhance student learning" (p. 144). Hopefully, if writing is taught as a way of learning throughout the school, all students are continuously engaged in both instruction and practice with all teachers.

While we recognize that teachers often see themselves as specialists in specific subject areas, writing promotes, develops, organizes, and enhances all learning, and every subject has its own literature—from mathematics to sports. Writing defines subject areas, deepening one's knowledge and recall (Kennedy, 1996). The sports writer, for example, touches upon statistics, history, geography, health, character behaviors, and values. As stated by Nancy Atwell, "Writing is basic to thinking about and learning knowledge in all fields as well as communicating that knowledge" (1998, p. xiii).

The first indicators of good instruction throughout a school are the walls. The slogan "the walls talk" reflects an active visualization of what students are doing and learning. Commercial posters and signs on the walls tell one story about instruction, while students' writings and projects tell a different story. Educators, parents, and other visitors should be able to walk into a classroom after the students have left and know from the walls what the students have learned. A classroom should be a living panorama where the visitor is invited to comment and marvel at the students' work, especially at what students have written about their learning or their insights into their learning. The classroom and hallway walls are the visual representation of what has been taught and what has been learned.

## STRATEGIES FOR WRITING

Today most schools accept writing as a process, in contrast to the older rule-bound, product-oriented approach in which the student writes and the teacher corrects (Kennedy, 1996). In a process environment, students are guided through successive, and possibly recursive, steps of prewriting, drafting, revising, editing, and if possible or appropriate, publishing. This arrangement of steps is probably a good description of what a writer might do in the development of a piece of writing, but what is often missing are the instructional strategies that guide the student toward the fulfillment of these steps.

Some questions are central to this process. What is prewriting? Does it mean discussion? Research? Interviewing? Outlining? How does a writer organize material before drafting? How does a student write a draft, and what are the elements of a good draft so that it becomes an excellent final product? What steps of the writing process does the student have to practice? Expansion of ideas? Use of transitional words? Reduction of clutter? How does one *teach* the concept of voice?

One way to think of writing is as a way of generating meaning through fluency plus organization. A writer needs the words and the organizational structures that convey the ideas or message coherently (Spivey, 1996). The strategies outlined in this book build fluency for the topic or content and provide the students with organizational schemata for specific genres and various audiences. As the students learn and practice a strategy, they use and integrate one or more of these schemata to prewrite, plan, draft, and revise. In addition, students become aware that "writing is the process of selecting as well as organizing" (Spivey 1996, p. 38).

To build these factors of fluency, organization, development, and coherence, students need to start with

- A Notebook specifically for writing and keeping track of strategies, illustrated in Figure 1.1.
- An understanding of genres and their organizational formats (see Figures 1.2 and 1.3).
- Slogans for strategies and displays of writing (Figure 1.4).
- Nontechnological and technological materials (Figures 1.5 and 1.6).
- Topics for writing (Figures 1.7–1.9).

- Resources for writing (Figure 1.10).
- Guidelines for writing a draft copy (Figure 1.11).
- Guidelines for editing (Figure 1.12).
- Skills for writing on the computer (Figure 1.13).

By providing students with the above materials and information, the classroom becomes a workshop for teaching and learning writing and makes writing the centerpiece for instruction.

## SETTING UP THE NOTEBOOK

Even with a computer, a writer still needs a notebook for keeping track of and easy referral to information relating to writing. Because the Notebook is so essential to writing, we have capitalized the word—Notebook—which is how it is written throughout this book. Provide your students (or have them get) a simple composition book, preferably *not* spiral, and begin your writing instruction by giving students the directions below for using the Notebook (Figure 1.1):

**Figure 1.1**    Setting Up the Notebook

| | • TABLE OF CONTENTS • | | |
| --- | --- | --- | --- |
| Date | Topic or Subject | Strategy | Page |
| 9/12/year | Weather, Science | Taxonomy of Terms | 8 |
| 9/15 | Weather, Science | Composing With Keywords | 10 |
| 9/19 | The Early Greeks, Social Studies | Metacognition on Ancient Greece | 12 |
| 9/22 | Myth of the Sun, Reading | Defining Format—What is a Myth? | 14 |
| 9/27 | Vocabulary on Weather, Science | Taxonomy of Weather Terms | 16 |

- Open the composition book to the first page opposite the cover.
- Number that page 1, and continue numbering on both sides of each page until you get to page 9. (Later you will continue to number the pages as needed.) All of these pages will be used for the Table of Contents.
- Go back to page 1 and head it *Table of Contents*.
- Under *Table of Contents,* write the following headings with spacing as illustrated and examples of entries. (Note that all entries follow the Table of Contents and begin on even-numbered pages and use a double-page spread—even number on the left, odd number on the right. For example, the first entry after the Table of Contents would begin on page 10.)

# THE GENRES OF WRITING

All writing of consequence has what is called *genre* or *form* that follows a recognizable organizational scheme. A genre refers to a specific, definable type of writing (or art) with noticeable attributes. A novel is organized quite differently from a research paper. A haiku is set up differently from a ballad. Writing genres may be fiction, nonfiction, or poetry. Experienced writers learn to mix their genres, so that in addition to myth, legend, fairy tale, novel, essay, and so forth, there is biographical fiction, descriptive narrative, and personal essay.

Despite the need for understanding and writing within a genre, many students remain unaware of genre formats and how to write within the parameters of their structures. Many times this lack of awareness results from being assigned writing topics such as, "Write an essay about . . . ," which either is too global or lacks format specificity. Such topics cause students to be uncertain as to whether the essay is to be persuasive, explanatory, or personal.

When students are asked, without instruction, to write about a famous person, they often end up creating a piece that strings facts together and is likely to resemble an obituary. Writing assignments that begin with words such as *discuss, tell,* or *describe* often result in students rambling, digressing, switching voices, or changing from objective to personal or vice versa. Writers must learn what genres are and how they are structured or organized. Learning about genres is developmental, so that young writers (and probably inexperienced writers) are limited in what they can write. Even at adult levels, few people can write well in a variety of genres. Nevertheless, in a school with a systematic, strategy-based writing program, students can learn to write fables, legends, news reports, plays, and other genres.

Figures 1.2 and 1.3 show two lists, or Taxonomies, that contain examples of the types of genres that students can learn to write. One list contains fiction and nonfiction formats, and the other list has different poetry genres. The lists can be used by teachers as planning and organizational tools. You may also want to have your students enter these genres in their Notebooks. (Follow the plan for entering Taxonomies given in Chapter 2). You can add other genres to these lists and place checkmarks in the "Plan to Teach" column.

**Figure 1.2**    Fiction and Nonfiction Genres

|   | Genres | Appropriate Grades | Plan to Teach |
|---|---|---|---|
| A | autobiography<br>animal story (fiction)<br>animal story (factual)<br>ABC book<br>adventure story | 3+<br>1+<br>1+<br>1+<br>3+ | |
| B | biography<br>business letter | 3+<br>4+ | |
| C | comedy skit<br>character sketch<br>comics | 5+<br>3+<br>3+ | |

**Figure 1.2** (Continued)

| | Genres | Appropriate Grades | Plan to Teach |
|---|---|---|---|
| D | descriptive essay | 3+ | |
| E | explanatory essay<br>editorial | 4+<br>5+ | |
| F | fairy tale<br>folk tale<br>friendly letter | 2+<br>2+<br>1+ | |
| G | ghost story<br>greeting card | 2+<br>1+ | |
| H | humorous story<br>how-to piece<br>history article | 1+<br>1+<br>3+ | |
| I | interview<br>instructions | 3+<br>2+ | |
| J | jokes<br>journal | 1+<br>1+ | |
| K | | | |
| L | legend<br>laboratory report<br>learning log | 4+<br>4+<br>1+ | |
| M | mystery<br>myth<br>metacognitive statement | 3+<br>3+<br>1+ | |
| N | novel<br>narrative | 7+<br>2+ | |
| O | opinion statement | 1+ | |
| P | personal essay<br>persuasive essay<br>play | 2+<br>3+<br>3+ | |
| Q | | | |
| R | research report<br>recipe | 4+<br>1+ | |
| S | short story<br>script<br>science fiction<br>speech | 6+<br>3+<br>4+<br>2+ | |
| T | travelogue<br>technical report<br>tall tale | 3+<br>6+<br>3+ | |
| U | | | |
| V | | | |
| W | wildlife story | 3+ | |
| X, Y, Z | | | |

**Figure 1.3** Poetry Genres

|  | Genres | Appropriate Grades | Plan to Teach |
|---|---|---|---|
| A | acrostic | 1+ | |
| B | ballad | 3+ | |
| C | couplet<br>cinquain | 1+<br>2+ | |
| D | diamante | 2+ | |
| E | epic | 4+ | |
| F | free verse | 1+ | |
| G | | | |
| H | haiku | 2+ | |
| I | | | |
| J | | | |
| K | | | |
| L | lyric(s)<br>limerick | 4+<br>3+ | |
| M | | | |
| N | | | |
| O | | | |
| P | | | |
| Q | quatrain | 3+ | |
| R | rap | 4+ | |
| S | sonnet | 6+ | |
| T | | | |
| U | | | |
| V | | | |
| W | | | |
| X, Y, Z | | | |

With the classroom as a showcase of student accomplishment, all work is displayed aesthetically and invitingly. A simple frame of construction paper and a statement about the work announces the importance of what is being displayed. The suggested phrases for bulletin board displays shown in Figure 1.4 serve as both announcements and invitations to writers and observers alike. Many students enjoy creating their own witty or catchy phrases, and teachers can encourage student suggestions and provide opportunities for brainstorming bulletin board captions.

**Figure 1.4**     Bulletin Board Invitations for Students' Writing

| | |
|---|---|
| Writers Under Construction | Need a Good Definition? Ask a Writer. |
| Writers Meet Here | Powerful Persuasions and Exacting |
| Author's Column |     Explanations |
| Writers' Convention—Stop and Browse | Writers Never Forget. |
| Mathematicians' Write-Abouts | Need a Friend? Write a Letter. |
| Writers Wanted—Space Available | Write? Right! |
| Writer's Scene | Write Today. Write Tomorrow. |
| A World of Writers |     Write Forever. |
| Publisher's Place | We're in the Write Company. |

## TOOLS AND MATERIALS FOR WRITING

The easy availability or accessibility of writing tools and materials is essential to helping students write better and maintain motivation for ongoing writing. Some writers need different kinds of writing paper—yellow pads for drafts and white or special paper for final and published copies. Most writers need and love different kinds of writing implements—well-sharpened, good lead pencils, easily flowing pens, and colored markers. And, of course, there is the computer, with its word processing and graphics programs—and the Internet. All of these features are easily accessible and user-friendly tools for writing. Writers also need spell-checkers, age-appropriate and unabridged dictionaries, atlases, globes, and reference material.

Of course, not all classrooms or schools may be able to provide all of these tools, but having them should be a goal. Think of how difficult writing is without them. Imagine building a house without plans and with only a small hammer and a few nails. Without the necessary tools, writing can be equally difficult. Figures 1.5 and 1.6 provide suggestions for the basic writing materials needed to support good writing instruction. Adjustments and substitutions will need to be made based upon available resources and budgetary constraints. Figure 1.5 lists items that a school should provide for elementary students. While materials for writing are often the responsibility of the students themselves in middle and high school, whenever possible schools should supply the basic writing materials needed to provide motivation for writing for publication or presentation to other students. The materials listed in Figure 1.6 are also helpful.

**Figure 1.5** Nontechnological Materials to Support an Instructional Writing Program—Elementary Grades

Draft paper—yellow and white pads

Final copy paper—white, lined and unlined

Publishing paper—colored construction paper

Writing implements—soft-lead pencils, pens and markers of various colors

Spiral notebook(s) for journals, lists, and writing strategy models

Grade-appropriate dictionaries and thesauruses

Unabridged dictionary (for grades 3 and up)

Wall of topics

Story frames and sentence starters

Charts of editing and proofreading rules

Labels, sticky notes, and glue sticks

Files of magazines and pictures

Blank greeting cards and envelopes

Blank bound books

Bookbinder and laminator

Anthologies of nursery rhymes, fairy tales, myths, folk tales, and legends

Globes and maps

Wall of words, including months, days of the week, seasons, colors, animals, names of classmates, mathematical terms, occupations, or whatever is needed for the students' writing

**Figure 1.6** Nontechnological Materials to Support an Instructional Writing Program—Middle School and High School

| | |
|---|---|
| Unabridged dictionary | Books of word histories and origins |
| Style manuals | Globes and maps |
| Alphabetical thesaurus and topic thesaurus | Book of concise biographies |
| Spell-checkers | Appropriate magazines, periodicals, and newspapers |

## WHAT SHOULD I WRITE ABOUT?

William Zinsser has stated that "the only way to write is to force yourself to produce a certain number of words on a regular basis" (1980, p. 53). To many teachers, this statement, while probably correct, may seem absurd or impossible: "I'm a mathematics teacher with a year's curriculum to cover" or "My students are just learning to read and can barely hold a pencil" or "Zinsser is talking about professional writers, not young students." Yet, one learns to write by writing, just as one learns to bowl by bowling. Following are suggestions to get students to want to engage in the practice of writing.

First, have students create a list (called a Taxonomy in this book—see Chapter 2) early in the school year of topics they might write about in class. Obviously, the list will vary depending on whether the class is a second grade class or a high school chemistry class. Have the students set up the list alphabetically as shown in Figure 1.7, and ask them to brainstorm for topics. Ask students what they think they will learn about, and have them turn their answers into topics. A third grader might answer, "How to multiply." Under M, the student would write "multiplication." In a chemistry class, suggested topics could be "contributions of chemists," "discoverers of elements," "alchemy and chemistry," and "careers in chemistry." Lists of possible writing topics can be generated at the beginning of the year or course and modified, updated, and otherwise revised throughout the year or program. Figures 1.7–1.9 show three samples of lists of topics.

**Figure 1.7**    Suggested Topics for Primary Grades

| • TAXONOMY • | |
|---|---|
| A | autumn, animal habitats |
| B | baby animals, books, baseball |
| C | cats, cars, colors, Christmas |
| D | dreams, dogs, dinosaurs |
| E | Easter |
| F | friends, farms, food, family |
| G | games, gifts |
| H | home, houses, helping, holidays, Halloween, Hanukkah |
| I | ice skating, insects, Indians, ice cream |
| J | jokes, jobs |
| K | kites, kittens, Kwanzaa |
| L | ladybugs |
| M | music |
| N | names, numbers |
| O | owls |
| P | pets, Passover |
| Q | questions |
| R | reading, running, Ramadan |
| S | swimming |
| T | television, trucks, teachers |
| U | uncles and aunts |
| V | visitors, valentine's day |
| W | weather, water, whales |
| X | xylophones, x-rays |
| Y | yesterday |
| Z | zero, zoos, zippers |

**Figure 1.8** Suggested Topics for Intermediate Grades

### • TAXONOMY •

| | |
|---|---|
| A | Africa, Antarctic, Asia, art, animals of the jungle, astronomy |
| B | basketball, books, babies, birds, butterflies |
| C | cats, cars, Christmas, cities, climate, cameras |
| D | dreams, dogs, dinosaurs, deserts |
| E | Easter, explorers, Eskimos |
| F | friends, farms, food, family |
| G | games, gifts, geography, geometry |
| H | home, houses, helping, Halloween, Hanukkah, health, horses |
| I | ice skating, insects, Indians |
| J | jokes, jobs, jogging |
| K | kites, kittens, kings, karate |
| L | leaders |
| M | music, musical instruments, mathematics |
| N | names, nocturnal animals |
| O | oceans, oceanography |
| P | pets, Passover, plants |
| Q | questions, quilting |
| R | reading, running, rivers, Ramadan |
| S | swimming, senses, sports, songs |
| T | television, transportation |
| U | uncles and aunts, United States of America |
| V | values |
| W | weather, water, whales, Washington, DC |
| X | xylophones, x-rays, xeriscapes |
| Y | yachts |
| Z | zero, zoography |

**Figure 1.9** Suggested Topics for Chemistry

### • TAXONOMY •

| | |
|---|---|
| A | agriculture and chemistry, atoms in our lives |
| B | blood chemistry |
| C | chemistry in the news, chemists of accomplishment, chemical warfare |
| D | DNA in medical treatment, detectives and chemistry, drug abuse |
| E | elements and their names |
| F | forensics, food chemistry |
| G | gold as a commodity of greed, gold as a commodity of medicine |
| H | history of chemistry |
| I | inventions of chemists |
| J | jokes for chemists |
| K | krypton as material and as birthplace of Superman |
| L | luminescence in our lives |
| M | mathematics and chemistry |
| N | nuclear chemistry |
| O | osmosis for living |
| P | plastics—past and future |
| Q | quinine and the story of malaria |
| R | radiation and cancer |
| S | silicones in the news |
| T | turpentine—home and medicine product |
| U | uranium and its discovery |
| V | vitamins for health |
| W | whiskey—product and history |
| X | xerography |
| Y | yeast for the baker |
| Z | zinc for health |

Students also need to know the resources for writing and becoming a writer—tools beyond the encyclopedia and copying articles off the Internet. Figure 1.10 shows a Taxonomy for these resources.

## THE STUDENT AS WRITER

Perhaps the greatest benefit derived from the shift of the teacher-correction model of writing to the writing process has been the teachers' and (hopefully) students' understanding that a writer is his or her own editor—at least initially. Many persons can probably remember receiving writing assignments that they wrote under duress, either in class or at home, and then handing in what they presumed were finished copies. Then, unless they were both gifted writers and mind readers, many got their papers back from their teachers red-inked with uncomplimentary comments on their grammar, spelling, and organization (or lack thereof). Hopefully, most teachers today have rethought this unpleasant and unhelpful system and see themselves as writing mentors, coaches, and counselors.

In order to facilitate writing and move students from draft to publication, several procedures are essential. First, students need to understand the concept of a draft copy. A draft copy is an initial effort and implies that the writer has done little or no editing. On the other hand, it is not, as some teachers indicate, a "sloppy copy." A draft copy is a work in progress that temporarily frees the writer from worrying too much about the conventions of spelling, grammar, and format. It also may free the writer from worrying about appropriate or upgraded word choices, so that she or he can just get the essential ideas down. Draft writing also allows the writer, as Zinsser states, to "summon out of the brain some cluster of thoughts or memories" (1980, p. 57) that previously had not been anticipated. It is important to distinguish between a draft copy and a sloppy copy. Good draft writing results in a well-thought-out piece that is organized and ready for improvement. Figure 1.11 provides a sample set of basic guidelines for writing a draft copy that can be given to students at the beginning of the school year.

**Figure 1.10**   Resources for Writing

| • TAXONOMY • | |
|---|---|
| A | articles, advertisements, aunts |
| B | books |
| C | catalogs, colleges, commercials, citizens, cousins, custodians |
| D | documentaries |
| E | editorials |
| F | family members, friends, field trips, filmstrips, firefighters |
| G | grandparents, guest speakers |
| H | how-to manuals, health professionals |
| I | Internet |
| J | journals |
| K | |
| L | letters, libraries |
| M | movies, magazines |
| N | newspapers, neighbors, neighborhood stores |
| O | |
| P | parents, police officers |
| Q | |
| R | relatives |
| S | siblings, seniors, security guards, stores, street signs |
| T | television, teachers |
| U | uncles |
| V | visitors, videos |
| W | |
| X | |
| Y | yellow pages |
| Z | |

**Figure 1.11**    To the Student: Guidelines for Writing a Draft Copy

---

The draft copy is the first of several copies you will use in your writing. After you have written your draft copy, you may go on to revise your draft either by hand or by computer. You might have one or two more revisions before someone else edits it. Then you may be ready for a final or even published copy. The number of copies you write depends on the importance of the piece of writing to you personally, to getting a certain grade, or to being recognized as a good writer. To get started in this writing process, you should begin with the best possible draft you can write. Here are some guidelines to help you.

1. Mark your paper "Draft Copy" so that the reader knows you have a work in progress.

2. If you are writing by hand, be sure to skip lines on your paper. If you are writing with a computer, set the computer file for double line spacing.

3. Before beginning to write, prepare some "notes," such as a web or cluster, Taxonomy, Defining Format, Profile, Essay outline, Venn diagram, or whatever else you know or your teacher has shown you.

4. Review and keep in mind the guidelines for the assignment: its length, audience, purpose, and any elements you are asked to include.

5. If you are writing by hand, cross out your changes and avoid erasing. Erasing interrupts your thinking and keeps you from moving ahead. Remember, you are making a draft copy, so you don't have to worry too much about neatness.

6. Read your draft copy aloud to anyone willing to listen, keeping a pencil or pen in your hand to make changes.

7. Ask someone you know to read your paper aloud to you. After it is read, make any desired changes as soon as possible.

8. Listen to suggestions for improving your writing, and make the changes you agree with. You also might want to get a second opinion on some suggestions.

9. Above all, be patient with yourself and your writing. You will be rewarded with having written great pieces.

---

## GUIDELINES FOR REVISING AND EDITING

Everyone who has written knows that almost as much time must be devoted to the editing process as to the writing itself. Teachers who assign writing and collect their students' papers to "correct" them also know that they are in for a tiring and tedious job that rarely is appreciated by the students, except possibly for those who get high grades. In Chapter 14, we focus on how to teach students strategies to incorporate editing with writing and also how to help teachers lighten their own editing role while helping their students become better writers. A summary of these guidelines is in Figure 1.12 on the next page; the details are in Chapter 14.

**Figure 1.12**    To the Student: Guidelines for Revising and Editing

Ask yourself these questions when you are revising and editing your writing:

Did I keep to the topic?

Do I have an order or sequence that my reader can follow?

Have I given my reader details and information?

Have I used the written conventions of capitalization and punctuation?

Have I checked my spelling?

Have I checked my grammar for the voice I want to use (formal or informal)?

Use these improvers to revise and edit your writing:

Add words, phrases, and punctuation that you have missed the first time.

Delete or remove words, phases, and punctuation that are unnecessary or repetitious.

Substitute words that will make your writing more interesting or stronger.

Move or rearrange words, phrases, or sentences that will help your reader better understand your writing.

## WRITING AND THE COMPUTER

It is almost impossible to imagine any writer of the future not using a computer. Although the common writing implements—pens and pencils—still have a place, today's students will be, at least until the next monumental invention, computer-bound. Hopefully, all schools are providing computers and computer instruction, especially in word processing, graphics, and using the Internet.

As teachers begin their writing programs, it is useful for them, or the computer specialists, to introduce students to what is truly the writer's best friend—the word processor. Although teaching word processing is beyond the scope of this book, introducing some basic word processing skills to students using computers to compose will help them learn to use the computer with ease. Figure 1.13 lists many skills students should have in order to write using a computer. Students who know these computer functions will learn to accept writing as a process that moves from draft copy to publication. With mastery of word processing, students will be less likely to hand in draft copies filled with spelling, grammar, and other errors that require the markings of the teacher's dreaded red pen. And for the teacher, there is the glory (or at least the pleasure) of the reduction of eyestrain brought on by unreadable handwriting.

**Figure 1.13**    What You Need to Know for Writing on the Computer

| | |
|---|---|
| Setting margins | Using spelling and grammar checkers |
| Line spacing | Using the thesauruses |
| Paragraph formatting | Knowing how to highlight, cut, copy, and paste |
| Keyboarding capital and lowercase letters | Creating and saving files |
| Setting font styles and sizes | Printing documents |

# CHAPTER TWO

Strategies, Genres,
Topics, and Tools

**Words Are Free!**

Have Words,
Can Write

Writing Is Thinking

Write to a Martian

Every Word
Has a Story

Organize
Your Writing

Know Who You
Know and Know
Who You Are!

Think in Threes

Everybody Has
to Be Someplace

Let's Make
a Movie!

Words Inspire

Know Thyself

Writers Are Editors

A Goal for
Every Student

# Building Vocabulary With Taxonomies

## Words Are Free!

*The meaning of even a single word is rather more complex than one might imagine.*

~Editors of the
*American Heritage Dictionary*, 1980, p. viii

## THE GIFT OF WORDS— CREATING TAXONOMIES

Writers need words. What is most wonderful about words is that they are free and in the public domain. When students realize that words can be shared and received from others—that people both receive words and give words—they discover that accumulating words is much easier than they thought. This belief in the power of having words is the basis of the first strategy—building Taxonomies.

## THE POWER OF WORDS (AKA VOCABULARY)

Knowing a lot of words is a major benefit to becoming a good reader and writer. Yet we know that students come to school with vast differences in their word knowledge, and we know that difference is often the cause of what we now call the achievement gap (Alvermann, 2005). In a powerful article, "Scaffolding Vocabulary Learning," Judith A. Scott advocates a "call to action, a call for teachers to actively and passionately embrace a curriculum that promotes accelerated and generative word knowledge for students who *depend* (our italics) on schools and on teachers to teach them how to use words effectively" (2004, p. 275).

In the work and writings of Eric Cooper (2004), executive director of the National Urban Alliance, we read and hear the words "school dependent children"—poor or segregated children who have a deep need for teachers who can be instrumental in closing the educational gap between them and those more affluent and with access to schools of diversity. Part of this closing of the gap can occur in the teaching of vocabulary (Scott, 2004), a premise these authors heartily endorse. Regardless of the circumstances that students bring to school, teaching vocabulary is essential to effective education. Marzano's (2004) research confirms the negative influence of poverty on academic performance.

Before we move on, we need to consider why knowing words—lots of them— makes such a powerful difference in a person's ability to read increasingly difficult text and to write more cogently, creatively, powerfully, and interestingly. We list our own reasons in Figure 2.1 and you, undoubtedly, can add several of your own.

**Figure 2.1**     Why Do You Need to Know Lots of Words?

Here are some excellent reasons. You can also add your own reasons.

Add to your knowledge of a subject—Example: Knowing the word *addend* means you know something important about addition.

Provide you with another or alternative way to say or write an idea—Example: The elephant is big (large, enormous, gigantic).

Help you better understand a piece of text or reading—Example: The principal *exhorted* the students to study hard so they would reach the *pinnacle* of success.

Write more interestingly—Example: The dog went home (written in simple vocabulary). The *Labrador retriever bounded* home (upgraded vocabulary).

Be more specific—Example: Lots of people in the place were looking at different books (least specific). Many customers in the store were browsing for books on diverse subjects (more specific). Dozens of customers in Ben Franklin's Literary Emporium were browsing for academic and literary texts in geography, literature, mathematics, and science (most specific).

Have many "voices"—Example: I want to go soon (least urgent voice). I would like to leave within the hour (more urgent voice). I urgently need to depart by midnight (most urgent voice).

## ORGANIZING STUDENT VOCABULARY

In *Writing as Learning*, we focus on three specific strategies that will help your students learn how to build and use a powerful vocabulary. These strategies are Taxonomies, Defining Format, and Morphology and Etymology. When all three are integrated, practiced, and applied, your students will develop a "power system" for writing (and reading).

We begin with the building of *Taxonomies*, a term we use to refer to a list of words related to a specific topic or subject area. A person can build a Taxonomy of terms related to waterways, geometry, capital cities, animals, or any other category. Categorization of words is important for both retention and retrieval of vocabulary.

Furthermore, it enables students to see the relationships among words. A major purpose for building Taxonomies is to provide the writer (student) with the terms or words that she or he might need for writing about a certain topic. Taxonomies also provide each student with a personal thesaurus.

## The Building of the Personal Thesaurus

To make the Taxonomy manageable and organized, we set it up alphabetically. By using the alphabet as the placeholder for the words, the students have several major advantages. First, words can easily be found or retrieved as in any alphabetical system. A second, and very valuable, advantage of using the alphabet is that it motivates students to search for words beyond the ordinary or expected. Students often want to look up words in the dictionary that begin with the letters *Q*, *X*, and *Z* to complete their Taxonomies. While this completion is not the purpose for the Taxonomy, students nonetheless get the benefit of finding words such as *quiescent*, *xenophobic*, and *zoography* and then deciding if these words relate to their topic. In addition, an alphabetical list serves as a mnemonic device or a way to think of words specifically with that letter on that topic. For example, in creating a Taxonomy on rivers, the student might think of the Ganges River because of the letter *G*.

As the students build their Taxonomies across the curriculum, they are creating personal thesauruses that they can add to or refer to on a continuous basis as they acquire knowledge. Beginning in either second or third grade, students should use Notebooks (see Chapter 1) to keep track of the numerous Taxonomies that relate to their subject areas and growing interests. By entering the Taxonomies in the Notebook, the students have an ongoing retrieval system. Figure 2.2 illustrates examples of Taxonomies students might have in their Notebooks interspersed over time with the other strategies.

**Figure 2.2**    Examples of Taxonomies of an Intermediate Grade Student Over Several Months

| Date | Topic/Subject | Page |
|------|---------------|------|
| Sept. 14 | Types of Numbers—Mathematics | 8 |
| Sept. 26 | Rain Forests—Science | 14 |
| Oct. 8 | Explorers—Social Studies | 18 |
| Oct. 15 | Halloween—Holidays | 22 |
| Nov. 1 | Geometric Terms—Mathematics | 26 |
| Nov. 10 | The Pilgrims—Social Studies | 28 |
| Nov. 13 | Thanksgiving—Holidays | 30 |
| Dec. 3 | Healthy Foods—Health | 36 |
| Dec. 12 | Helen Keller—Reading | 40 |

In addition to the creation of the personal thesaurus, Taxonomies can be used for the following purposes:

- Advance organizing and assessment of prior knowledge
- Continuous note taking
- Advanced vocabulary development
- Development and assessment of new knowledge
- Starting to write

You will find the steps shown in Figure 2.3 useful in initially showing your students how to set up their Taxonomies in their Notebooks. As the students become proficient in using this strategy, you can vary the procedures. Throughout this book, there are many suggestions based on the purpose and need for the Taxonomy in conjunction with the other strategies. Another major asset of Taxonomy building is its natural use of cooperative or collaborative learning. Johnson and Johnson (1999) define five elements of cooperative learning, all of which emerge when students create Taxonomies as outlined in Figure 2.3:

1. Positive interdependence

2. Face-to-face interaction

3. Individual and group accountability

4. Interpersonal and small group skills

5. Group processing

In addition to the above benefits, cooperative and collaborative learning have been shown to result in significant achievement gains when compared to individual and competitive learning (Marzano, Pickering, & Pollock, 2001).

## ADVANCE ORGANIZING AND ASSESSMENT OF PRIOR KNOWLEDGE

E. D. Hirsch Jr. stated that "we use past knowledge to interpret [our] window of experience" (1987, p. 48). In his extensive discussion of the structure of background knowledge and its importance for developing new knowledge, he stresses the essentialness of *schemata,* or organizational formats to achieve meaningful learning. He points out that through schemata, we "store knowledge in retrievable form" and "organize knowledge in more and more efficient ways so that it can be applied rapidly and efficiently" (p. 56). He further states that one's personal background knowledge allows for understanding and communication through spoken and written language.

Marzano (2004, p. 1) adds that "the research literature supports one compelling fact: What students already know about the content is one of the strongest indicators of how well they will learn new information relative to the content." He devotes a substantial portion of his book, *Building Background Knowledge for Academic Achievement,* to the importance of direct vocabulary instruction, because research links vocabulary instruction to building background knowledge and then, in turn, to higher academic performance.

**Figure 2.3**     Setting Up Taxonomies in Your Notebook

In your Notebook, enter the topic, subject, and strategy, for example, "Animal Habitats," "Science," or "Taxonomy."

Enter the page number, which should be an even number on the left side of the page. All your page entries will start on even-numbered pages so that you will always have a double-page spread for your strategies and writing.

Turn to the pages where you will enter your Taxonomy, for example, pages 8 and 9. In the wide top margin of these two pages, write, "Taxonomy of Animal Habitats" (or whatever your topic is).

On the even-numbered page, write the letters *A* to *M* on the left of the red margin line, skipping a line for each letter. You may need to double up letters *J* and *K* (as an example) so you can fit 13 letters on the page. On the odd-numbered page, write the letters *N* to *W*, skipping lines and ending with *X, Y,* and *Z* together. You are now ready to build your Taxonomy.

First, you will work *solo,* by yourself. Think of a word that belongs with your topic. For Animal Habitats, a word might be "nest." Write "nest" next to the letter it begins with. Work for about five minutes, writing as many words as you can think of that fit in your category or Taxonomy. You may write more than one word for each letter. Stop when your teacher tells you to stop.

Now pair up with a partner. You will *collaborate* by sharing your words and adding to your own Taxonomy. For example, if you have written "river" and your partner doesn't have "river," tell your partner, who then adds "river" to her or his Taxonomy. Then your partner will share her or his words, and you add those to your Taxonomy. Thank your partner for sharing words with you. Stop when your teacher tells you to stop.

Your class is now ready to *cross-pollinate.* Your teacher will have prepared a master Taxonomy of the topic and will ask you to contribute a term on the topic to the master Taxonomy. The teacher might say, "Who can contribute a term on the topic of _____ to the Taxonomy. Raise your hand, and if called on, say, "I would like to contribute the term _____."

Add all the terms from the master Taxonomy to your Taxonomy. Then, as you learn more about the topic, you can keep adding more words. You will soon have your own personal thesaurus on all the topics you are studying and learning about.

Remember that Words Are Free!

Teachers are certainly aware of the importance of background knowledge, yet they may not always have efficient means for assessing what their students know about a given topic before they introduce the topic. One way to assess background or prior knowledge might be to give a pretest, but this can be cumbersome and time consuming, especially for young students. The Taxonomy, as a preassessment tool, can serve effectively as the advance organizer that provides a window for glimpsing what students individually and collectively already know about what you want them to know (Robinson, 1993; also see Chapter 4).

Figure 2.4 (on the next page) shows the collected prior knowledge on deserts of a fourth grade class at the onset of the unit, and Figure 2.5 shows the addition of new terms collected as the students read and discussed this topic. You can initially put the words of the topic on a master Taxonomy and then keep adding words as the students learn more. We also suggest that students enter the words in their Notebooks and keep the Taxonomy growing.

**Figure 2.4** Deserts

| | TAXONOMY |
|---|---|
| A | |
| B | |
| C | camel, cactus |
| D | dry |
| E | |
| F | |
| G | |
| H | hot |
| I | |
| J | |
| K | |
| L | little rain |
| M | |
| N | |
| O | oasis |
| P | |
| Q | |
| R | |
| S | sand |
| T | |
| U | |
| V | |
| W | |
| X | |
| Y | |
| Z | |

**Figure 2.5** Deserts Expanded

| | TAXONOMY |
|---|---|
| A | arid, Arabia, Africa, Asia |
| B | Bactrian camel, Bedouins |
| C | camel, cactus, California desert, cool nights |
| D | dry, dromedary |
| E | Ethiopia, Egypt |
| F | |
| G | Gobi |
| H | hot days |
| I | Israel |
| J | |
| K | Kalahari |
| L | little rain |
| M | Mojave |
| N | Negev, nomads |
| O | oasis |
| P | Painted Desert, palm trees |
| Q | |
| R | |
| S | sand, Sahara, Sinai, sparse |
| T | tents, treeless |
| U | |
| V | |
| W | watering holes, wadi |
| X | xeriscapes |
| Y | Yemen |
| Z | |

## Continuous Note taking

As students study a topic from their textbook, research materials, or discussion, they use their individual Taxonomies for note taking and for adding new terms that reflect their growing knowledge. The value of note taking has never been in doubt. Marzano, Pickering, and Pollock (2001) substantiate its value with three specific guidelines for students (p. 44):

1. Notes should be considered a work in progress.

2. Notes should be used as study guides for tests.

3. The more notes that are taken, the better.

By the end of the unit, the students have a Taxonomy that represents what they have learned or should know. The Taxonomy is now available for continuous amending, can be used for review, and can serve as the basis for moving into other writing strategies.

Upon the completion of the unit on deserts, there might be a class Taxonomy that looks like the one shown in Figure 2.5. Students may have slightly different Taxonomies resulting from individual choices.

## Vocabulary Development

As the students build their Taxonomies in different subject areas, they learn and define new terms. As students initially learn a word, they may, at first, have only a basic definition. By having their words on the Taxonomy, they have both the starting point for getting new knowledge and an indication of what they need to know about the topic. Once students become accustomed to Taxonomy building, they will have a complete vocabulary of all the topics and units they have studied in the course of a school year, plus lists of topics that personally interest them.

Taxonomies also can be used to increase students' vocabularies beyond the usual ways, such as teaching words in a prereading lesson or having students read more stories or books. One vocabulary-building strategy related to retaining and using high-level words is to have students learn selected words alphabetically. If a student could learn one new word a week, starting with an *A* word and ending with a *Z* word at the end of 26 weeks, the student obviously would know 26 new words. Then the cycle could start again and repeat itself—52 words, then 78 words, and so forth. Twenty-six words may not seem like much, but each word in this Taxonomy has related words. In Chapter 6, we show how learning one word (e.g., *progress*) leads to knowing many derivative words (e.g., *progressive, progressively, progression*), and this is followed by learning related words (e.g., *digress, egress, regress, transgress*).

One group of innovative teachers in a low-income school used this strategy by compiling a Taxonomy of Glorious Words from A to Z that they felt their students were not likely to know. They taught one word a week intensively—meaning consistently and repetitively in a variety of contexts and with the full morphology. For example, if the targeted word were *accurate,* the teacher would remind the students to do their work *accurately* and to check their work for *accurateness.* Furthermore, the "word of the week" was the word for the whole school, to be used in every classroom, announced by the principal over the public address system, and posted on the Taxonomy of Glorious Words poster in the entrance hallway or other visible area. Students were encouraged to use this word in their speech and their writing until it became a natural part of their language. By integrating Taxonomies with Morphology and Etymology, your students will indeed have a glorious vocabulary. Figure 2.6

**Figure 2.6**   Glorious Words

| • TAXONOMY • | |
| --- | --- |
| A | automatic, accurate, achieve |
| B | boisterous, belligerent, bombard |
| C | compliment, compromise, conscientious |
| D | defy, depart, diligent |
| E | emulate, examine, elegant |
| F | function, fraternize, formal |
| G | generate, govern, gravitate |
| H | habitat, harmony, hilarious |
| I | initiate, irritate, infinite |
| J | jovial, judge, jealous |
| K | knowledge, kindle, knead |
| L | lament, lenient, liquid |
| M | mature, metamorphosis, miniature |
| N | narrate, nurture, negotiate |
| O | object, operate, obstacle |
| P | prohibit, proceed, promote |
| Q | quarrel, quote, quiver |
| R | radiate, reconcile, redundant |
| S | sensitize, satisfy, superfluous |
| T | technique, terminate, tolerate |
| U | unite, unique, urgent |
| V | visualize, verify, verbatim |
| W | wily, warrior, wilderness |
| X | xenophobia, xeriscape, xanthous |
| Y | youth, yield, yearn |
| Z | zealous, zoology, zest |

shows the Taxonomy of Glorious Words selected by a committee of teachers. Of course, you can create your own Taxonomy too.

# DEVELOPMENT AND ASSESSMENT OF NEW KNOWLEDGE

As students are entering terms (or names) on their Taxonomies, they often are dealing with new information. They need to learn these terms' meanings and how they fit them into the schema of the topic. This learning, of course, will occur through the usual methods of practice, study, and memory. However, since creating Taxonomies requires continuous active student participation, cooperative involvement and discussion, and finally writing (as discussed in subsequent chapters), student learning is enhanced and more thoroughly developed.

When a lesson or topic is completed, the terms on the Taxonomy can be used for evaluation and review. For example, students can create postlesson Taxonomies by preparing a blank Taxonomy sheet and listing information about the topic. The quantity and relevancy of these terms are indicators of student learning and further serve as the basis for developing test-taking and study skills. Teachers can ask the students to put a checkmark next to those terms they are sure they know and a question mark next to those terms they need to study. Also, you can review the Taxonomy with the students to identify what terms are significant or essential and what terms are inconsequential or trivial. Students also can use the Taxonomies to plan or create a test that they think will be a fair assessment of what they have learned. You can then use this student-generated test as a study tool or adapt it as an actual evaluation.

Through the categorization system of Taxonomies, the students are involved in continuous development and assessment of new knowledge, bringing about what Hirsch points out is "active and constructive rather than passive and reconstructive" (1987, p. 55).

Figures 2.7–2.11 show several examples of Taxonomies representative of different grade levels and for different purposes. Incorporate, adapt, or innovate depending on your students' needs and curriculum. And as we said before, the glory of Taxonomies is that Words Are Free!

**Figure 2.7**    Roster of Names

| • TAXONOMY • | |
|---|---|
| A | Amanda |
| B | Bettina, Bacti |
| C | Christina, Carlos, Charlene |
| E | Ebony |
| F | |
| G | Germaine |
| H | |
| I | Ismelda, Ivan |
| J | Juan, Julissa, Jiro, Jose, James |
| K | Knokeia, Karl |
| L | Latoya |
| M | Megan |
| N | Naaz, Nemo |
| O | Omar |
| P | Pepi |
| Q | |
| R | Raoul |
| S | Sam, Shavone |
| T | Tabitha, Timothy, Tom |
| U | |
| V | Viktor |
| W | Willie, Willy |
| X | |
| Y | Yuri |
| Z | Zieba, Zena |

## Taxonomy Especially for Kindergarten and First Grade

On the very first day, or by the first week of school, set up a large chart with the alphabet written vertically. Head it "Roster of Names." Tell the students that this list (which you call a Taxonomy) is very important because it tells "who lives in this class." To develop the roster, ask each student to say her or his name using this form: "My name is Ebony and it begins with the letter E." Then write the student's name on the roster of names.

You can then use the roster to introduce initial letter sounds, variations in spelling, alphabetical order, and information that can be graphed. By asking students questions such as the following, they can obtain varied information from a simple roster.

- How many students are in this class?
- Which letter has the most names?
- Which letters have no names?
- Which names sound the same but are spelled differently?
- Who can read a name that begins with the letter ___?

## Building a Personal Identity Taxonomy

Personal Identity Taxonomies help prepare students for both autobiographical and biographical writing and will be referred to again in Chapter 8. However, you might want to introduce this Taxonomy early in the school year as a way of getting acquainted and personalizing this strategy.

A Personal Identity Taxonomy contains the words that answer the question, "Who am I?" To have the students create their Taxonomies systematically for use in writing, divide this Taxonomy into categories, such as family membership, geographic membership, and personal identity.

The first category is family membership. Students can identify themselves by words that identify family relationships, such as *daughter* or *son*, *sister* or *brother*, *niece* or *nephew*, *granddaughter* or *grandson*, *goddaughter* or *godson*, and *cousin*. Ask your students to start with, "I am a . . . ," and choose a family member designation such as *daughter, son, sister, cousin, grandson*, or something comparable. After the students have listed all their family membership names, add geographic information. A student will have many geographic identities; she or he might be a New Yorker, an American, a North American, and an Earthling. If the student cannot form an identity term with his or her state (e.g., Connecticut), she or he can complete the statement as "I am a Connecticut resident."

Students discuss these geographic terms, and each student adds to her or his list. When students come from countries other than the United States, encourage them to list their first country identity as well; for example, "I am a

**Figure 2.8**  Personal Identity of Vanessa

| | • TAXONOMY • |
|---|---|
| | I am a (an) |
| A | American |
| B | bicyclist |
| C | cousin, classmate |
| D | daughter |
| E | Earthling |
| F | friend |
| G | granddaughter, gymnast |
| H | helper |
| I | individual |
| J | jacks player |
| K | kid |
| L | lemonade lover |
| M | math expert |
| N | niece |
| O | |
| P | popcorn eater, pet owner |
| Q | |
| R | runner, reader |
| S | sister, student |
| T | Tacoma resident |
| U | |
| V | |
| W | Washingtonian, writer |
| X | |
| Y | youth |
| Z | zoo visitor |

Dominican," "a Russian," or "a Pakistani." These identities can serve as topics for the strategy Where in the World (Chapter 10) or as part of a multicultural program or study.

Another category is personal interests; for example, a student might be a ball player, dancer, singer, in-line skater, reader, or movie goer. Continue to guide your students using the starter, "I am a . . . ," and then adding their identity terms relating to personal interests or other categories. Figure 2.8 shows an example of a student's personal identity Taxonomy.

## Two Related Taxonomies

Figures 2.9 and 2.10 illustrate two different Taxonomies made by fourth grade students embarking on a study of animals of the woods and jungles. The teacher had the students create Taxonomies on animals of the woodlands and jungle and on animal habitats to get an in-depth vocabulary of the subject. Notice how Figure 2.10, Animal Habitats, relates to Where in the World (Chapter 10). Through this categorization of related topics, the students are involved in continuous development and

**Figure 2.9**    Animals of the Woodlands and Jungle

• TAXONOMY •

| | |
|---|---|
| A | apes, antelopes |
| B | bears, beavers, baboons |
| C | cheetahs. chimpanzees, chipmunks |
| D | deer |
| E | elks, eagles |
| F | foxes, field mice |
| G | giraffes, gorillas |
| H | hyenas, hippopotamuses, hares |
| I | iguanas |
| J | jaguars |
| K | koala bears |
| L | lions, leopards |
| M | monkeys, moles |
| N | newts |
| O | ocelots, opossums, orangutans |
| P | porcupines, panthers, parrots, pandas |
| Q | |
| R | rabbits, raccoons |
| S | squirrels, skunks, snakes |
| T | tigers |
| U | |
| V | |
| W | woodchucks |
| X | |
| Y | |
| Z | zebras |

**Figure 2.10**    Animal Habitats

• TAXONOMY •

| | |
|---|---|
| A | aerie |
| B | burrow |
| C | cave |
| D | den |
| E | |
| F | forest |
| G | grass |
| H | hole, hill, hive |
| I | |
| J | jungle |
| K | |
| L | lake |
| M | mountain |
| N | nest |
| O | ocean |
| P | pond |
| R | ravine |
| S | swamp, stream, sand |
| T | tree |
| U | |
| V | valley |
| W | woods |
| X | |
| Y | |
| Z | |

assessment of new knowledge, bringing about what Costa and Kallick call "thinking interdependently" (2000, p. 13).

## Taxonomies in the Upper Grades Through High School

While Taxonomies are valuable in all grades, they are essential in the upper grades, as they become the word carriers for the topic. In the upper grades, therefore, students should maintain Taxonomies across the curriculum, from mathematics through music, and for every topic that requires in-depth factual knowledge. Figures 2.11–2.14 are four Taxonomies that are representative of subject area information in middle and high schools. These Taxonomies are not complete, but they show the possibilities for keeping track of information.

**Figure 2.11** Who's Who in Astronomy, Flight, and Space?

• TAXONOMY •

| A | Aristotle, Aldrin, Armstrong |
| B | Brahe, Borman, Braun (Von), Bluford |
| C | Copernicus, Cochran, Carpenter, Chaffee |
| D | |
| E | Eratosthenes, Euclid, Earhart |
| F | |
| G | Galileo, Goddard, Gargarin, Glenn, Grissom |
| H | Hypatia, Halley, Herschel, Hubble, Hughes |
| I | |
| J | |
| K | Kepler |
| L | Lindbergh |
| M | Mitchell, McAuliffe |
| N | Newton |
| O | |
| P | Ptolemy, Penzias |
| Q | |
| R | Ride, Resnick |
| S | Shapley, Schirra, Shepard, Scott, Sikorsky |
| T | Tereshkova-Nicolayeva |
| U | |
| V | |
| W | Wright (Wilbur, Orville), Wilson, White |

**Figure 2.12** Terms for Polygons and Polyhedrons

• TAXONOMY •

| A | angle |
| B | bilateral |
| C | cube, cylinder |
| D | decagon, dodecahedron |
| E | |
| F | |
| G | geodesic dome |
| H | hexagon, hexahedron, hexagram, heptagon |
| I | |
| J | |
| L | |
| L | |
| M | |
| N | nonagon |
| O | octagon, octahedron |
| P | plane, pentagon, pentangle, pentahedron, pentagram, parallelogram, prism, pyramid |
| Q | quadrangle, quadrilateral |
| R | rectangle, rhombus |
| S | sphere |
| T | triangle, trapezoid, trihedral, tetragon, tetrahedron |
| U | unilateral |

**Figure 2.13**  Geographers' Battlefields

| | | |
|---|---|---|
| • | **TAXONOMY** | • |
| A | Acre, Austerlitz, Alamo |
| B | Borodino, Bunker Hill, Bikini Atoll |
| C | Chateau-Thierry |
| D | Dunkirk, Dien Bien Phu |
| E | El Alamein |
| F | Fort Sumter |
| G | Gettysburg, Gallipoli, Guadalcanal |
| H | Hastings |
| I | Iwo Jima |
| J | |
| K | |
| L | Little Big Horn, Lexington |
| M | Marne, Marathon |
| N | Normandy |
| O | |
| P | Port Arthur, Pearl Harbor |
| Q | |
| R | |
| S | Salamis, Saratoga, Somme, Stalingrad, Seoul, Saigon, Sarajevo |
| T | Thermopylae, Trafalgar, Tannenberg |
| U | |
| V | Verdun |
| W | Waterloo |
| X | |
| Y | Yorktown, Ypres |
| Z | |

**Figure 2.14**  Hablo Español

| | | |
|---|---|---|
| • | **TAXONOMY** | • |
| A | arroz, adobe, amigo |
| B | burrito |
| C | caballero |
| D | dinero |
| E | enchilada |
| F | fiesta |
| G | guacho, gracias, gusto |
| H | hacienda, hermano, hermana |
| I | infante |
| J | junta |
| K | kilogramo, kilometro |
| L | libertad, lagrima, leutes |
| M | muchacho, muchacha, mañana, mesa, mucho, momento, madre |
| N | niño, niña |
| O | oficina |
| P | patio, pollo, padres, pescado |
| Q | queso |
| R | ranchero, redondo |
| S | señorita, sol, sueño |
| T | taco, tortilla, tío, tía, tapas |
| U | ultimo |
| V | vaquero |
| W | |
| X | xenofobia |
| Y | yanqui, yo |
| Z | zapato |

# INTERNET LINKS

http://iteslj.org/links/ESL/Vocabulary/Lists/

http://dmoz.org/Reference/Dictionaries/Vocabulary_Lists/

http://www.tampareads.com/vocabulary/4thgrade/index4.htm

http://www.esl-lab.com/vocab/index.htm

http://school.discovery.com/puzzlemaker/wordlists/

# CHAPTER THREE

# Composing With Keywords

## Have Words, Can Write

Strategies, Genres,
Topics, and Tools

Words Are Free!

**Have Words,
Can Write**

Writing Is Thinking

Write to a Martian

Every Word
Has a Story

Organize
Your Writing

Know Who You
Know and Know
Who You Are!

Think in Threes

Everybody Has
to Be Someplace

Let's Make
a Movie!

Words Inspire

Know Thyself

Writers Are Editors

A Goal for
Every Student

*By words the mind is excited and the spirit elated.*

--Aristophanes

## HAVE WORDS, CAN WRITE

Teachers and researchers have long noticed and known that words define knowledge (Scott, 2004; Stahl & Fairbanks, 1986). As students build vocabulary, they know more or understand more about the topic or concept. Virtually all school testing involves word knowledge, and students with extensive vocabularies have the advantage of being better readers and *writers*. However, in order for vocabulary knowledge to impact on writing, we again emphasize the importance of *teaching* students how to use this [word] knowledge to compose.

## WHAT IS COMPOSING WITH KEYWORDS?

In the strategy Composing With Keywords, students use the words from their Taxonomies, reading material, and content areas to compose sentences, paragraphs, and full-length pieces in a variety of ways. It is a strategy that provides students with the practice they need before they can effectively write lengthy pieces and create writings in complex genres. Composing With Keywords focuses on providing students with the skills to

- Develop a variety of sentences and paragraphs.
- Write factual and fictional pieces.
- Write creative pieces on word play and humor.
- Respond to new learning.
- Expand vocabulary knowledge.

In a study by Bereiter and Scardamalia (1985), students were asked to think of keywords they might use in an essay. Then, the students wrote an essay in which they used those words. Not surprisingly, the students had more to say and wrote more cohesively than similar-age students who were merely given a topic without this instruction. The findings in this study have been upheld in more recent studies, notably in the research of Langer (2000), who cites the features of classroom instruction that correlate with improved test performance. Composing With Keywords focuses on three of these features:

1. Making connections across instruction, curriculum, and life

2. Using creative thinking

3. Working collaboratively

Many students, on their own, have discovered the strategy of using words to compose better sentences, most noticeably when teachers have (unwisely) asked them to write one sentence for *each* spelling word. These students then (wisely) ask if they can use *more than one* spelling word in their sentences. What they have discovered is that they are not short-circuiting the assignment, but are able to write more interesting and substantive sentences. However, words on spelling lists generally are not grouped around a topic but rather around some phonemic or syllabic element, and they are not particularly useful for writing essays or stories.

Composing With Keywords is an across-the-curriculum strategy applicable in every grade. It can be used by students in a social studies class who have compiled a Taxonomy of major rivers of the world. With this topic, you might ask the students to select three or four of the rivers in Europe and write a statement about each one, telling its location, source, and mouth. In another class, the students may have compiled a Taxonomy on Halloween words. Here, the writing assignment might be to write Halloween sentences or a story using as many words as possible or as needed. From a Taxonomy of verbs to use for "said," students can write a story about two or three characters who never "say" anything: They only *whisper, shout, laugh, murmur, bellow,* or *giggle.*

Composing With Keywords provides students with opportunities to actually write and gain practice as writers without worrying about the more difficult aspects of topic selection or initially attending to the conventions of style and form. Students can share their writings in small groups and have them posted on bulletin board displays, thereby gaining a concept of themselves as writers with something worth saying and worth sharing.

## INTRODUCING COMPOSING WITH KEYWORDS

Teachers can introduce Composing With Keywords by the middle of first grade when students are reading stories of 30 to 50 words, and it should be continued throughout the upper grades and subject areas. Figure 3.1 on the next page illustrates one way of getting your students started on this strategy, using a previously developed Taxonomy. Be sure the students enter this strategy in their Notebook and write the name of the topic and *Composing With Keywords.* Always have the students use a *double-page spread* (two pages facing each other with the even

**Figure 3.1**     Composing With Keywords by Using Words From a Taxonomy

---

### Writing, Sharing, and Nominating

Select three words from your Taxonomy on _____. Write these words on the left-hand page of your Notebook.

Compose one sentence that tells something about the topic in which you use all three words. You may change the form of the words (e.g., verb form, singular to plural, etc.) and you may use the words in any order you wish. Remember to start your sentence with a capital letter and end with punctuation.

After you have composed your sentence, meet with a partner or small group and take turns reading your sentences. Nominate one member of your group to read her or his sentence aloud to the class. Each time you practice Composing With Keywords, different students will be nominated.

---

number on the left-hand page and the odd-number on the right-hand page).

We illustrate the power of combining a Taxonomy with Composing With Keywords in Figures 3.2 and 3.3. Figure 3.2 is a Taxonomy developed in a primary grade class based on the story *Five Little Monkeys* (Christelow, 1998). After the students had written and reviewed these words, the teacher asked them to create their own sentences following the procedures outlined in Figure 3.1.

You will notice that by combining the two strategies, the students have the words they need for retelling or summarizing. With the task of composing only one sentence, they can also focus on simple punctuation—a capital letter and a period. By checking the master Taxonomy that you have created, the students can also check their spelling for the keywords. From this activity, they are beginning the process of editing.

Use Composing With Keywords by combining this strategy with a listening activity and a Taxonomy as illustrated in Figure 3.4. Remember to use the Notebook.

After you have introduced the above activity, you can follow the procedures in Figure 3.3, making the following suggestions: Using three words from the story, compose a sentence that you think is funny, imaginative, or exciting. Write a sentence that you believe no on else in the class might think of.

**Figure 3.2**     Words from *Five Little Monkeys*

| • TAXONOMY • | |
|---|---|
| A | all |
| B | bedtime, bath, bed |
| C | |
| D | doctor |
| E | |
| F | four, five, fell |
| G | go |
| H | head |
| I | in |
| J | jumping |
| K | |
| L | little |
| M | Mama |
| N | never |
| O | one |
| P | pajamas |
| Q | |
| R | |
| S | said |
| T | two, three |
| U | |
| V | |
| W | |
| X | |
| Y | you |
| Z | |

**Figure 3.3**    Creative Sentences From the Words in *Five Little Monkeys*

---

The doctor told Mama not to let the monkey jump on the bed.

One little monkey broke his head because he was jumping too high.

Before bedtime the monkeys took a bath and then put on pajamas.

---

**Figure 3.4**    Writing Keywords While Listening to a Story

---

Teacher:

I am going to read you the same story twice. The first time, I will read the whole story while you just listen. (Read the story as you usually do. Then follow these steps for the second reading, which can be a day or two later.)

Now I am going to read you _____, which you heard the other day. This time set up a double-page spread for building a Taxonomy in your Notebook. In the meantime, I will write the name of the story, which you should put in the top margin of your Notebook.

When you are ready, I will read you the story, but you will have to listen very carefully. I will emphasize certain words by saying them louder. These are the keywords.

When you hear the emphasized word, write it on your Taxonomy, next to the letter with which the word begins.

Spell the words as best you can, and you can fix them later by looking at the master Taxonomy that I will post in the classroom.

---

# PROCEDURE FOR SHARING SENTENCES

Reading their writing aloud is essential for students. First, by reading their work aloud, they have a real audience. In addition, reading aloud to fellow students often brings approval and (if encouraged) positive commentary. When reading aloud, the writer often improves the writing by saying or noting changes that will make the sentence better. Finally, reading aloud develops reading fluency. Figure 3.5 shows a simple way for students to read aloud the sentences they have composed.

**Figure 3.5**    Reading Your Sentence

---

First, say to your audience, "Here are my words: _____, _____, _____."

Then say, "This is my sentence: _____."

---

In a second-grade class, the teacher guided the students in creating a Taxonomy of tasks from which they wrote their own stories. First, the teacher asked the students to orally state what they do at home to help. A student responded, "I feed my dog." The teacher then focused on the word *feed* and wrote it on the Taxonomy. From each sentence a student said, the teacher extracted the verb. She then asked the students to think about what tasks and chores other family members do (e.g., my mother drives me to school) and again focused on the verbs. Then the teacher gave the following instructions: Write a story about tasks or chores that you and your family do. Use as many of the words from the Taxonomy as you want to help you write the story. You can add your own words to this list. You can make your stories true or make believe.

Figure 3.6 shows a Taxonomy of tasks that is a composite of words generated by the students.

The teacher in this class then compiled a book of the students' stories, and the students titled it *Tasks I Do at Home.* Here are representative stories from the second grade students:

First I go to the store and buy cat food.

I feed the cat and then clean the litter box.

I then help my mother cook dinner.

I like to go shopping at the mall. We drive to the mall from my house.

Sometimes I buy a Nintendo game. When I get home, I sweep the steps.

I walk my dog and take out the garbage before I go to school.

I also wash my daddy's car and he gives me a dollar.

Sometimes my dad lets me mow the grass.

**Figure 3.6**   Tasks

| • TAXONOMY • | |
| --- | --- |
| A | ask |
| B | bring, bake, buy |
| C | cut, cook, clean, care |
| D | drive, dust |
| E | eat |
| F | find, feed |
| G | give, get, go |
| H | help, hold |
| I | |
| J | |
| K | know, keep |
| L | leave, listen, let |
| M | make, mix, mow |
| N | |
| O | open |
| P | paint, plant, play |
| Q | |
| R | read, ride |
| S | sweep, shop |
| T | take |
| U | use |
| V | |
| W | water, wait, walk |
| X | |
| Y | |
| Z | |

## COMPOSING WITH KEYWORDS FOR BOTH FACTUAL AND FICTIONAL WRITING

In the primary grades, teachers can have students create Taxonomies of words from nursery rhymes and fairy tales. For example, one Taxonomy could contain the names of characters—Boy Blue, Bo-Peep, Goldilocks, Humpty Dumpty, and so forth. From this Taxonomy, students have the names of different characters for sentence or story writing. A second Taxonomy could contain places mentioned in the rhymes or fairy tales—corner, hill, moon, wall, and so forth. The third Taxonomy would be of objects and items mentioned—crown, curds and whey, fiddle, kettle, tea, hood. Students would then be asked to select one character, one place, and one object or item and compose sentences using their three words.

Using nursery rhymes and fairy tales with Taxonomies and Composing With Keywords creates a naturally integrated curriculum of reading and writing and can be used throughout the primary grades and even with older students for an advanced study of the nursery rhyme and fairy tale genre. Figures 3.7–3.10 are examples of Taxonomies and student writing using the words from these Taxonomies. The sentences that the students write can further serve as story starters for tales of imagination and creativity.

Notice that the boldfaced words in the following writing sample come from each of these three Taxonomies related to the nursery rhymes:

**Little Bo-Peep** took her **fiddle** and climbed up the **hill.**

I asked **Humpty Dumpty** to get off the **wall** and make me some **tea.**

**Little Boy Blue** sat in the **corner** with a **crown** on his head.

This activity that combines rhymes, reading, vocabulary building, and writing can lead to projects that involve illustrating sentences, making dioramas, and creating books with new titles such as *Mixed-Up Rhymes and Fairy Tales* or *Hey Diddle, Diddle, Bo-Peep,*

**Figure 3.7**   Nursery Rhyme and Fairy Tale Characters

### • TAXONOMY •

| | |
|---|---|
| A | |
| B | Beauty, Beast, Boy Blue, Bo-Peep |
| C | Cinderella |
| D | Dick Whittington |
| E | |
| F | Frog Prince |
| G | Goldilocks, Gingerbread Boy, Gretel |
| H | Humpty Dumpty, Hansel |
| I | |
| J | Jack Sprat, Jack (Nimble), Jack Horner, Jack and Jill |
| K | King Cole, Knave of Hearts |
| L | |
| M | Mother Goose, Mary (Quite Contrary), Miss Muffet |
| N | |
| O | |
| P | Peter Pumpkin Eater, Polly |
| Q | Queen of Hearts |
| R | Rapunzel |
| S | Snow White, Sleeping Beauty, Suki |
| T | Tom Thumb |
| U | |
| V | |
| W | Wee Willie Winkie |

**Figure 3.8**   Places in Nursery Rhymes and Fairy Tales

### • TAXONOMY •

| | |
|---|---|
| A | |
| B | barn |
| C | corn, castle, cottage, corner, castle |
| D | |
| E | |
| F | fireplace |
| G | gingerbread house, garden |
| H | hill |
| I | |
| J | |
| K | |
| L | lane |
| M | meadow, moon |
| N | |
| O | |
| P | pumpkin shell |
| S | |
| T | town, treetop, tower |
| U | |
| V | |
| W | wall, woods |
| X | |
| Y | |
| Z | |

*and the Fiddle.* By combining the strategies of Taxonomies and Composing With Keywords in this activity, the focus is placed on all of the following:

- Character names
- Settings
- Names of objects and items
- Innovative sentence composing
- Publication and presentation formats

## COMPOSING WITH KEYWORDS AS A RESPONSE TO NEW LEARNING

By consistently combining Taxonomies and Composing With Keywords, students can move on to becoming independent writers, especially since they will also be adding new strategies as they continue to develop their writing (see subsequent chapters). From each Taxonomy, they can compose sentences, stories, or summaries that relate to the topics in their curriculum. An extra benefit of this writing is that it provides an opportunity for the students to more easily revise their initial pieces (drafts) as they add more words to the Taxonomies. Figure 3.10 is an example of the first draft of a sixth grade student's summary of Robin Hood, followed by a more detailed piece that included added keywords gathered from the original story.

**Figure 3.9**    Objects in Nursery Rhymes and Fairy Tales

| • TAXONOMY • | |
|---|---|
| A | apple |
| B | bread crumbs, bread, bowl, basket |
| C | crown, candlestick, cradle, curds, clothes |
| D | dish |
| E | |
| F | fiddle |
| G | glass slipper, gown, goodies |
| H | honey, parlor |
| I | |
| J | |
| K | kettle |
| J | |
| M | money |
| N | |
| O | |
| P | pebbles, pie, plum |
| Q | |
| R | rye |
| S | spoon, sixpence |
| T | tarts, tea, tuffet |
| U | |
| V | |
| W | wool, water, whey |
| X | |
| Y | |
| Z | |

## COMPOSING WITH KEYWORDS IN THE CONTENT AREAS

Numerous researchers have written about the value of summarizing as a key to learning, remembering, and re-creating (Marzano et al., 2001; Robinson, 1993; Strong, Silver, & Perini, 2001). Summarizing requires the student to ask, "What information is important here?" and "How can I paraphrase this information?" (Robinson, p. 81). Yet, teaching students how to respond to these two important questions can be challenging. However, by using Composing With Keywords, students have a starting point for selecting key elements. From these key elements they compose in their own syntax and are not dependent on paraphrasing, which for many students is very close to copying.

When students begin by selecting and then composing with content-specific vocabulary, they, in effect, summarize their knowledge. They can use their Taxonomies of mathematical terms to create factual writing that states and reinforces their mathematical understanding. When studying verbs, students can compile Taxonomies of different types of verbs (see Chapter 6) and then compose using these verbs to achieve deep meaning as well as to write with clarity and creativity.

Here are five examples that represent student writing in content areas developed by Composing With Keywords (Figures 3.11–3.15). The bolded words were on the students' Taxonomies.

**Figure 3.10**    First and Second Drafts

---

**First Draft**

Robin Hood was an outlaw who lived with his Merry Men in Sherwood Forest. Some of his Merry Men were Alan-a-Dale, Will Scarlet, and Little John. Maid Marian was his girlfriend. All of Robin Hood's men were good with a bow and arrow, but Robin Hood was the best archer of all.

**Second Expanded Draft**

When Robin Hood was nineteen years old, the king's forester challenged him to an archery match to see who could shoot a deer from a hundred yards. Robin Hood won and made the forester very angry. From that time on, King John declared that Robin Hood was an outlaw and told the Sheriff of Nottingham to find and hang Robin Hood. The king said that challenging anyone who worked for him was an act of treason and punishment was death. But Robin Hood and his men were clever and tricky and always managed to outwit the Sheriff and King John.

---

**Figure 3.11**    My Summary Statement on Fractions

---

Fractions are special kinds of numbers. They have a numerator and denominator and are not whole numbers. They are also different from integers because an integer can only be one, two, three, and so forth. Sometimes a fraction is actually an improper fraction when the numerator is larger than the denominator. If you want to add fractions, you must be sure that they have common denominators. To do this, you need to find the factors for each fraction you are adding.

—Sixth Grade Student

---

**Figure 3.12**    Composing With Verbs of Movement

---

Each animal has its own way of moving. A horse can trot, canter, or gallop. A cat might run, scoot, or climb. Birds hop, fly, glide, and soar. Elephants usually lumber, but when they are trained to be in the circus, they dance, prance, and twirl. Monkeys lope and swing, ducks waddle and swim, and jaguars speed and pounce. Humans can move in almost as many ways as the animals, but they are not always as fast or as graceful as the animals.

—Fifth Grade Student

---

**Figure 3.13**    Understanding and Accepting Differences

---

Even though people may look and act differently, they also are alike in many ways. They may have different religions, speak different languages, and have different skin colors, but they do many of the same things. They live in family groups, love their children, and have spiritual beliefs. By looking at how we are the same instead of how we are different, we learn to accept and respect each other.

—Seventh Grade Student

**Figure 3.14**    Writing a Travelogue With Earth Science Words

Take a trip in a small, low-flying airplane and you will see a landscape of forms and shapes that are either below sea level or soar high into the atmosphere. If you are flying over New Mexico, you will see the flat-topped mesas above the dry arroyos and the stretches of desert. Then head north to Colorado to glimpse the Grand Canyon and continue towards the Rockies. Take out your binoculars and peer into sharp-cut gorges and deep valleys surrounded by snow-capped peaks. Beneath the snow line of the mountains are evergreen forests looking down upon the river banks that are waiting for the river to flood and quench their parched soil.

—Collaboration of Eighth Grade Students

**Figure 3.15**    Mathematics in the Language Arts Class

Five years ago my family moved to Division Street, about ten kilometers away from the first house we lived in. Nearby was a Seven-Eleven gas station where my mother could fill up her car. I was glad the gas station was near because sometimes my mother would let the gas go down to zero. Sometimes she would forget to add water to the car engine and the temperature would rise. I liked living on Division Street because it was in the center of town. The street intersected with Eighth Avenue and was close to Circle Drive. On all these streets there were numerous stores that sold hundreds of items. I calculated that if I lived in this neighborhood for five years, I could spend my total salary buying thousands of items and never saving a penny. My bank account would have nothing and I would be minus money.

—Ninth Grade Student

# ADDITIONAL STUDENT WRITING USING COMPOSING WITH KEYWORDS AT DIFFERENT GRADE LEVELS

We believe this strategy is a perfect fit for creating what Tomlinson calls the "differentiated classroom" (Tomlinson, 1999). One mark of a differentiated classroom is that each student "learns as deeply as possible and as quickly as possible" and "consistently experiences . . . success" (p. 2). Because writing is often difficult for many students, especially those who have fallen behind in reading or are second-language learners or do not have a way with words, teachers need to provide every student with a no-fail writing activity or strategy (Gomez & Madda, 2005). The examples in Figures 3.16–3.18, showing student writing from different grades using keywords as the starting point, illustrate the potential of this strategy as a beginning point for learning to write.

# COMPOSING WITH KEYWORDS FOR SPECIFIC VOCABULARY BUILDING

Figures 3.17 and 3.18 are two writing examples, one by a sixth grade student who was studying weather in a science class and the other by a high school student who had to read *The Pearl* by John Steinbeck (1947/1990). Bolded words are from the students' texts.

**Figure 3.16**    Composing With Keywords Using Foods

My mother tells me that I have to eat vegetables like broccoli and string beans and red peppers because they have lots of vitamins. But I like foods like pizza and fries and hamburgers. So my mother and I made a deal. Every time I got to eat pizza, I would eat some broccoli with it. My mother promised to make the broccoli taste good so she added some salt, and olive oil, and garlic. It didn't taste too bad, especially when I took a bite of the pizza right after. Now I have to work on eating string beans and red pepper. My mother is looking for a good recipe for me.

—Fourth Grade Student

**Figure 3.17**    Weather Vocabulary

**Meteorologists** know exactly how much **humidity** there is by using an instrument called a **hygrometer**. A **hygrometer** uses hair that stretches when it's **wet** and shrinks when it's **dry**. In **winter**, everyone complains because of high **winds, cold weather fronts**, and **ice crystals** on the trees. Now the **meteorologists** are using instruments like **anemometers** to **measure wind speed, barometers to measure air pressure**, and **satellites** to track **air movements** and **storms**.

**Figure 3.18**    Vocabulary From *The Pearl* by John Steinbeck

The story *The Pearl* is considered a **parable**, a story that teaches a moral lesson. The lesson is about the **avarice** or greed of a rich doctor who refuses to help cure a poor couple's baby because they haven't the money to pay him. The couple is too proud to beg for **alms**—food or money. They do not want to be considered **supplicants**—beggars without a trade. Yet the couple is terrified that their baby, who has been bitten by a **scorpion**, will die without medicine. They stand outside the **church** and pray that the **priest** will offer a **benediction**, a blessing, on their child even though they are poor.

# INTERNET LINKS

http://www.users.qwest.net/~rwhancock/PoemsASunintent.htm

http://www.eslbee.com/topic_sentences.htm

http://www.writingfix.com/rightbrain/!Great_Sentence_Creator_Home.htm

# *M*etacognition

## Writing Is Thinking

Strategies, Genres,
Topics, and Tools

Words Are Free!

Have Words,
Can Write

**Writing Is Thinking**

Write to a Martian

Every Word
Has a Story

Organize
Your Writing

Know Who You
Know and Know
Who You Are!

Think in Threes

Everybody Has
to Be Someplace

Let's Make
a Movie!

Words Inspire

Know Thyself

Writers Are Editors

A Goal for
Every Student

*I write entirely to find out what I'm thinking. . . .*

~Joan Didion
(http://en.thinkexist.com/quotes/joan_didion, July 9, 2006)

## WHAT IS METACOGNITION?

Metacognition refers to the conscious awareness of thinking, or, as Costa and Kallick state, "thinking about thinking" (2000, p. 99). Costa and Kallick include Metacognition as one of the essential characteristics of intelligent human behavior that, together with curiosity and wonderment, motivate people to seek additional knowledge. The concept of Metacognition is elaborated upon by David Perkins, who defines four levels of metacognitive learners: tacit learners who are unaware of their knowledge, aware learners who know about some of the kinds of thinking they do, strategic learners who are problem solvers and decision makers, and, finally, reflective learners who "ponder their strategies and revise them" (Perkins, 1992, p. 102).

Teachers generally find that successful or achieving students are aware of what they already know about a particular topic (prior knowledge), they recognize what they have learned that they didn't know before (new knowledge), and they identify what they need to know to meet requirements or standards (expected knowledge). Another definition of metacognition, therefore, can be "thinking about knowing," a definition that comes close to that given in *Random House Unabridged Dictionary* (2003), where *cognition* means the act or process of knowing, and *meta*—a loan form from Greek, means *beyond* or *about*. Finally, we want to add the definition of Livingston, who refers to Metacognition as "higher order thinking which involves active control over the cognitive processes involved in learning" (1997, p. 1)

We have purposely cited several definition(s) of Metacognition, because by recognizing its expanded meanings, we can develop a powerful strategy for learning. Many teachers already use the concepts underlying metacognition when they teach KWL, a procedure developed by Donna Ogle (1986) that asks students to identify for themselves "what I know," "what I want to know," and "what I have learned." Through this procedure, the learner can conceptualize or visualize what she or he already understands and then keep track of new understandings that accrue. Metacognition incorporates a person's conscious awareness of what she or he knows deeply and what she or he only knows on the surface. Metacognition strategies include reflection, keeping track, monitoring, concentrating, and planning ahead (Brown, Bransford, Ferrara, & Campione, 1983; Ertmer & Newby, 1996).

# METACOGNITION FOR WRITING OR WRITING FOR METACOGNITION

In defining Metacognition as a strategy for writing as learning, we focus on students' awareness of their knowing or learning. Again, we cite the insightful work of Robinson in *What Smart Students Know* (1993). What they know, among many things, is what they already know, what they need to know, and how they might go about knowing it.

A simple and effective strategy is to have students write what they believe they already know about a specific topic. This writing is often in contrast to what happens in school, especially in the middle and high school grades, when students are *asked* or *assigned* to write on topics they often know very little about. Many of us already know the disastrous results of these assignments, bringing about cutting, pasting, and just plain plagiarism.

We therefore begin with the following procedures and structures, which have given students of different abilities success in writing about what they know, what they have learned, and what they expect or hope to learn. Students who use Metacognition before, during, and after learning a new topic develop a skill for acquiring and applying knowledge, thereby making the move from being passive learners to becoming active and reflective learners. Following is our Metacognition plan, which includes teaching students how to

- Activate prior knowledge and acquire new and advanced knowledge.
- Use specific strategies for writing and achieving writing goals.
- Combine Taxonomies and Composing With Keywords to enable metacognitive thinking.
- Integrate metacognitive writing with subject areas.

In addition, introduce the slogan "Writing Is Thinking" as part of the Metacognition strategy.

## Getting Started With Prior Knowledge

To make students aware of their prior knowledge, we suggest you build a master Taxonomy titled *Metacognition: I Know That I Know Something About* _____. Have the students write this Taxonomy along with you in their Notebooks. You can follow the procedures of Taxonomy building outlined in Chapter 2 if you wish (i.e., solo, collaborate, cross-pollinate). Figure 4.1 on the next page is an example of a Taxonomy of primary grade students; Figure 4.2 illustrates topics of middle grade students after the teacher prompted them to think about what they know about social studies.

**Figure 4.1**    I Know That I Know Something
About _____.

| | TAXONOMY | |
|---|---|---|
| A | apples |
| B | babies |
| C | cars, cats |
| D | dogs |
| E | eating |
| F | friends |
| G | grandmas, grandpas |
| H | helping, house |
| I | ice cream |
| J | jump rope |
| K | kittens |
| L | lemonade, love |
| M | mommies |
| N | nighttime, neighbors |
| O | owls |
| P | paper, pizza, pets |
| Q | quilts |
| R | running |
| S | school |
| T | television |
| U | umbrellas |
| V | voices |
| W | water |
| X | x-rays, xylophones |
| Y | yellow |
| Z | zoos, zebras |

**Figure 4.2**    I Know That I Know Several Facts or
Ideas About _____.

| | TAXONOMY | |
|---|---|---|
| A | algebra |
| B | Bill of Rights |
| C | Constitution |
| E | elections |
| F | farms |
| G | ghettos, gold |
| H | Holocaust, hurricanes |
| I | Indians, igloos |
| J | Japan, jazz |
| K | King, Martin Luther, Jr.; Kennedy, John F. |
| L | Louisiana |
| M | Mexicans, Mississippi River |
| N | New York City |
| O | oil |
| P | Puerto Rico |
| Q | Queens (borough of New York City) |
| R | recycling |
| S | slavery, Somalia |
| T | taxes |
| U | United States |
| V | voting |
| W | wars |
| X | |
| Y | Yorktown |
| Z | |

## Writing Metacognition Statements

Once the students have entered their Metacognition Taxonomy, you can teach them how to write their Metacognition Statements. Once again, have them enter the information in the Table of Contents with the topic as "I know that I know something about _____" and the strategy as "Metacognition." Figure 4.3 shows more specific instructions.

Have your students set up their Metacognition page in the Notebook as illustrated in Figure 4.4.

**Figure 4.3**    Instructions for Writing a Metacognition Statement

- Open to a new double-page spread in your Notebook.

- In the top margin, across both pages, write the word "Metacognition."

- Under that word, write "Draft Copy." Be sure to skip lines when you write.

- On the left-hand, even-numbered page, write the sentence: "I know that I know something about," and write in your topic. (This can be whatever you are teaching or it can be a topic of the student's choice.)

- Skip a line, and write the word "First" with a comma after it.

- Find the middle of the page, and write "In addition," with a comma after it.

- Go to the top of the odd-numbered page and write "Finally" with a comma after it.

- Go to the middle of the odd-numbered page or slightly below, and write, "Now you know something that I know about" and write your topic again.

**Figure 4.4**    Metacognition Page in a Notebook

| | META | COGNITION |
|---|---|---|
| | Draft | Copy |
| I know that I know something about _____. <br><br> First, | | Finally, |
| In addition, | | Now you know something that I know about _____. |

A simple Metacognition Statement is illustrated in Figure 4.5. Notice that now the student has an organizational template for adding details about the topic. This template can be made more complex, as Figure 4.5 shows, and it can provide students with both an ever-ready means for thinking about topics, ideas, or concepts and a procedure for recording this information.

**Figure 4.5**    Fxample of a Metacognition Statement

> **Dogs**
>
> I know that I know something about dogs.
>
> First, a dog can be a very good friend.
>
> In addition, I know that you need to take your dog to the veterinarian for a checkup.
>
> Finally, you should feed your dog good food and give it lots of love.
>
> Now you know something that I know about a dog.

From this basic or simple statement, your students can now proceed to expanded writing that illustrates their growing knowledge, which can be further developed by adding "thought processing" starters in more complex templates. Figures 4.6–4.8 illustrate example of three Metacognition Statements—those of prior knowledge, new knowledge, and advanced knowledge—written in a fifth grade class.

After studying the Mississippi River through readings and class discussions, the students add to the Taxonomy and continue to Compose With Keywords. They then wrote a Metacognition Statement to indicate new knowledge, as shown in Figure 4.7.

**Figure 4.6**    Metacognition—Prior Knowledge

> I know that I know something about the Mississippi River. First, it is a very long river in the United States. In addition, I know it is in the state of Mississippi. Finally, I know that many boats travel on this river. Now you know something that I know about the Mississippi River.

**Figure 4.7**    Metacognition—New Knowledge

> After reading my social studies book and looking at a map of the United States, I now know more about the Mississippi River than I knew before. I also understand why the Mississippi River has been so important in the settling of America. This river flows through many states such as Minnesota, Wisconsin, Michigan, Iowa, Illinois, Missouri, Kentucky, Tennessee, Arkansas, Mississippi, and Louisiana. It meets the Ohio River in southern Illinois and empties into the Gulf of Mexico in New Orleans. I now know a lot of important information about this Mississippi River.

**Figure 4.8**    Metacognition—Advanced Knowledge

> I further know that other rivers besides the Ohio flow into the Mississippi. They are the Missouri, the Red, and the Arkansas rivers. The Mississippi River is 3,779 kilometers or 2,348 miles long. The more I learned about this river, the more I understood about rivers. For example, many cities are on the river. Some of these cities are St. Paul, Dubuque, Hannibal, St. Louis, Memphis, Vicksburg, Baton Rouge, and New Orleans. Cities often begin where there is a river because in the early days cities needed rivers for travel and trade.
>
> Many boats still travel on the river today, not only steamboats. Sometimes the Mississippi has terrible floods that destroy homes and farms. When Hurricane Katrina came in 2005, it destroyed the levees in New Orleans, and the Mississippi River flooded the city. I'm glad we studied about this because I now know much more about the Mississippi River than anyone else in my family.

For the final piece of writing (Figure 4.8), the students were asked to think about the importance or value of having this knowledge and also to add any new information they had learned.

## Using Pre- and Postmetacognitive Writing

Students at the middle school or high school level often remember more and have better understanding of topics when they write premetacognitive statements, later followed by postmetacognitive statements. While similar to the previously mentioned prior knowledge statements, these differ in that students write two Metacognition Statements, which allow them to compare what they knew before the lesson(s) and after the lesson(s). These pre- and poststatements are excellent for students to use in small cooperative groups of three or four, where they can discuss what they first thought about the topic and what they have since learned. Figure 4.9 is an example of pre- and postwriting of a high school student.

**Figure 4.9**    American History

Teacher Prompt: Today we will be discussing the Reconstruction period after the Civil War. Using the Metacognition strategy, write what you think happened in America during this period of time.

**Student's Response Before Teacher's Presentation**

I know that after the Civil War the former slaves could not find jobs. They had no skills except what they did as slaves, which was picking cotton or working in the master's house. The government would have to find a way to help both the slaves and the soldiers who had fought in the war. I think this is why this time was called Reconstruction.

—Eleventh Grade Student

**Student's Response After Teacher's Presentation**

In today's class discussion, I learned that the southern governments that were in the Civil War passed laws that were called Black Codes. These laws made Blacks pay high taxes if they worked at jobs that were not on a farm or plantation. These taxes made Blacks go back to where they lived before the war and do the same kind of work. There were many other laws against Blacks. They could not buy land or own guns or even dogs. The worst thing was that their children could be taken from them if their old masters said they were unfit parents. Then the children would practically be slaves again to the masters who had taken them away from their family. I now realize that even though slavery was supposed to end because the North won the Civil War, Blacks were not yet free or better off.

—Eleventh Grade Student

## Starting Sentences for Metacognitive Writing

Have your students begin their writing with simple sentences. Beginning writers and writers who have trouble thinking of what to write will always do better when given a start. You can provide students with a list of sample starting sentences, or you can brainstorm starting sentences with students. Post the starting sentences in the classroom as part of your word wall. Your students will be grateful, and you will have the pleasure of reading better writing. Figures 4.10 and 4.11 illustrate different starters that are particularly useful for metacognitive writing.

**Figure 4.10** Try These Starters to Write What You Know

I know that I know a lot about _____.

I know that I know something about _____.

I know many things about _____.

I need to know more about _____.

I know very little about _____.

I know almost nothing about _____.

I would like to know more about _____.

**Figure 4.11** Sentences to Get You Started Writing About What You Know, Understand, Remember, and Would Like to Know

Before I read _____ , I only knew these facts (or this information).

As I listened (read, watched) _____ , I better understood (realized, learned) _____.
_____

After I heard _____ , I remembered (thought about, considered) _____.

As a result of reading (hearing, listening to, studying, observing) _____ , I now can
_____.

## COMBINING TAXONOMIES, COMPOSING WITH KEYWORDS, AND METACOGNITION

As soon as students are able to write, they can compose Metacognition Statements based on the many things they already know about and the new information they are learning.

With the Notebook providing a personal thesaurus, students can select topics and concepts to write about and can share information with classmates. Figure 4.12 shows examples of student writing from different grades that were developed from the words and topics in related Taxonomies.

**Figure 4.12**    Examples of Student Writing Developed From Taxonomies

I know that I know something about ice cream. It can be chocolate or vanilla. If you're a grown up it can be something like pistachino [*sic*] which is green. It comes in a cone or a cup or sometimes on a stick. Now you know something about ice cream.

—First Grade Student

My teacher read us *Charlotte's Web* and now I know what a runt is. It's a baby pig that is too small to live. So sometimes the farmer wants to kill it before it dies by itself. Wilbur was a runt, but Fern saved him from dying. Now I know what a runt pig is.

—Third Grade Student

**Figure 4.13**    The Sad Vocabulary of Loneliness

| • TAXONOMY • | |
| --- | --- |
| A | alone, alienated, abandoned, avoided |
| B | bored, bereft |
| C | |
| D | depressed, detached, disconnected, desolate |
| E | |
| F | friendless, forsaken |
| G | |
| H | homesick, helpless |
| I | ignored |
| J | jilted |
| K | |
| L | lonely |
| M | melancholy |
| N | |
| O | ostracized |
| P | |
| Q | |
| R | removed, rejected |
| S | sad, solemn, solitary, shut-in, shunned |
| T | tired |
| U | unfulfilled |
| V | vexed |
| W | weary |
| X | xenophobic |
| Y | |
| Z | |

With the Taxonomy as the holder of the terms or vocabulary of a topic, the students have words for writing. Now they must select or draw upon those words that they find meaningful or significant to the topic. The students are becoming cognitive decision makers, making decisions as to what they will write about. Thus, with the words they have selected from the Taxonomy and with the starting Metacognition Statement, students have what to say and a format for saying it. This arrangement is especially comfortable for students who ordinarily find writing difficult.

The following example is from a literature class studying Paul Zindel's novel *The Pigman* (1978). Here the students used the strategy Composing With Keywords to write Metacognition Statements that expressed their insights on loneliness as it related to the central character in the story, Mr. Pignati. The students first created a Taxonomy of words that describe loneliness (Figure 4.13).

Next, the students selected three terms from the Taxonomy and wrote what they knew or understood about Mr. Pignati's loneliness (Composing With Keywords). Figure 4.14 shows an example written by an eighth grade student.

**Figure 4.14**    Loneliness

The three words of loneliness that help me better understand Mr. Pignati are alienated, ostracized, and unfulfilled. To be alienated means to be unattached to the world, something like an alien. That is how Mr. Pignati feels after his wife dies. He seems to have very little understanding of what people outside of his world do or feel is correct. Because he can't relate to other people and they can't relate to him, he is ostracized, meaning that no one, except Lorraine and John, want to associate with him. Finally I know that he is unfulfilled in his hopes and dreams. No one appreciates his collection of pigs or can even understand what this collection means to him. I feel sad for Mr. Pignati because I know and feel what loneliness does to destroy a person's feeling of importance.

—Eighth Grade Student

# USING METACOGNITIVE WRITING TO CONSOLIDATE WRITING WITH SUBJECT AREAS

By the middle grades, students can reinforce their learning by writing Metacognition Statements on a daily basis and for a variety of subject areas. You can post a chart or agenda for the day that shows topics to write about to sum up what they know, have learned, or need to learn. Figure 4.15 shows what these assignments may look like, while Figure 4.16 provides some phrases to help students get started.

**Figure 4.15**    Metacognition Assignments for Thinking and Knowing

Mathematics: After you have finished adding fractions with mixed denominators, write a Metacognition Statement telling what you now know about fractions.

Social studies: We will be starting a unit on the Constitution. Write a Metacognition Statement telling about three ideas that you believe are in the Constitution.

Science: After you have read the section "How Plants Make Their Food," write a Metacognition Statement telling of three new ideas that you learned as a result of your reading.

Literature: Now that you have read the story of "Arachne and Athena," write a Metacognition Statement with this opening: "Before I read this story I did not know (or understand) _____. However, I now know (or understand) _____.

**Figure 4.16**    Metacognition Starters for Easy Writing

What Do I Know That I Know?

I know that I know something about _____.

First, I know _____.

I also know _____.

Finally, I know _____.

Now you know something that I know about _____.

*(Continued)*

**Figure 4.16** (Continued)

What Would I Like to Know?

I would like to know more about _____.

First, I would like to know why _____.

Then I would like to know where _____.

Last, I would like to know when _____.

These are some of the things I would like to know about.

What Do I Need to Know?

I need to know how to _____.

Then I would be able to _____.

I would also be able to _____.

Finally, I could _____.

These are the reasons I need to know how to _____.

I Know What I Know

In my (subject area) class, I understand several important ideas.

First, I understand _____.

In addition, I _____.

Furthermore, I _____.

I am now prepared to _____.

As a Result of _____, I Now _____.

As a result of (reading, studying, listening, discussing), I now (realize, recognize, think about, dream of) _____.

I better understand _____.

Furthermore, I believe _____.

Above all, I _____.

This new (knowledge, discovery, idea, thought) will help me _____.

Present Knowledge to Future Knowledge

In my class, I have been studying (learning) _____.

When I began this topic, I knew

1. _____

2. _____

3. _____

Over the next few weeks (months), I expect to know

1. _____

2. _____

3. _____

This new knowledge will _____.

As students develop the habit of writing Metacognition Statements, they gain a greater sense of ownership of their learning. They have a tangible representation of how much knowledge they started with and how much knowledge they are adding and can add. Metacognition writing can be compared to setting up one of those charts or "thermometers" that is used to record fundraising results: "Here is where I began, here is how much I have achieved to date, and here is where I have to go."

## INTERNET LINKS

http://www.ncrel.org/sdrs/areas/issues/students/learning/lr1metn.htm

http://www.gse.buffalo.edu/fas/shuell/CEP564/Metacog.htm

http://chiron.valdosta.edu/whuitt/col/cogsys/metacogn.html

http://coe.sdsu.edu/eet/Articles/metacognition/start.htm

http://www.psyc.memphis.edu/trg/meta.htm

http://www.usask.ca/education/coursework/802papers/Adkins/SEC1.HTM

http://members.iinet.net.au/~rstack1/world/rss/files/metacognition.htm

Strategies, Genres,
Topics, and Tools

Words Are Free!

Have Words,
Can Write

Writing Is Thinking

**Write to a Martian**

Every Word
Has a Story

Organize
Your Writing

Know Who You
Know and Know
Who You Are!

Think in Threes

Everybody Has
to Be Someplace

Let's Make
a Movie!

Words Inspire

Know Thyself

Writers Are Editors

A Goal for
Every Student

CHAPTER FIVE

# Defining Format

## Write to a Martian

*The race is not to the swift, but to the verbal.*

~Steven Pinker (1994, p. 3)

## DEFINING OUR WORDS AND CONSTRUCTING MEANING

A visitor from another planet (e.g., a Martian) might assume that a classroom is a type of questioning machine. Throughout the day, the Martian hears teachers asking students questions such as "What is (a) . . . ?" as in "What is a river?" "What is a mammal?" "What is a triangle?" "What is a fable?" and so forth. The Martian is then likely to hear the students struggle to explain the term, giving answers such as "A river is water *like* a lake but different," "A mammal is an animal *with* fur," or "A triangle is *something* with three sides." When the teacher asks for elaboration, many students simply add more "pieces" in haphazard order: "Well, a river is long, not round like a lake." "A mammal also has live babies." "A triangle has three angles." When students try to define common terms, they often have great difficulty. A pencil is defined as "something to right [*sic*] with"; rain is "water falling from the sky"; and a flag is "what waves."

We might assume that the Martian finds that there is something missing in these partial responses. The problem with these responses is they are partial, and while they may be a clue that the student knows something about the word, these simplistic definitions leave out the deeper or complete meaning of a word or term; they lack an expression of cognition or metacognition.

Yvette Jackson, in her extensive work with underachieving students, uses the phrase "competence and confidence" to frame what all students need to meet the standards of current education. She defines *competence* as "fluency in the language . . . , ability to construct meaning [from text] and ability to communicate meaning [constructed from the text]" (2005, p. 205). These three aspects of competence are indeed hallmarks of student achievement, yet many students fail to achieve this competence because they are uninstructed. This lack of instruction is not by design, but comes about by assumption, the same assumption that has resulted in *asking* students to write, rather than *teaching* them to write.

The ability to define a term (e.g., *river*) requires thought, knowledge, and *instruction*. Looking up a word in a dictionary or glossary, while a good practice, often fails to provide the student with more than a surface or cursory understanding. Only when the student constructs the meaning, and begins to expand the meaning, does knowledge and understanding begin to become internalized and make an academic impact (Vygotsky, 1962).

## WHAT IS DEFINING FORMAT?

Defining Format is a strategy for defining terms that provides the student with a constructive format consisting of three parts:

- Asking a *question*—what term do I want to define? (e.g., what is (a) _____?)
- Responding by finding the *category* to which the term belongs (e.g., a river is in the category *body of water*; a pencil is in the category *writing tool*; addition is in the category *mathematical operation*)
- Stating the essential *characteristics* that separate that term from other terms belonging to the same category (e.g., a river and a lake are both bodies of water, but with different characteristics)

In Defining Format, we ask the student (writer) to imagine that the audience is a Martian, someone who is totally unfamiliar with the term being defined, who needs a clear, unambiguous definition. Figure 5.1 illustrates the template for Defining Format with the question, "What is a river?"

Figure 5.1

**What Is a River**

| Question | Category | Characteristics |
|---|---|---|
| What is a river? | | |
| A river is a | body of water that | 1. flows into another body of water, such as a lake, a bay, a gulf, or the ocean.<br>2. has a source and a mouth.<br>3. forms banks on each side.<br>4. begins with fresh water that may become brackish and then salty.<br>5. may flow north or south.<br>6. may have rapids or meander. |

• DEFINING FORMAT •

In Defining Format, the student turns the question into a statement that begins "A _____ is a _____" (e.g., "A river is a"). The article "a" (or "an") is essential to state the category (e.g., A river is a body of water"). Following the category, the student numerically lists the characteristics of the term being defined. Notice the detailed information that the writer provides to the "Martian."

Once a student has defined one term in a category, he or she can define other terms in the same category. For example, the student who defines a river could subsequently define a lake or bay or ocean by stating that these too are bodies of water but with different characteristics or qualities. When two or more terms in the same category are defined using the Defining Format strategy, the student can use the defining information to compare the items, as shown in the following example written by a sixth grade student that compares a river and a lake.

> We can compare a river with a lake in several ways. Both are bodies of water, but with different characteristics. A river begins at a source that is usually in high land and flows north or south towards its mouth. The mouth is where it empties into another body of water such as a lake, a bay, or the ocean. A lake is a body of water that is surrounded on all sides by land and may get its water from a river flowing into it. Rivers are thought of as long and lakes are thought of as large. Both rivers and lakes can have fresh water, brackish water, or salt water.

Student instructions for setting up the Defining Format in the Notebook are in Figure 5.2. Remind students to enter this strategy in the Table of Contents. An easy word to start with as an example is *cat* or another word for a pet.

Guide your students in stating the characteristics that can be very simple for young students or quite advanced by the upper grades. Figure 5.3 shows a *composite response* representing students from primary grades to middle school.

**Figure 5.2**    Setting Up for Defining Format

- Go to the next double-page spread in your Notebook.
- In the top margin, across both pages, write Defining Format
- Divide the left-hand, even-numbered page in half. Keep the right-hand page unfolded.
- Write the word "Question" in the first column on the even-numbered age.
- Write the word "Category" in the second column.
- Write the word "Characteristics" on the right-hand or odd-numbered page.
- Draw a line across both pages under all three words.
- Under Question, write the question "What is a cat?
- Draw a line again across both pages.
- In the Question column, begin your answer with the words "A cat is a(n) . . ."
- In the Category column, write the words "animal that"
- Go to the Characteristics column, and write the number 1

Figure 5.3

What Is a "Cat"?

| • DEFINING FORMAT • |||
|---|---|---|
| Question | Category | Characteristics |
| What is a cat? | | |
| A cat is an | animal that | 1. says meow.<br>2. has fur and a tail.<br>3. can be a pet.<br>4. catches mice.<br>5. has babies called kittens.<br>6. has claws and whiskers.<br>7. is a feline.<br>8. is a mammal.<br>9. has been domesticated.<br>10. is related to bobcats, tigers, and other felines. |

# USING DEFINING FORMAT IN ALL GRADES AND SUBJECTS

Defining Format can be introduced as early as the first grade and continued throughout the grades. The teaching aspect of this strategy is guiding or directing the students toward stating the category rather than using the word *something*. For example, in response to the question, "What is a jacket?" a student might answer, "A jacket is a type of clothing" (not "something you wear"). By helping students to state the category, the teacher shows them how items can be classified or categorized. An excellent way to begin Defining Format is to have the students create a Taxonomy of words related to a category that you might be teaching (e.g., types of clothing).

We also suggest that you post a model template of a Defining Format and continue to emphasize "writing to a Martian"—someone who is not likely to know what these terms mean. As students learn more about the topic or item, they add this information to the Defining Format template so that it provides an ongoing note-taking system. When the students have completed their Defining Format(s), they can write a Metacognition Statement using the information they have gathered:

**A simple starter can be,** "As a result of writing a Defining Format about a dog, I know five important facts that I would tell to a Martian."

**At a higher level of writing,** a student could add, "While all these facts or characteristics fit a dog, the most important characteristic is that it can be domesticated, which means. . . ."

**A more advanced level** of writing might include the sentence, "Dogs are a member of the canine family and trace their lineage to the wolves."

**A conclusion** that shows Metacognition (reflection and understanding) might be, "Until I studied about dogs, listed their characteristics, and compared them to other animals, I was unaware of their history and changes. My next search will be about the Scottish Terrier, which is the breed of my own dog, Barney."

# TEACHING CATEGORIES

Students often have difficulty stating the category and need assistance. The suggestions and activities below can be adapted for different grade levels so that your students can create Defining Format templates in all subject areas.

Set up a master Taxonomy of categories that relate to your subject and curriculum. Have your students write this Taxonomy in their Notebooks, adding to it as new categories are created. With frequent use of the Defining Format, your students will become more skilled in defining a term by stating its category and listing its characteristics. A sample list of categories is shown in Figure 5.4, and additional Taxonomies of categories are shown in Figures 5.5–5.7.

**Figure 5.4**    Categories and Examples

**• TAXONOMY •**

| | | |
|---|---|---|
| A | animal | bird |
| B | building | Empire State Building |
| C | clothing | shirt |
| D | dwelling | cabin |
| E | emotion | happiness |
| F | fruit | orange |
| G | game | chess |
| H | holiday | Fourth of July |
| I | instrument | violin |
| J | jazz | blues |
| K | kingdom | Great Britain |
| L | liquid | water |
| M | monarch | king |
| N | number | zero |
| O | ornamentation | Christmas wreath |
| P | precipitation | rain |
| Q | | |
| R | religion | Islam |
| S | subject | geography |
| T | timepiece | clock |
| U | | |
| V | vehicle | truck |
| W | woodwind | oboe |
| X | | |
| Y | | |
| Z | | |

**Figure 5.5**    Object Categories

**• TAXONOMY •**

| | |
|---|---|
| A | art form |
| B | building |
| C | communication device, clothing, container |
| D | divider, dwelling |
| E | eating utensil |
| F | furniture, footwear, farm equipment |
| G | gemstone, geometric shape |
| H | headwear, habitat |
| I | illumination |
| J | jewelry |
| K | |
| L | |
| M | musical instrument, mineral, measuring device |
| N | numerals |
| O | |
| P | pictorial representation, partition |
| R | reference book, recording device |
| S | symbol, sports equipment, sailing vessel |
| T | timepiece, tool |
| V | vehicle |
| W | writing tool, writing surface, window covering |
| X | |
| Y | |
| Z | |

**Figure 5.6**   Animal Categories

• TAXONOMY •

| | |
|---|---|
| A | amphibian, arachnid, arthropod, annelid |
| B | bird, biped, bovine |
| C | canine, cattle, carnivore, crustacean |
| D | domestic, dinosaur, diurnal, desert |
| E | equine |
| F | farm, feline, fish, fowl |
| G | grazing |
| H | herbivore |
| I | invertebrate, insect |
| J | jungle |
| K | |
| L | lepidoptera |
| M | mammal, mollusk, marsupial, mountain |
| N | nocturnal |
| O | omnivore, one-celled |
| P | primate, predator, pet |
| Q | quadruped |
| R | reptile, rodent, rain forest, ruminant |
| S | sea mammal |
| T | timberland |
| U | ungulate, ursine |
| V | vertebrate |
| W | worm, woodland, waterfowl |
| X | |
| Y | |
| Z | |

**Figure 5.7**   Occupational Categories

• TAXONOMY •

| | |
|---|---|
| A | author, artist, athlete, actor |
| B | business tycoon, boxer |
| C | community helper, civil rights activist |
| D | doctor of medicine, dancer |
| E | entrepreneur, explorer |
| F | farmer |
| G | general |
| H | health worker, horticulturist |
| I | investigator, illustrator |
| J | journalist |
| K | knight, king |
| L | legislator |
| M | musician, mountain climber |
| N | national leader, naturalist |
| O | opera singer, ornithologist, orator |
| P | poet, philanthropist, philosopher |
| Q | queen |
| R | religious leader |
| S | social activist, sculptor, scientist, social worker, senator |
| T | teacher, talk-show host |
| U | union leader |
| V | veterinarian |
| W | writer, wrestler |
| X | x-ray specialist |
| Y | youth leader |
| Z | zoologist |

An additional way to help students better understand categories is to set up a chart showing how a category connects two related items (Figure 5.8). By using this chart, students can write a comparative statement such as "An almanac and a dictionary are both types of reference books but contain different information." They can then set up the Defining Formats for listing the shared and dissimilar characteristics of different reference books.

## USING DEFINING FORMAT FOR MORE COMPLEX TERMS

As students move into the intermediate grades and middle school, they are inundated with content area terminology, especially in social studies and science. Words such as *colony, state, country, pioneer,* and *revolution* become part of the expected vocabulary terrain of middle grade students. Some students will grasp the full meanings of

**Figure 5.8**    Category Terms as Connectors

| Item | Category | Item |
|------|----------|------|
| cup | container | bucket |
| cottage | dwelling | mansion |
| boot | footwear | sandal |
| rectangle | polygon | parallelogram |
| ruler | measuring device | meter stick |
| wall | partition | fence |
| flag | symbol | wreath |
| bat | sports equipment | hockey stick |
| dictionary | reference book | almanac |
| clock | timepiece | sundial |

these words. Unfortunately, others will have only a vague or superficial understanding of where one term ends and another begins. Many students remain fuzzy about even commonly used words. When students in a sixth grade class were asked to define the word *planet*, some students responded by saying, "It's a big round ball in the sky," and "It's something [that word again!] that goes around the sun." Of greater significance, many students, when given a list of words to define, assume that *define* means *copy*. Using a glossary or a dictionary, they merely transfer to their notebooks what they have trouble understanding in the first place. One student in a social studies class, when asked to define *referendum,* copied the meaning verbatim from the textbook's glossary and when asked to explain the meaning in her own words, was startled by the question. Her answer was, "It's what it says it is in the glossary."

By high school, students should be accustomed to setting up their definitions of content area terms using the Defining Format. They will think in terms of categories rather than discrete items, so that for each content area, they define terms based on the categories specific to that content area. For mathematics, students would define a written number as a symbol, addition as an operation, a trapezoid as a polygon, and so forth. In geography and earth science, students would think in terms of landforms or bodies of water; in health, they would classify terms by body systems or chemical substances. The literature teacher points out the literary genres, and the art teacher can have the students group and define by art genres.

Figures 5.9–5.14 are examples of several Defining Formats for terms students frequently encounter in their studies but rarely define with clarity.

## DEFINING FORMAT APPLICATION

In addition to guiding students toward separating the category from the specific characteristics, Defining Format can serve several writing and learning purposes.

### Note taking and Outlining

Students can use Defining Format's three-part structure to gather the essential elements of a word or term and then observe or analyze its components.

Figure 5.9

| What Is a Colony? | | |

| • DEFINING FORMAT • | | |
| --- | --- | --- |
| Question | Category | Characteristics |
| What is a colony? | | |
| A colony is a | type of community that | 1. may be composed of people who have chosen to live together for a common purpose or goal.<br>2. may be formed by a more powerful country for its own needs.<br>3. may have its own local form of government but is generally governed by a larger or more powerful government.<br>4. may be composed of one or several settlements.<br>5. was formed in the early years after the discovery of the American continents. |

Figure 5.10

| What Is a Slave? | | |

| • DEFINING FORMAT • | | |
| --- | --- | --- |
| Question | Category | Characteristics |
| What is a slave? | | |
| A slave is a | person who*<br><br><br><br><br>*Note the use of "who" for a person instead of "that." | 1. is owned by another person and is property.<br>2. is unable to own his or her possessions.<br>3. works without wages, but is provided with food, clothing, and shelter according to the owner's wishes.<br>4. does not have rights as a parent to raise or keep his or her children.<br>5. can be bought and sold at the owner's desire. |

## Paragraph Development

After using the three parts of this strategy to define a term, students can use the information to write the term's meaning in paragraph form:

A slave is a person who is owned by another person and is considered to be property that can be bought and sold. Slaves are generally unable to

Figure 5.11

| What Is a Planet? | | |
|---|---|---|
| • DEFINING FORMAT • | | |
| Question | Category | Characteristics |
| What is a planet? | | |
| A planet is a | body in space that | 1. orbits around the sun.<br>2. is made of gases and other related matters.<br>3. may rotate on its axis.<br>4. may have moons or rings. (add more) |

Figure 5.12

| What Is a Cell? | | |
|---|---|---|
| • DEFINING FORMAT • | | |
| Question | Category | Characteristics |
| What is a cell? | | |
| A cell is a | structural unit that | 1. is the basis of all plant and animal life.<br>2. may be a complete organism or a part of other organisms.<br>3. has a surrounding membrane and a substance called cytoplasm.<br>4. contains the genetic material known as DNA.<br>5. is composed of oxygen, hydrogen, carbon, and nitrogen. |

Figure 5.13

| What Is Addition? | | |
|---|---|---|
| • DEFINING FORMAT • | | |
| Question | Category | Characteristics |
| What is addition? | | |
| Addition is a | mathematical operation that | 1. requires two or more numbers, called addends, to get a sum.<br>2. may be written horizontally $(2 + 6 = 8)$ or vertically.<br>$$\begin{array}{r} 2 \\ + 6 \\ \hline 8 \end{array}$$<br>3. when written vertically is written with one number under the other by place value, plus sign, an equal sign, or an underline bar.<br>4. is the basis of multiplication.<br>  *For more examples of Defining Format in mathematics, see Rothstein, Rothstein, & Lauber (2006). |

Figure 5.14

| | • DEFINING FORMAT • | | |
| --- | --- | --- | --- |
| **Question** | **Category** | **Characteristics** | |
| What is a fable? | | | |
| A fable is a | type of literary genre that | 1. teaches a moral or lesson.<br>2. generally uses animals as characters for humans.<br>3. is short and to the point. | |

What Is a Fable?

own their homes or belongings. They get their food, clothing, and shelter from their owners, but they work without wages and usually for long hours. Worst of all they do not have rights as parents and their children can be sold separately to other slaveholders.

## Comparing and Contrasting

After students have written definitions for two items belonging to the same category, they easily can compare the two items by matching characteristics that are similar or different. For example, after defining a triangle and a rectangle, students can write a paragraph by composing basic sentences that describe the corresponding characteristics for both objects. They follow the format outlined in the Defining Format visual organizer. Following is a student example showing the first few sentences that compare a triangle and a rectangle:

We can compare a triangle with a rectangle. Both are polygons, but with different characteristics. A triangle has three sides that equal 180 degrees, while a rectangle is four-sided with angles equaling 360 degrees.

The compare/contrast aspects of Defining Format also can be used in conjunction with Venn diagrams and the "Double Bubble Maps" created by David Hyerle (1995, pp. 1–10). Double Bubble Maps are graphic organizers that help students visualize the relationship between two items belonging to the same category. These visual organizers can be used either before or after setting up Defining Format. By using the Venn diagram or the Double Bubble Map first, the students go from picture to words. As a follow-up activity, the students go from words to picture. Both strategies are important and offer students flexibility in thinking and constructing. Figure 5.15 shows a Venn diagram comparing a triangle and a rectangle. Figure 5.16 shows the same information in a Double Bubble Map.

## Expanded Explanations

Each characteristic in the Defining Format has the potential to be expanded as a detailed paragraph.

In writing about addition, for example, the student might elaborate on its first characteristic of requiring two or more numbers to get a sum:

Figure 5.15

**Venn Diagram of Geometric Shapes**

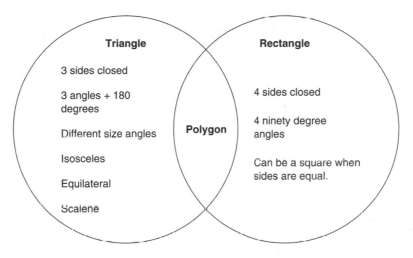

Figure 5.16

**Double Bubble Map**

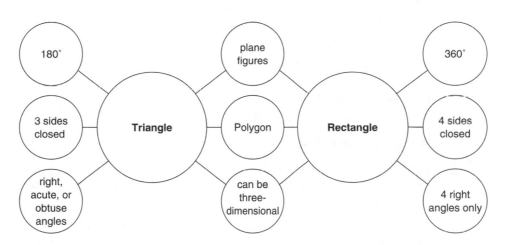

Figure 5.17

**What Is a Quadrilateral?**

| • DEFINING FORMAT • | | |
|---|---|---|
| Question | Category | Characteristics |
| What is a quadrilateral? | | |
| A quadrilateral is a | polygon that | 1. has four sides closed and four angles.<br>2. may be a rectangle, square, parallelogram, or trapezoid.<br>3. has angles equaling 360 degrees. |

Figure 5.18

| What Is a Meter? | | |
| --- | --- | --- |

| • DEFINING FORMAT • | | |
| --- | --- | --- |
| Question | Category | Characteristics |
| What is a meter? | | |
| A meter is a | type of measurement that | 1. is 100 centimeters.<br>2. is one-tenth of a kilometer.<br>3. is equal to 39.38 United States inches.<br>4. has been defined as equal to one ten-millionth of the distance from the equator to the pole measured on a meridian. |

Any amount or type of number can be added. We can add four place numbers, fractions with the same or different denominators, negative and positive numbers, prime numbers, and odd or even numbers. We always get a sum, which is usually more than we started with, except when we add negative numbers. Then we seem to get less.

When students use Defining Format to define all subject-area terminology, they have a permanent template for organizing factual information that they can use for reports, presentations, and explanatory writing.

## Combining and Reviewing

Students can create their own books of Defining Formats with titles such as *Occupations From A to Z, The ABC Book of Animal Categories, Landforms and Waterways,* and so forth. These can be a combination of definitions with drawings for young students or full paragraph writings for older students. Another activity is to have students create their own glossaries for particular units that they then can use for review of important terminology.

Defining Format is the strategy that helps students write clearly and concisely on specific subject matter. It enables them to explain a term to a distant audience that knows very little about the topic. It also is a strategy that requires the student to organize through classification and to pay attention to the details that separate one item or concept from a similar item or concept. Finally, Defining Format allows students to write a cohesive paragraph with a clear opening statement and a support structure. From this strategy, students can backtrack to Taxonomies (for categories) and to Metacognition to express their knowledge and thinking.

## INTERNET LINKS

http://en.wikipedia.org/wiki/Semantic_feature

http://www.intelligent-systems.com.ar/intsyst/definit.htm

# CHAPTER SIX

# Morphology, Etymology, and Grammar

## Every Word Has a Story

Strategies, Genres,
Topics, and Tools

Words Are Free!

Have Words,
Can Write

Writing Is Thinking

Write to a Martian

**Every Word
Has a Story**

Organize
Your Writing

Know Who You
Know and Know
Who You Are!

Think in Threes

Everybody Has
to Be Someplace

Let's Make
a Movie!

Words Inspire

Know Thyself

Writers Are Editors

A Goal for
Every Student

*They've a temper, some of them—particularly verbs: they're the proudest—adjectives you can do anything with, but not verbs—however, I can manage the whole lot of them! Impenetrability! That's what I say!*

~Humpty Dumpty in *Through the Looking Glass* (Lewis Carroll, 1871/1965, p. 94)

## MORPHOLOGY, ETYMOLOGY, AND GRAMMAR—A TRIPLEX IN THE SCHEME OF WRITING

We are including these three aspects of language for the fifth strategy of *Writing as Learning,* because we firmly believe that students who know *about* words and who know *about* language (which includes grammar) can learn to write *better.* We use the word *better* in the context of students being able to express themselves fluently, interestingly, and creatively in a variety of genres, voices, and *language registers.* By language registers, we mean the ways in which humans can communicate, especially in writing; examples include informal, conversational, colloquial, formal, and friendly communication.

We believe that students become *better* writers when they are on friendly terms with language and comfortable with all aspects of it—dialects, slang, idioms, vernacular, jargon—as well as with the academic language that is promoted in school.

To bolster this statement of belief, we begin by defining the three terms of this chapter, because each term promotes and enhances language or linguistic understanding and knowledge. The strategies and activities in this chapter also draw upon what has been previously presented and will consolidate and enhance your students' ability to write and learn from writing. We strongly recommend that you include as much of the material on this topic as you can or as fits your students' needs.

**Morphology** is the study of patterns of word formation in a particular language, including inflection, derivation, and composition.

**Etymology** is the study of the derivations of words, the historical changes in individual words, and the way words are used in different contexts and cultural settings.

**Grammar** is the study of the way the sentences of a language are constructed, including its morphology, and the rules that the speakers of that language have internalized.

## THE ROLE OF GRAMMAR IN TEACHING WRITING

The word *grammar* is likely to conjure up a whole range of different opinions and emotions. Generally, English teachers embrace it, while mathematics teachers are likely to shun it. But, whatever are the beliefs about grammar (which includes morphology and etymology), we know from research and observation that it is taught spottily in American education and rarely, if at all, in any subject other than English or language arts (Weaver, 1996).

One serious problem that we have encountered as teachers and consultants in schools across the county is that the teaching of English grammar is stuck in a time warp based on eighteenth-century notions of what English should be rather than what English is. In the delightful and well-researched book *The Mother Tongue: English and How It Got That Way*, Bill Bryson states:

> English grammar is so complex and confusing for the one very simple reason that its rules and terminology are based upon Latin—a language with which it has precious little in common. . . . Making English grammar conform to Latin rules is like asking people to play baseball using the rules of football. It is patently absurd. (1990, p. 137)

Yet, when established linguists and other language experts point out the foolishness of trying to teach English grammar through Latin, many teachers reply that they have to follow the English book, and even if the book is wrong, they have no choice, since the students will have to take a test and answer wrongly stated information correctly.

Before reading on, we would like you to take the following test on nouns (Figure 6.1). When you have completed this test, ask yourself: Does the traditional definition of a noun make sense?

Frustrated with the previous task? Try the one in Figure 6.2 and see if it works any better.

**Figure 6.1** Defining Nouns

Directions: A noun (according to traditional school grammar books) is a person, place, or thing. All the bolded words in the passage below are nouns. Decide which nouns are persons, which are places, and which are things. Sort them in the table that follows the passage.

The new **employee** displayed her **anger** and **indignation** to her **boss**. "We've never had a **discussion** about my **terms** of **employment**. First, you make me an **offer** of a **salary**; then you decide to give me only a **commission**. Finally, you ask me to hand in my **resignation**. Your **behavior** shows **arrogance**, **indifference**, and a total **lack** of concern for my **needs**. I have two **plans**—to look for another **job** immediately or to file **suit** against your **company**."

| Persons | Places | Things |
|---------|--------|--------|
|  |  |  |
|  |  |  |
|  |  |  |
|  |  |  |
|  |  |  |
|  |  |  |
|  |  |  |
|  |  |  |
|  |  |  |
|  |  |  |

**Figure 6.2** Verbs and Prepositions

Directions: Many school grammar books classify words such as *up, out, before, down* and *by* as prepositions, meaning that they indicate the location of he noun that follows it (e.g., *in* the sky; *up to* the house; *before* the class). In the passage that follows, underline all the verbs plus the words that traditionally are classified as prepositions. Are they prepositions? What part of speech would you call them?

"Wake **up**," Mother called **out**. "Straighten **up** your room before you go to school. Get **down** on your knees, and make sure that you clean **up** the mess. I will not let you get **by** with a dirty room. Hurry **up**, because I have to back **out** my car from the garage. Dad needs to get **out** early for his meeting. Later this afternoon, we'll pass **by** your grandma's house and catch **up** on what she's been **up** to.

Teaching grammar serves a useful purpose when it helps students write (or possibly speak) better (McWhorter, 1998; Pinker, 2000). However, making students classify words such as *anger, discussion, possibility,* and *industrialization* as "things" will in no way improve their word knowledge or their writing. Reciting that "a verb is a word of action," and "an adjective describes" provides no power to the student writer. Underlining the subject once and the predicate twice in the sentence "It is raining" can hardly improve a student's communication skills. Weaver (1996) points out that the reason traditional teaching of grammar has little transfer to learning is that it is based on the false notion that skills practiced in isolation will be applied in relevant situations, despite the overwhelming evidence that this doesn't work. Yet, in hundreds of classrooms, teachers display products purchased at teachers' stores that tell students these shibboleths of nouns, verbs, adjectives, and sentences and other grammatical inaccuracies. No wonder Humpty says, "They've a temper" (Carroll 1871/1965, p. 94).

Yet, there is an important place for grammar in the scheme of writing, learning, and acquiring a deep and lasting understanding of language as wonderfully and wittingly written by authors such as Bryson (1990), Lederer, (1994, 1998), and Pinker (2000). By teaching Grammar (capitalized from now on as a strategy for writing) and including Morphology and Etymology, you can provide lessons and activities that encourage students to think about English as it is and that show students how to create meaningful, well-constructed, information-bearing sentences in their writing. Grammar, as described in *Standards for the English Language Arts* (National Council of Teachers of English & International Reading Association, 1996), defines "what one knows about the structure and use of one's own language and leads [the student] to its creative and communicative use" (p. 72).

We have organized learning this structure through the following activities and strategies:

- Categories of nouns (Figures 6.3–6.5)
- Categories of verbs (Figures 6.6 and 6.7)
- Categories of adjectives (Figures 6.8–6.10)
- Sentence Stretchers for creative sentences (Figures 6.11–6.13)
- Defining Format for parts of speech
- Morphology for the formation of words
- Etymology for words and their stories
- ABC stories for sentence variety and structure

## Categories of Nouns

Now that you have realized, by taking the "test" in Figure 6.1, that nouns go far beyond "things," you can introduce your students to the wide, wide world of nouns in the English language. Begin with Figure 6.3, the first step in the Categories of Nouns activity. This activity can be taught with students starting in the third grade (and possibly before) and used throughout all grade levels as an extension of vocabulary building. In the Notebook, have students enter the topic (Categories of Nouns); then, on a double-page, have them divide their papers into four columns, one marked "Persons," one marked "Places," one marked "Objects," and the last one marked "Other." Then have students follow the instructions in Figure 6.3.

Figure 6.3    Categories of Nouns

Introduction: I am going to say many words that are called nouns. Some nouns will refer to persons or people, some will tell the names of places, some will be objects. I will also say nouns that fit in none of these categories. Write those words in the column marked "Other." I will help you with spelling if you need it.

| Persons | Places | Objects | Other |
|---|---|---|---|
| author | avenue | ax | anger |
| barber | building | ball | behavior |
| child | church | card | Christmas |
| designer | den | dress | dog |
| electrician | elevator | egg | effort |
| friend | farm | fork | friendship |
| grandparent | garden | glass | golf |
| helper | home | hat | housework |
| Indian | igloo | iron | illness |
| janitor | jail | jacket | joy |

Even when students are not sure about the meanings of the words that are not persons, places, or objects, they usually know that such words are not "things," a term many school grammarians use as a substitute for the word *object*. When students are given the option to put words in a list marked "Other," they immediately know that a dog is an animal and Christmas is a holiday. Some students realize that joy is a feeling or emotion. Although some school grammar books have added "idea" as part of the definition of noun, this still doesn't enable students to identify a dog, joy, or Christmas, as a person, place, thing, or idea, since a dog and joy can hardly be thought of as ideas, and Christmas is a holiday or celebration.

You can now expand the classification of nouns to include other categories, such as animals, emotions, and school subjects, again leaving a place for "Other." After a while, the list of nouns might look like the one shown in Figure 6.4 on the next page. Note that the Taxonomy format of listing the letters vertically has been added to this table.

Before continuing to the next group, noun categories, we suggest that students compose sentences using the strategy Composing With Keywords, as described in Chapter 3. Students select three words from three different noun categories, one of which should be from the "Other" column. They then compose a sentence using the three words in one sentence, with the option to change the forms of the words if necessary. Here are several examples taken from students in different grades:

- My grandma bought me a monkey that had a bad temper.
- I get a lot of pleasure when my teacher tells me that I got an A in mathematics.

**Figure 6.4**     Expanded Categories of Nouns

**• TAXONOMY •**

| | Persons | Places | Objects | Animals | Emotions | Subjects | Other |
|---|---|---|---|---|---|---|---|
| A | author | avenue | ax | ape | anger | art | action |
| B | barber | building | ball | bear | | biology | beauty |
| C | child | church | card | cheetah | concern | carpentry | charm |
| D | designer | den | dress | dog | desire | design | depth |
| E | educator | eatery | emerald | eagle | envy | education | energy |
| F | friend | farm | fork | fox | fear | forensics | finality |
| G | grandma | garden | glass | goat | gladness | geometry | greed |
| H | helper | home | hat | hare | happiness | health | helplessness |
| I | Indian | igloo | iron | iguana | indignation | ichthyology | inaction |
| J | janitor | jail | jacket | jaguar | joy | | joke |
| K | kid | kennel | kettle | kangaroo | kindness | kinetics | karma |
| L | leader | laundry | lamp | lion | love | literature | lesson |
| M | master | market | mirror | monkey | misery | mathematics | melody |
| N | neighbor | Norway | nutcracker | newt | nervousness | nutrition | nod |
| O | owner | orchard | opener | owl | | ornithology | opportunity |
| P | pal | pool | pin | panda | pleasure | psychology | position |
| Q | queen | quagmire | quilt | quail | queasiness | quilt making | quest |
| R | runner | restaurant | ring | rabbit | | radiology | rumor |
| S | student | school | sock | skunk | sympathy | science | song |
| T | teacher | tent | table | tiger | terror | technology | temper |
| U | umpire | United States | umbrella | unicorn | | | unit |
| V | violinist | vineyard | vase | vixen | | | vision |
| W | waitress | wadi | watch | whale | worry | weaving | wisdom |
| X | xylophonist | Xanadu | xylophone | | | | x-factor |
| Y | youth | yard | yardstick | yak | | | youthfulness |
| Z | zookeeper | zoo | zither | zebra | | zoography | zero |

- I sang a song of happiness to the queen.
- There was a rumor that the skunk was in the restaurant.
- Some students in my geometry class have a lot of wisdom.

By generating their own sentences, students not only learn about the variety of nouns but also begin to use more advanced vocabulary and develop flexibility in their sentence composing skills. In contrast, when nouns are only "things," everything can be anything, with nothing much mattering.

Once students have an understanding of what a noun is, they are ready to learn about noun endings, called *affixes*; this instruction can be started as early as fourth grade. The most common of these affixes are *-ness -ion*, *-ment*, *-ence/ance*, *-ity*, *-ism*, and *-ship*, as shown in Figure 6.5. These high-level words can be used for vocabulary and sentence development and can be integrated with teaching Morphology and Etymology in virtually every subject area.

**Figure 6.5**     Noun Affixes

| | | -ness | -ion | -ment | -ence/-ance | -ity | -ism | -ship |
|---|---|---|---|---|---|---|---|---|
| | | **· TAXONOMY ·** | | | | | | |
| A | | attractiveness | attention | advancement | attendance | activity | absolutism | authorship |
| B | | boldness | bastion | bereavement | benevolence | brevity | Buddhism | |
| C | | carelessness | commotion | commitment | credence | Christianity | capitalism | clerkship |
| D | | darkness | detention | department | difference | deity | Darwinism | |
| E | | eagerness | elation | engagement | exuberance | | extremism | |
| F | | friendliness | fraction | fragment | forbearance | fragility | feudalism | friendship |
| G | | gentleness | generation | government | governance | gratuity | gigantism | |
| H | | helpfulness | humiliation | harassment | hindrance | humanity | humanism | hardship |
| I | | inventiveness | information | instrument | intelligence | individuality | individualism | |
| J | | judiciousness | juxtaposition | judgment | jurisprudence | joviality | Judaism | judgeship |
| K | | kindness | | | | | | kinship |
| L | | loneliness | lamentation | ligament | | lucidity | | ladyship |
| M | | maliciousness | motion | monument | magnificence | magnanimity | minimalism | |
| N | | neatness | notion | | | nobility | nepotism | |
| O | | openness | operation | | opulence | opportunity | opportunism | |
| P | | playfulness | perforation | parliament | permanence | perspicacity | populism | partnership |
| Q | | quietness | question | | quintessence | quantity | | |
| R | | ruthlessness | radiation | rudiment | radiance | radioactivity | rationalism | relationship |
| S | | sweetness | situation | sentiment | significance | sensitivity | sensationalism | statesmanship |
| T | | timeliness | temptation | temperament | temperance | timidity | Taoism | |
| U | | usefulness | usurpation | understatement | | utility | utilitarianism | |
| V | | viciousness | variation | | vehemence | veracity | | |
| W | | wastefulness | wonderment | | | | | worship |
| X | | | | | | | | |
| Y | | youthfulness | | | | | | |
| Z | | zealousness | | | | | Zoroastrianism | |

## Categories of Verbs

The verb, like the noun, is often given short shrift as teachers tell their students that "a verb is a word of action." Sentences such as "Nothing exists," "It is not important," and "There are six people in the room" defy this explanation. Some teachers tell us that sentences such as these are about the "action of nonexistence" or "a state of being" or "a state of not being." Or something like that. These explanations (if they can be called that) come from grammar based on an eighteenth-century perspective that has wormed its way into school grammar books.

The distinguished Robert Claiborne, in *Our Marvelous English Tongue—The Life and Times of the English Language*, points out how the Latinists saddled "English with quite a few arbitrary rules" and "literary prissiness" through their "attempt to jam English into the Procrustean bed of Latin rules that managed to confuse generations of schoolchildren" (1983, p. 186). This misplaced teaching certainly has given a temper to the verbs by asking students to parse the English verbs that have the same structure as the Latin word *amare,* with its elaborate forms of infinitives, gerunds, participles, and subjunctives, as well as past, present, and future tenses and whatever else belonged to Latin, but not English.

Students can become better writers if we introduce them to the variety of verbs and verb structures they need as writers. For example, in writing, they need to replace tired verbs such as *think, say,* and *go* with more varied, vivid words. They need to have a personal thesaurus of verbs of different categories (see Figure 6.6) so that they have an extensive vocabulary to draw upon when writing. Begin with the activity in Figure 6.6 (good from third grade and up) and follow through with the subsequent activities that will enhance writing in all genres. Use the Notebook and enter the title Categories of Verbs in the Table of Contents. This activity will take several days; there is no rush.

The above Categories of Verbs can become a starting point for classification that provides students with an ongoing resource of vocabulary. Additional classifications for verb Taxonomies include verbs for expressing

- Gesture (frown, nod, point, smile)
- Caring and feeling (admire, believe, care, enjoy, love)
- Dislike (abhor, distrust, detest, envy, hate)
- Subject areas (e.g., mathematics: add, borrow, calculate, divide)

By classifying verbs, students have a vocabulary for expressing not merely action, but behaviors that can be mental, vocal, physical, and emotional.

**Figure 6.6**     Taxonomies of Verbs of the Mind, Vocalization, and Locomotion

**Directions:**

- Open to a double-page spread in your Notebook. Fold your even-numbered and odd-numbered pages in half so you have four columns. You will also use the margin on the left-hand page.

- Write all the letters of the alphabet in the left-hand margin. You can combine *X, Y,* and *Z* if you can't fit all the letters.

- In the first column, draw a full-length person with a face, a neck, and a body. Write the word "I" above this figure.

- Label the second column "The Mind," the third column "Vocalization," and the fourth column "Locomotion." Make sure you put these headings above the letter *A.*

- Verbs of the mind will be for verbs that are about thinking, so put the letter *T* in the head of your figure. Verbs of vocalization are verbs that refer to sounds you can make from vocal chords, so put the letter *V* in the neck of your person.

- Verbs of locomotion are verbs that are about moving or getting from one place to another, so put the letter *L* in the body.

- We will now collect verbs that fit into these three categories. I will begin with the example of "I think." Write the word *think* in the column labeled the mind. Now we will think of other verbs of the mind by starting with the word *I* and listing them in our Taxonomy.

- In a short time, we will have a large collection of verbs to help make our writing vivid, exciting, interesting, and clear to our audiences.

**Figure 6.6** (Continued)

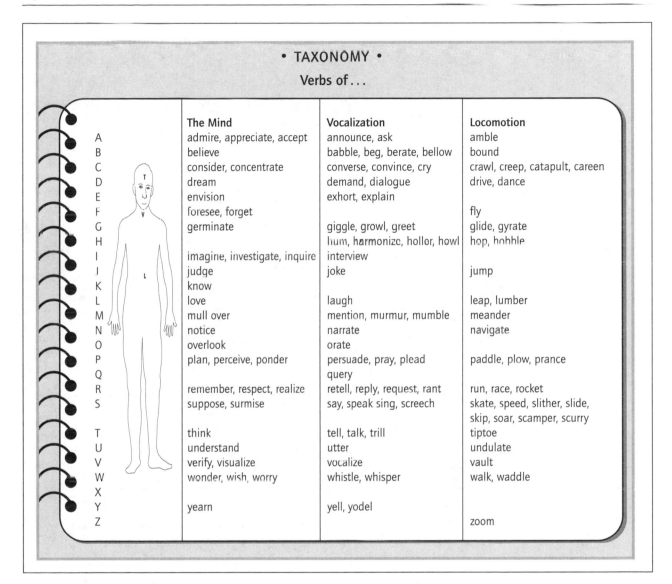

• TAXONOMY •

Verbs of . . .

| | The Mind | Vocalization | Locomotion |
|---|---|---|---|
| A | admire, appreciate, accept | announce, ask | amble |
| B | believe | babble, beg, berate, bellow | bound |
| C | consider, concentrate | converse, convince, cry | crawl, creep, catapult, careen |
| D | dream | demand, dialogue | drive, dance |
| E | envision | exhort, explain | |
| F | foresee, forget | | fly |
| G | germinate | giggle, growl, greet | glide, gyrate |
| H | | hum, harmonize, hollor, howl | hop, hobble |
| I | imagine, investigate, inquire | interview | |
| J | judge | joke | jump |
| K | know | | |
| L | love | laugh | leap, lumber |
| M | mull over | mention, murmur, mumble | meander |
| N | notice | narrate | navigate |
| O | overlook | orate | |
| P | plan, perceive, ponder | persuade, pray, plead | paddle, plow, prance |
| Q | | query | |
| R | remember, respect, realize | retell, reply, request, rant | run, race, rocket |
| S | suppose, surmise | say, speak sing, screech | skate, speed, slither, slide, skip, soar, scamper, scurry |
| T | think | tell, talk, trill | tiptoe |
| U | understand | utter | undulate |
| V | verify, visualize | vocalize | vault |
| W | wonder, wish, worry | whistle, whisper | walk, waddle |
| X | | | |
| Y | yearn | yell, yodel | |
| Z | | | zoom |

## Categories of Adjectives

Students are traditionally taught that an adjective is a word that *describes* a noun, or in more traditional schools, students are told an adjective *modifies* a noun. There is a certain truth to this, but we believe that students learn more (about almost anything) when they explore the organization first and develop the rules after. We begin by having the students use the template below to list words (adjectives) that have a base, the *-er* affix, and the *-est* affix as illustrated in Figure 6.7. Have your students build a three-part template in their Notebooks to keep track of adjectives that use affixes to express *comparison*. By adding to this template, they will realize that a major definition of an adjective is "a word that compares" or simply means *more* or *most*. (You will find more information on defining parts of speech later in this chapter.)

As you know, there are other adjectives (e.g., *courageous*) that are preceded by the words *more* or *most* to form the comparison. But adjectives are not only words that describe and compare. They are a body of words that are formed by a large variety

**Figure 6.7**    Three-Part Adjectives in the English Language (add more)

| Base | -er | -est |
|---|---|---|
| big | bigger | biggest |
| deep | deeper | deepest |
| easy | easier | easiest |
| friendly | friendlier | friendliest |
| great | greater | greatest |
| hard | harder | hardest |

of affixes as shown in Figures 6.8–6.10. You will notice that these words represent a wide range of vocabulary levels and are presented here as a resource from which you can pick and choose depending on the grade and development of your students.

**Figure 6.8**    Adjectives That End in *-y* and *-ly* (add others)

| | | -y | -ly |
|---|---|---|---|
| | A | antsy | ably |
| | B | busy, bony | bubbly |
| | C | crazy, cozy | costly |
| | D | dizzy, dusty | daily |
| | E | easy | |
| | F | funny | friendly |
| | G | greedy | |
| | H | hazy, happy | |
| | I | itchy, icy | |
| | J | juicy | |
| | K | | |
| | L | lazy | lovely, lonely |
| | M | merry | |
| | N | needy | |
| | O | | only |
| | P | pretty | pearly |
| | Q | | |
| | R | rosy, rusty | |
| | S | scary, sassy, sunny | |
| | T | tiny | |
| | U | | ugly |
| | V | | |
| | W | | |
| | X | | |
| | Y | | |
| | Z | | |

NOTE: Generally, adverbs have the *-ly* affix, but a few adjectives have it as well, as illustrated. Some of these adjectives also have the *-er* and *-est* affixes.

**Figure 6.9**    Adjectives Formed by the Affixes -al, -ic, -ive, and -ent (add others)

| | -al | -ic | -ive | -ent |
|---|---|---|---|---|
| A | antithetical | alcoholic | appreciative, attractive | ambient, apparent |
| B | bilateral | balsamic | | beneficent, benevolent |
| C | comical | comedic | cooperative | convergent |
| D | dialectical | despotic, demonic | divisive, distributive | divergent |
| E | ethereal | empathetic, energetic | elusive | emergent |
| F | federal | frenetic | furtive, figurative | |
| G | gradual | genetic | generative | |
| H | hysterical | Homeric, horrific | | |
| I | inimical, infinitesimal, intellectual | | imperative, investigative | impertinent, intelligent |
| J | judicial | | | |
| K | | | | |
| L | lackadaisical | laconic | | latent |
| M | musical, magical, maniacal | metric | massive | magnificent, malevolent, maleficent |
| N | numerical | | | nascent |
| O | occasional, oppositional | opportunistic | oppressive | |
| P | peripheral prepositional | philanthropic, peripatetic, pathetic | permissive, persuasive | persistent |
| Q | quizzical | quixotic | quantitative | quiescent |
| R | rhetorical, rhythmical | romantic | restive, reclusive, responsive, retentive | reticent |
| S | sensational, spherical | sympathetic, sybaritic | supportive, subjective | sentient |
| T | temperamental, tyrannical, transcendental | toxic | transformative, tentative, transformative | |
| U | universal | | | |
| V | visual | | vituperative | vehement |
| W | | | | |
| X | | | | |
| Y | | | | |
| Z | | | | |

**Figure 6.10**  Adjectives Formed by the Affixes *-ous, -ory, -ary,* and *-able/-ible* (add others)

|  | -ous | -ory | -ary | -able/-ible |
|---|---|---|---|---|
| A | amphibious, ambiguous, abstemious | anticipatory | antiquary | able |
| B | bituminous | | binary | |
| C | cautious, capacious | | cautionary, contrary | capable, comprehensible |
| D | deleterious, delicious, delusional | defamatory, declamatory | | desirable, dependable, destructible |
| E | envious, enormous, efficacious | expository, explanatory | exemplary | expendable |
| F | famous, fractious | | | formidable |
| G | generous, gracious | | | |
| H | humongous, horrendous, herbivorous | | | hospitable |
| I | infectious, infamous, industrious | inflammatory | | impossible, inflammable, indestructible, invisible, insupportable |
| J | judicious | | | |
| K | | | | |
| L | laborious | | | lamentable, lovable |
| M | monstrous, magnanimous | mandatory, migratory | | malleable, manageable |
| N | noxious, numerous, notorious | | | notable |
| O | ostentatious | obligatory | | |
| P | poisonous, pernicious | participatory, preparatory | proprietary | possible, permissible |
| Q | | | | |
| R | ravenous, rapacious | | | reprehensible, responsible, remarkable |
| S | supercilious, stupendous, serious, specious, serendipitous, synchronous | satisfactory, statutory | stationary | supportable |
| T | timorous, tenacious, tendentious | | temporary | tenable |
| U | unctuous | unsatisfactory | | understandable |
| V | vicious, vicarious, voluminous | | | visible |
| W | | | | washable |
| X | | | | |
| Y | | | | |
| Z | | | | |

## Sentence Stretchers

You can move next to showing students how verbs, nouns, and other word categories form the sentence structures of English. A lively, no-fail activity is Sentence Stretchers, which teaches students how to write expanded sentences using major parts of speech. This activity requires the use of an eight-slot chart which is explained in Figure 6.11, with the slots referring to the places where certain parts of speech are most likely to fit. The directions involve a variation in the use of the Notebook. Because Sentence Stretchers need eight slots, we have the students do this activity on legal size or drawing size paper. They can then fold the paper and tape it into their Notebooks. Remember to put the name and page of this activity in the Table of Contents.

Figure 6.12 shows how the eight slots are used to create the sentence.

Students are now ready to replicate this activity in a variety of ways. Once the students know the procedure, they can write an infinite number of expanded sentences while adding to their own Taxonomies of adjectives, animals, verbs of locomotion, and adverbs. They will have delightful, humorous sentences to illustrate and share.

**Figure 6.11**   Sentence Stretchers

---

**Directions:**

- Hold your large size paper horizontally. Fold it in half, then into fourths, then into eighths. You will have eight slots or columns. Number each slot at the top of the page.

- Go to slot 4. Label the slot "Animal." Then make the word plural by adding *-s* (*bear/bears*) or changing the form (*wolf/wolves*).

- Go to slot label 5 and label it "Verb." Enter a verb of locomotion, which you can select from your Categories of Verbs. Keep the verb in the base form (e.g., *stalk, pounce, fly*).

- Go to slot 3. Label it "Adjective." Enter an adjective. Think of a powerful adjective such as *dangerous, courageous, graceful, peaceful,* or *fierce.* You can select from your Taxonomy of Adjectives in your Notebook.

- Go to slot 2. Label it "Determiner." The word *determiner* is used to determine the amount or number. A determiner can be an exact number such as three, or it can be an inexact number represented by words such as *some, many, several,* or *numerous,* or a phrase such as *a pack of.* (Make sure students do not confuse adjectives with determiners, since they each serve different purposes.)

- Go to slot 6. Label it "Adverb." Enter an *-ly* adverb. An *-ly* adverb is an adjective to which *-ly* has been added (*angry/angrily, brave/bravely/graceful/gracefully*).

- Go to slot 1. Label it "When." Write when this event occurred (e.g., *at the stroke of midnight*). Be sure to begin with a capital letter. You must also go to slot 5 and check that the verb is in the right form or tense, and change it if necessary (*dance/danced*).

- Go to slot 7. Label it "Where." Write where this event is taking place (e.g., *in the playground*).

- Go to slot 8. Label it "Punctuation." Put in punctuation.

- Let's hear these wonderful, expanded sentences.

After students have practiced Sentence Stretchers using verbs of locomotion, proceed with two variations—one with persons and verbs of vocalization and one with persons and verbs of the mind—using the arrangements shown in Figures 6.13 and 6.14.

In the Sentence Stretcher that uses verbs of the mind (Figure 6.14), the students add their own endings.

**Figure 6.12**    Sample Sentence Stretcher

| 1 | 2 | 3 | 4 | 5 | 6 | 7 | 8 |
|---|---|---|---|---|---|---|---|
| When | Determiner | Adjective | Animal | Verb of Loco-motion | Adverb | Where | Punctuation |
| Early this morning | several | brilliant | giraffes | danced | gracefully | over the hills | [.] |
| | | | | | | | |
| | | | | | | | |
| | | | | | | | |

**Figure 6.13**    Sentence Stretcher With Persons and Verbs of Vocalization

| 1 | 2 | 3 | 4 | 5 | 6 | 7 | 8 |
|---|---|---|---|---|---|---|---|
| When | Determiner | Adjective | Person | Verb of Vocalization | Adverb | Where | Punctuation |
| As the curtain opened | twenty | delightful | students | chanted | gloriously | on the stage | [.] |
| | | | | | | | |
| | | | | | | | |

**Figure 6.14**    Sentence Stretcher With Persons and Verbs of the Mind

| 1 | 2 | 3 | 4 | 5 | 6 | 7 | 8 |
|---|---|---|---|---|---|---|---|
| When | Determiner | Adjective | Person | From Where | Verb of the Mind | Add Your Own Ending | Punctuation |
| Last winter | a group of | courageous | teachers | living in Australia | decided | | [.] |
| | | | | | | | |
| | | | | | | | |

## Understanding Parts of Speech by Using Defining Format

The theme of this book—writing as learning—emphasizes that when students construct meanings through writing, they understand what they are trying to understand. So it is with explaining language, especially English, which has the largest known vocabulary of any of the world's languages (a vocabulary that is drawn from numerous other languages), and a grammar system that has developed and reformed for over a thousand years. No wonder teachers are on slippery terrain when they try to explain English parts of speech. However, after students have explored aspects of the English language through the activities that have been previously suggested, they can then try to pin down some explanations though Defining Format. The examples shown in Figures 6.15–6.17 define *noun, verb,* and *adjective*—three terms, among others, that traditional school grammar books have failed to examine carefully or explain accurately.

Figure 6.15

| What Is a Noun in the English Language? | | |
|---|---|---|
| • **DEFINING FORMAT** • | | |
| **Question** | **Category** | **Characteristics** |
| What is a noun? | | |
| A noun is a | word that | 1. names many categories, including persons, places, objects, animals, emotions, and whatever can be named.<br>2. may have specific endings: *-ion, -ment, -ence/-ance, -ness, -ity, -ism. -ship.*<br>3. may be singular or plural: girl/girls, mouse/mice, wolf/wolves, sheep/sheep, alumnus/alumni, addendum/addenda.<br>4. may be formed from verbs:<br>I played in a play.<br>Playing is fun.<br>5. may be paired with a verb, but is distinguished by stress:<br>I don't want to subject you to this subject.<br>We have to reject all rejects.<br>I have to record the record. |

Figure 6.16

---

**What Is an Adjective in the English Language?**

**• DEFINING FORMAT •**

| Question | Category | Characteristics |
|---|---|---|
| What is an adjective? | | |
| An adjective is a | word that | 1. compares or contrasts the quality or appearance of a noun:<br>The beautiful (i.e., not ugly) dress<br>The brave (i.e., not cowardly) soldier<br>The white (i.e., not brown) horse<br>2. may add the inflections *-er and -est:* big, bigger, biggest.<br>3. may be preceded by *more* or *most; less* or *least; quite, rather,* or *very:*<br>More dangerous, least dangerous<br>Quite dangerous, rather dangerous<br>Very dangerous<br>4. usually precedes the noun (fierce storms) or follows the "be" verb. (The storms were fierce.) |

Figure 6.17

---

**What Is a Verb in the English Language?**

**• DEFINING FORMAT •**

| Question | Category | Characteristics |
|---|---|---|
| What is a verb? | | |
| A verb is a | word that | 1. has four forms, also called its *conjugation:*<br>Base—I work. I speak.<br>Verb + *s*—She works. She speaks.<br>-ing—She is working. She was speaking.<br>Past—She worked. She spoke.<br>2. may have a fifth form: *-en*—I have spoken.<br>3. forms the past in several ways:<br>By adding *ed,* with several pronunciations—I worked [t]. She sighed [d]. He painted. [•d]<br>By vowel change—We ran. They gave. He saw. She took.<br>With no change—Today I quit. Yesterday I quit.<br>4. may serve in the noun or adjective position:<br>Singing is fun for singing waiters.<br>Traveling with traveling musicians makes a lively journey.<br>5. can be combined with other verbs to indicate time or tense:<br>We should have stayed in the park.<br>From the moment I met her, I knew she was going to be my friend. |

# MORPHOLOGY—THE STUDY OF THE FORMATION OF WORDS

Morphology literally means the study (*-logo*) of the shapes (*morph-*) of words, a term derived from the Greek god of dreams, Morpheus, who had the ability to assume different shapes or appearances. English is a highly morphological language, meaning that a large number of its words can have affixes (e.g., girl, girls, girlhood; play, playful, playfulness) and only a very small number of words, called *function words,* cannot have affixes (e.g., the, but, and, some, all, this).

From the very beginning of reading instruction, teachers point out the plural formation of certain nouns and the verb endings (technically called *inflections*). By second grade, therefore, most students are able to understand how a word can have more than one form or shape and are ready to learn morphology. Figure 6.18 introduces students to setting up a Morphology Chart—an organizational template for sorting words into nouns, verbs, adjectives, and adverbs. While we recognize that labeling words as parts of speech can have pitfalls because of usage, the Morphology Chart can serve as a representation of how one word can have many forms and can be used in different parts of a sentence.

**Figure 6.18**   Morphology Chart Template

Directions:

- After you have folded your double-page spread so that you have four columns, label them "Noun," "Verb," "Adjective," and "Adverb."

- Write the word "play" in the "Verb" column, as in "I play."

- We will now add all the other forms of play:

  o Plays (as in "she or he plays")

  o Playing (as in "now we are playing")

  o Played (as in "yesterday they played")

- You have just written the four forms of a verb; this is called its *conjugation.*

- Sometimes in English, a verb can serve as a noun.

  o Write the word "play" in the "Noun" column. When the word is a noun, it can mean, "I watched a play."

  o Under it, write the word "plays." We now have a plural noun, as in "We watched two *plays* in school." We can form a sentence that uses both the verb and the noun in the same sentence, as in "I played in a play."

- There is another noun formed with the word *play.* Write the word "player" in the "Noun" column. Then write its plural, "players." You can now write a sentence that says, "I played in a play with many other players."

- Go to the column that is labeled "Adjective." Write the word "playful." Words that end in *-ful* are adjectives, such as *wonderful, helpful,* and *careful.*

- Move to the column that is labeled "Adverb." Many adverbs can be formed by adding *-ly* to an adjective. You now have *playfully.* You can now write a playful sentence such as "I playfully played in a play with many other playful players."

*(Continued)*

**Figure 6.18** (Continued)

- Go back to the "Noun" column. Write the word "playfulness." You will discover that all words that end with the affix -*ness* are nouns, such as *joyfulness, carelessness, helplessness,* and *loveliness.*
- Write your own morphological sentence using as many forms of the word *play* as you can.

Illustration of Completed Morphology Chart for the Word Play

| Morphology Chart—Completed | | | |
|---|---|---|---|
| Noun | Verb | Adjective | Adverb |
| play | play | playful | playfully |
| plays | plays | | |
| | playing | | |
| player | played | | |
| players | | | |
| | | | |
| playfulness | | | |
| | | | |

## Notes on Verbs

The linguistic terms for various forms of verbs are the *base* (e.g., play, jump, run), the *verb+s* form (plays, jumps, runs), the *verb+ing* form (playing, jumping, running), and the *past* form (played, jumped, ran). There are two complications related to verbs. One is that the past form of the verb has several variations, unlike the other three forms that are invariant. In addition, many words in English that are born verbs serve as nouns, such as the word *play*. And words that start out as nouns can become verbs: For example, a *table* is a piece of furniture, but a committee can also *table* a motion.

Using morphology with students requires teachers to become aware of words with expansive morphologies and makes students aware of the various patterns of affixes (prefixes, suffixes, and inflections) in the English language. Figure 6.19 shows a dual Taxonomy of words that you can use for your morphology lessons. It is divided into two levels of difficulty. Following this Taxonomy are examples of the morphologies of different words (Figures 6.20–6.23).

## The "Be" Verb

This verb differs from all the other verbs of English in that it has a two-part system. The base word, *be*, has forms that contain the base itself:

We will *be* there soon.

*Being* on time is important.

I have *been* visiting my friends.

Only three (out of five) conjugation forms are currently used in standard written English: *be, being,* and *been.* In certain dialect forms, however, the other two forms of this conjugation are still in use:

She bes good (verb+s).

We beed here a long time (past).

These last two forms may be used in the speech dialects of certain communities and can be heard in the emerging speech of young students. If judgments are not

**Figure 6.19**   Verbs for Studying Morphology

The following verbs are those that can become other parts of speech such as nouns, adjectives, and adverbs. Introduce them based on your students' levels of vocabulary or grade level.

| Level I | | Level II |
|---|---|---|
| A | add, act, agree, attract | admire, anger, argue, appreciate, adore |
| B | boast, believe | beautify, befriend |
| C | care, comfort, copy | create, consider, civilize, circle |
| D | drive, delight, darken, disagree | decide, defend, decorate, design, depend |
| E | enjoy, eat, entertain, express | energize, endanger, endure, equal, enslave |
| F | fly, fool, free | frighten, finance, function |
| G | govern | generate, graph |
| H | help, hope | humanize, honor |
| I | imagine, improve, interest | invade, include, inquire, illustrate |
| J | jump | judge |
| K | know | |
| L | love | limit |
| M | move | multiply, manage, master, motivate |
| N | name | narrate, nationalize, note |
| O | open | organize, object, observe, occupy, offend |
| P | play, pay | progress, provide, possess, perceive |
| Q | question | qualify |
| R | rest, respect, run | reason, recognize, receive, reflect, repeat |
| S | speak, sweeten, serve, soften | sign, sympathize, secure, segregate |
| T | taste, transport, trick | terrify, transmit, tyrannize |
| U | use, understand | unite |
| V | | value, vaccinate, verify, vibrate |
| W | wonder, waste, warm, wash, work, whiten | |
| X, Y, Z | | |

made about correct use, one can see that the verb *be* follows the English verb conjugation system.

However, *be* has a second strand of conjugations: *am, is, are, was,* and *were.* These forms are commonly used and are considered to be part of standard usage when matched to the appropriate noun or pronoun: *I am,* but not *I is.* Many middle schoolers and high schoolers find this discussion of usage fascinating. For further information and background on this topic, refer to *The Story of English* (McCrum, Cran, & MacNeil, 1986) and *Mother Tongue: English and How it Got to Be That Way* (Bryson, 1990).

**Figure 6.20**    Morphology Chart for *Add*

| Noun | Verb | Adjective | Adverb |
|---|---|---|---|
| addition | add | additional | additionally |
| additions | adds | | |
| | adding | | |
| addend | added | | |
| addends | | | |
| additive | | | |
| additives | | | |
| addendum | | | |
| addenda | | | |

**Figure 6.21**    Morphology Chart for *Believe*\*

| Noun | Verb | Adjective | Adverb |
|---|---|---|---|
| belief | believe | believable | believably |
| beliefs | believes | | |
| disbelief | believing | unbelievable | unbelievably |
| | believed | | |

\*Notice that there is a consonant change from the verb to the noun—believe/belief.

**Figure 6.22**    Morphology Chart for *Defend*

| Noun | Verb | Adjective | Adverb |
|---|---|---|---|
| defendant | defend | defensible | defensibly |
| defendants | defends | defensive | defensively |
| | defending | indefensible | indefensibly |
| defense | defended | | |
| defenses | | | |
| defensiveness | | | |

**Figure 6.23**   Morphology Chart for *Sign*

| Noun | Verb | Adjective | Adverb |
|------|------|-----------|--------|
| sign | sign | | |
| signs | signs | | |
| | signing | | |
| signature | signed | | |
| signatures | | | |
| signal | signal | | |
| signals | signals | | |
| signatory | signaling | | |
| signatories | signaled | | |
| significance | | significant | significantly |
| | signify | | |
| signification | signifies | | |
| | signifying | | |
| | signified | | |

# ETYMOLOGY

Etymology—the study of the origin of words—is often given much less attention than it merits in the study of English. From its roots in India, the English language developed across Persia, up through the Germanic tribes into Scandinavia, and across to Britain. The spread of Christianity, the Norman Conquest, and the Renaissance added to the lexicon of English. English then expanded to the New World from England, while simultaneously spreading to Australia and into parts of Africa. So where in the world does the English language come from? Everywhere. Where in the world is the English language in use? Everywhere. We have added several activities to *Writing as Learning* that relate to the etymology of the English language, which resulted from its global travels.

## Words and Their Stories

An informative book for young students is *101 Words and How They Began* by Arthur Steckler (1979). This is a good starting book to make students aware that words are born or come from other words or other languages. Teachers can supplement the reading by having students create lists of words they learned about from the story; we call this a Taxonomy of Words With a Story (Figure 6.24). If possible, provide students with *Random House Webster's Unabridged Dictionary* (2003), which provides the origin of most words. Another valuable book is the *Dictionary of Word Origins* by John Aton (1990). Then assign each student a word from a popular Taxonomy, and have them write their words' histories for compilation into a book of word stories. You will find that once the students get hooked on etymology, they will become avid searchers for the origins of their names, their localities, the foods they eat, and the hundreds of other words that have stories.

## Borrowings and Lendings

Counter to the advice of Polonius in *Hamlet*, English has heavily borrowed from other languages and, in turn, has loaned its own words freely—a process that linguistically enriches all those who speak it. As students prepare their book of word stories, they will start to notice the variety of origins—French, Spanish, Greek, Latin, Hebrew, Native American, African, Arabic, and more. The Taxonomies below illustrate English words borrowed from India (Figure 6.25), words that come from ragtime, jazz, swing, and hip-hop (Figure 6.26), and words and place names from Native Americans (Figure 6.27). Students can also create Taxonomies of words from Spanish, French, and Yiddish that have become part of the English lexicon. Each of these Taxonomies can be used for Composing With

**Figure 6.24**   Taxonomy of Words With a Story

### • TAXONOMY •

| | |
|---|---|
| A | apron |
| B | bracelet |
| C | chair |
| D | dandelion |
| E | eight |
| F | factory |
| G | ghetto |
| H | hippopotamus |
| I | inch |
| J | January |
| K | knight |
| L | lamp |
| M | marathon |
| N | nickel |
| O | orange |
| P | pantry |
| Q | queen |
| R | report |
| S | Saturday |
| T | teddy bear |
| U | umbrella |
| V | vaccine |
| W | wall |
| X | xylophone |
| Y | Yankee |
| Z | zero |

**Figure 6.25**   Passage From India

### • TAXONOMY •

Directions: In the early 1600s, the British East India Company sent ships to India, and by the end of the eighteenth century, all major educational institutions in India used English as the primary language of instruction. But the English of India took on its own accents, idioms, and expressions. And, in turn, the native languages of the Indian people—Urdu, Hindi, Bengali, and Punjabi—gave their own words to English. Check out the meanings of the words you don't know and tell their stories.

| | |
|---|---|
| A | |
| B | Brahman, bungalow, bandanna |
| C | calico, coolie, curry, chintz, chutney, cummerbund |
| D | dhurrie, denim, dungarees |
| E | |
| F | |
| G | guru |
| H | |
| I | |
| J | jungle, jute |
| K | karma |
| L | |
| M | maharaja |
| N | nirvana |
| O | |
| P | |
| Q | |
| R | raja, rupee |
| S | |
| T | toddy |
| U | |
| V | verandah |
| W | |
| X | |
| Y | yoga |
| Z | |

**Figure 6.26**  And All That Jazz

• TAXONOMY •

Directions: From the early days of slavery to the present time, African Americans have used music to express their feelings, beliefs, and yearnings. From this music, English has enriched its vocabulary. Here are some of the words. Add others to this list, and write a story about jazz and other music using as many of these words as you need.

| | |
|---|---|
| A | |
| B | blues, boogie-woogie, break dancing, bebop |
| C | cool, cakewalk, chick |
| D | |
| E | |
| F | |
| G | groovy, gospel |
| H | hip, hip-hop, hepcat |
| I | |
| J | jam, jive, jitterbug |
| K | |
| L | latch on |
| M | mellow |
| N | |
| O | |
| P | pad |
| Q | |
| R | rap, riff |
| S | sharp, soul, solid, square |
| T | |
| U | |
| V | |
| W | |
| X | |
| Y | |
| Z | |

**Figure 6.27**  Word Contributions From Native Americans

• TAXONOMY •

Directions: Here is a sampling of English words and place names that come from the population who lived on the American continent before the arrival of the white settlers. Try to locate the place names on a map. Add your own names to this list.

| | |
|---|---|
| A | Alaska, Amagansett |
| B | |
| C | chipmunk, Connecticut |
| D | Delaware |
| E | |
| F | |
| G | |
| H | hominy, hogan |
| I | igloo |
| J | |
| K | kayak, Kissimmee |
| L | |
| M | moose, moccasin, Massachusetts |
| N | Neponset, Narragansett |
| O | opossum |
| P | powwow, papoose |
| Q | Quogue |
| R | raccoon |
| S | squash, squaw, skunk, Seattle, Seminole |
| T | teepee, totem, Tallahassee |
| U | Utah |
| V | |
| W | wigwam, wampum |
| X | |
| Y | |
| Z | |

Keywords or as the basis for research, discussion, and inclusion in numerous writing activities.

## British English and American English

Students are always interested in comparing British words with American words, and this topic can be introduced in social studies, English, or language arts classes to show the great variety of words in the English language. The Taxonomy shown in Figure 6.28 contains some British versus American variations of the language.

**Figure 6.28**    A Taxonomy of American English Words and British English Words

### • TAXONOMY •

Directions: Following are pairs of words that mean the same thing. However, the first word is commonly used in the United States, and the word in parentheses is used in the British Isles. Write a story in which you substitute the British words for the words you are more likely to use. For example, you might write about asking a bobby to direct you to a place where you can rent a flat in a building with a lift or get your driving license or have a meal of fish and chips.

| | |
|---|---|
| A | apartment (flat) |
| B | baby carriage (pram), beets (beet roots) |
| C | cookie (biscuit), crib (cot), cop (bobby), candy (sweets) |
| D | driver's license (driving license), dishwashing liquid (washing-up liquid) |
| E | elevator (lift), eggplant (aubergine), expressway (motorway) |
| F | fries (chips), fire department (fire brigade) |
| G | garden hose (hosepipe), garbage can (dustbin), gasoline (petrol) |
| H | hood of a car (bonnet), hardware (ironmongery) |
| I | |
| J | |
| K | |
| L | long distance call (trunk call), lawyer (barrister) |
| M | mail (post), muffler (silencer) |
| N | nail polish (nail varnish) |
| O | out of style (out of fashion) |
| P | pail (bucket), period (full stop), pitcher (jug), potato chips (crisps), popsicle (ice lolly) |
| Q | quotation marks (inverted commas) |
| R | refrigerator (fridge), railroad car (railroad carriage) |
| S | soda (fizzy drink), subway (underground or tube), sidewalk (pavement), stove (cooker) |
| T | thread (cotton), traffic circle (roundabout), trunk of a car (boot), truck (lorry), two weeks (fortnight) |
| U | |
| V | |
| W | windshield wiper (windscreen wiper) |
| X | |
| Y | |
| Z | |

# INTERNET LINKS

http://www.etymonline.com/

http://www.behindthename.com/

http://www.wordorigins.org/

http://eleaston.com/etymology.html

Strategies, Genres,
Topics, and Tools

Words Are Free!

Have Words,
Can Write

Writing Is Thinking

Write to a Martian

Every Word
Has a Story

**Organize
Your Writing**

Know Who You
Know and Know
Who You Are!

Think in Threes

Everybody Has
to Be Someplace

Let's Make
a Movie!

Words Inspire

Know Thyself

Writers Are Editors

A Goal for
Every Student

CHAPTER SEVEN

# Profiles and Frames

## Organize Your Writing

*Patterns give context to information that otherwise would be meaningless.*

~Eric Jensen (1998, p. 95)

## WRITING AND ORGANIZATION

In the previous chapters, we have focused mainly on building fluency by using specific organizers such as Taxonomies, Metacognition Statements, Defining Format, and Morphology Charts. In the strategy Profiles and Frames, we present two organizing formats that guide the students into research and developing full-length pieces. Organization (in writing) requires the writer to maintain a "progression, relatedness, and completeness of ideas, or simply put, making the writing unified and complete" (Public Schools of North Carolina, n.d.). Many students, especially in the upper grades, are asked or taught to make an outline to achieve this unity. While outlines are useful for writers who already have a good sense of composing, we have found Profiles and Frames to be particularly valuable for students who need specific guidance or steps to get started.

## WHAT IS A PROFILE?

A Profile is a visual outline that helps the writer organize information about a topic, such as animals, art, persons of accomplishment, or political and geographic entities. Profiles guide students in selecting specific information from written text, enabling them to restate or write the information in *their own words* without resorting to major copying. In fact, the only way that most people can truly paraphrase, or write in their own words, is to take notes and then restate from their notes. By using Profiles, students learn the technique of moving from notes to writing without having to copy text verbatim. You can create Profiles for almost any aspect of the content area. For example, Profiles can be created about a planet, country, city, colony, cultural group, geometric shape, element or compound, plant, character, and more.

## How to Use Profiles

Students can use Profiles templates to organize ideas prior to writing about them. The purpose of using a Profile is to highlight key information required for the writing piece. Profiles can be used to organize information in a variety of ways, for a multitude of subjects, and for writers at all grade levels. For example, the animal Profile shown in Figure 7.1 can be adapted for a specific grade level or content or to engage student interest. If you wanted your students to learn about the primary characteristics of an animal, you could modify this Profile, requesting information you wanted to focus on by adding

- Phylum, genus, and related species.
- Method of reproduction and gestation period.
- Weight, height, length, girth.

Figures 7.2 and 7.3 shows an animal Profile completed by a sixth grade student who used the textbook and the Internet to research her topic—Siberian tigers.

If you are using an animal Profile, you can have students develop specialized Taxonomies dealing with topics such as animal colors (e.g., amber, calico, pearl, salmon, tawny, umber, etc.) and verbs of animal locomotion (e.g., bound, careen, dart, lumber, pounce, etc.). These Taxonomies can provide the specialized vocabulary that relates to specific topics or concepts and gives the students additional information for writing in their own words.

You also may want to have students write Metacognition Statements indicating their prior knowledge of the topic. When the Profile is completed, students can add newly learned terms to their Taxonomies and revise their Metacognition Statements. Another option is for students to use the Profile as an outline, and write a report using the information they gathered or researched. If students have been using the Defining Format strategy (e.g., what is a tiger? see Chapter 5) prior to completing a Profile, they can add the appropriate information from the Defining Format into the Profile. Once students become familiar with Profiles, they can create their own, using previous Profiles as models. With this integration of strategies, students reinforce their *learning* of the content and continuously develop and practice their *writing* skills.

Figures 7.4–7.5 show Profiles that focus on topics in different content areas: art, careers, and sports and games. These Profiles can be adapted or modified as appropriate to your curriculum and grade level needs. Profiles for mathematics can be found in *Write for Mathematics* (Rothstein, Rothstein, & Lauber, 2006).

## Art Profile

To complete this template, shown in Figure 7.4, students should be involved in a curriculum that presents various works of art: paintings, sculpture, photography, ceramics, or any other artistic form. You may wish to use the Art Profile in conjunction with an artist of the month or art form of the month program, so that the students have ongoing opportunities to become familiar with different artists and their work. Students also could use this Profile to describe the artwork of their

**Figure 7.1**    Animal Profile

Directions: Select an animal that you like or that you are learning about, and complete the following Profile. When you have all the information, write what you now know about that animal.

Name of Animal

_____

Colors

_____

Size

_____

Special Markings (stripes, quills, spots, etc.)

_____

Sound Animal Makes

_____

Natural Habitats

_____

_____

Food(s) Animal Eats

_____

_____

Method of Getting Food

_____

Method(s) of Movement

_____

_____

Special Habits

_____

_____

Classification (fish, amphibian, reptile, bird, mammal, etc.)

_____

Other Classification (canine, feline, bovine, etc.)

_____

Other Information

_____

**Figure 7.2**     Animal Profile Completed by a Sixth Grade Student

Directions: Select an animal that you like or that you are learning about and complete the following Profile. When you have all the information, write what you now know about that animal.

| | |
|---|---|
| Name of Animal | *Siberian tiger* |
| Colors | *yellow orange* |
| Size | *13 feet long and weighs about 700 pounds* |
| Special Markings | *thick yellow fur with dark stripes* |
| Sound | *loud roars and growls* |
| Natural Habitat(s) | *Northern Asia in the mountains and up to the Arctic Circle* |
| Food(s) | *eats deer, cattle, snakes, termites, and carrion (animals that have been lying dead for a while)* |
| Method of Getting Food | *hunting and preying (animal is a predator)* |
| Method(s) of Movement | *runs, walks, prowls* |
| Special Habits | *prefers to be alone, is solitary* |
| Classification | *mammal* |
| Other Classification | *belongs to the Feline family and is also known as Panthera tigris* |
| Other Information | *is very rare and endangered; the mother has a litter of two or three cubs and the cubs stay with the mother for about a year* |

Following this Profile is the student's written paragraph about the animal.

**Figure 7.3**     Student Report

## My Report on the Siberian Tiger

The Siberian Tiger is the largest tiger in the world. It is thirteen feet long and weighs about seven hundred pounds. Its color is yellowy orange like other tigers and of course it has stripes on its thick fur. It lives in Northern Asia in Siberia, which is at the Arctic Circle, so the Siberian tiger is used to cold weather. The Siberian tiger is a mammal and also belongs to the feline or cat family.

This tiger is a predator. That means that it hunts other animals for its food. It will eat deer, cattle, snakes, and even termites. Sometimes it eats dead meat that has been lying around on the ground, called carrion. The Siberian tiger likes to be alone and only mates once a year with another tiger. When the mother has babies, she usually has two or three cubs and they stay with her for about a year. She teaches them to hunt so they can get their own food. The Siberian Tiger is endangered so we must not kill it or we will not ever be able to see this big tiger in person.

**Figure 7.4**    Art Profile

Directions: Select an art piece that interests you or that you are learning about, and complete the Profile. When you have all the information, write about that piece of art.

Title of Art _____

Name of Artist _____

Years of Artist's Life _____

Type of Art _____

Size of Art _____

Year Completed _____

Place Where Art Can Be Seen _____

Owner or Donor of Art _____

Description of Art _____

Subject or Theme _____

Materials Used _____

Colors _____

Other Information _____

My Reaction to this Artwork

_____

_____

_____

classmates. This personalization of art is particularly effective with young students who get to see themselves described as artists by their peers and whose artwork then is displayed with a completed Profile.

## Career Profile

From the middle grades through high school, students need to learn about careers, especially those that can be related to their school studies. Students often ask, "Why do I have to know this?" and while not all topics are career related, students often get a broader view of the work world and the related academic or subject-area requirements when the relationships between the two are demonstrated to them.

Before completing the Career Profile shown in Figure 7.5, have your students create a Taxonomy of occupations or careers. The Taxonomy can be a list of diverse occupations (e.g., author, baker, or carpenter) or it can be a list of specialized occupations in relation to a specific subject (e.g., science: astronomer, biologist, cardiologist, ecologist, or geneticist; mathematics: accountant, cartographer, economist, geographer, meteorologist, or navigator). Students can choose a career from their Taxonomies to research, using the career Profile for recording basic information.

**Figure 7.5**     Career Profile

Directions: Select an occupation or career and use the Profile to record your information. You may obtain information by interviewing a person who has that career, or you may check materials in the library or on the Internet. When you have completed the Profile, write a Metacognition Statement that tells why you think this career would be a good choice for you or might not be a good choice.

Name of Career or Occupation _____

Major Duties or Tasks _____

_____

Training Needed or Required _____

_____

Beginning Salary _____

Highest Range of Salaries _____

Personal Abilities Needed _____

_____

Places of Work (e.g., outdoor, indoors, foreign countries) _____

_____

Specializations Within Career (e.g., gym teacher, police detective, or technical writer)

_____

_____

Other Information _____

_____

_____

_____

_____

## Sports and Games Profile

Only occasionally does the health or physical education teacher ask students to write. An obvious reason is that students expect to *do* an activity, not write about it. Yet, the world of sports and games is full of writing—sports stories, instructions, events, awards, just to name a few. And since most students enjoy sports and games, they may enjoy or can come to enjoy writing about them. Writing about sports also creates an interdisciplinary opportunity.

Prior to doing a Profile, students can create a Taxonomy of sports and/or games. While this is an easy Taxonomy for students to do because they have so much prior knowledge, research adds a new dimension. For example, there are sports that are not well known in America, such as rugby, polo, and jai alai. Sports have histories, personalities, and specialized language that can interest and fascinate students. Figure 7.6 shows a sports and games Profile that is a starting point for writing about topics that often carry great interest for students.

**Figure 7.6**    Sports and Games Profile

Directions: Select a sport or game that interests you. Check books, magazines, and the Internet for information on that sport or game. When you have completed the Profile, write a sports article telling a person unfamiliar with the sport or game what she or he needs to know to understand it or play it.

Name of Sport or Game _____

Number of Players Required_____

Countries Where Popular _____

Equipment Needed _____

_____

_____

Uniform Items _____

_____

Names of Team Positions (e.g., pitcher, goalie) _____

_____

_____

*(Continued)*

**Figure 7.6** (Continued)

Scoring Terms _____

_____

Other Special Terms _____

_____

Object or Purpose (e.g., cross finish line first) _____

_____

Other Information _____

_____

_____

# WHAT IS A FRAME?

A Frame is another organizing template that provides students with a structure for writing a story, an explanation, or a narrative. It is a textual outline that helps students get started and to focus on the topic through use of transition words or narrative markers. A Frame is useful as an instructional approach to guide students in the early stages of writing, such as sentence and paragraph development. When students use Frames, they begin to internalize the formal structures that writing demands and, over time, move to independent writing while retaining organization and a consistent point of view.

The types of Frames used can vary depending on grade level(s) and or subject area(s). You and your students can create original Frames forming the structure and deciding the information the Frame should contain. As a starter, we offer a variety of Frames that can be used repeatedly and with a wide range of grade levels and abilities. Subsequent chapters also have Frames (as well as Profiles) that relate to the topics in these chapters. Feel free to modify them to meet your students' needs.

## Frames for Primary Grades

Young students do particularly well when they use Frames as the springboard for organized and, eventually, detailed writing. Since many writers worry so much about spelling and format, they feel more secure when they have a plan to follow and know that their writing sounds "good." Figure 7.7 (see page 100) shows a Frame adapted from an old jump rope rhyme known as "A, My Name Is _____" (To make it easier for young students, we have not used the original alphabet format of this Frame, but you can certainly go back to that one if you wish.)

Students can complete the Frame with a classmate and share their completed writing with the class. After the students have completed the Frame, you can assemble all of the Frames in a book that the students illustrate with drawings of themselves, their friends, and whatever else they might like. As an extension, this Frame can be used to set up a Taxonomy of places the students come from as the start of a geography lesson or activity. The Frames shown in Figures 7.8–7.10 are also simple organizers for young or emerging writers.

Use these examples as models to design your own Frames, making them more complex as your students' writing skills develop.

**Figure 7.7**     A Frame for the Primary Grades

> Hi, my name is... [Evan],
>
> My friend's name is... [Nora],
>
> We come from... [Los Angeles],
>
> And we like... [swimming].

**Figure 7.8**     Meet My Teacher

My teacher's name is _____

She teaches me many things.

First, _____

_____

Second, _____

_____

Third, _____

_____

I think _____

_____

_____

**Figure 7.9**     People I Love

There are many people I love.

First, _____

because_____

Second, _____

especially_____

Third, _____

who _____

These are some of the people who I love.

**Figure 7.10**     Then, Now, Later

Directions: Complete the first four lines of the Frame with important events that happened to you at different times in your life. Then complete the last two lines with what you think will happen when you grow up.

When I was small I _____

I also _____

Now I _____

I also _____

When I grow up I will_____

I will also _____

## Frames for the Intermediate Grades and for Middle and High School

Frames can be used to ensure that students follow a writing plan, use transitional markers, and keep to the topic—the three essential rubrics of quality writing. An easy way to develop one's own Frames for content areas is to use the starting or topic sentences of books or texts the students are using. Then create the Frames that will allow students to write (in their own words) the significant information you want them to know. For example, your students can be given a starting sentence such as, "Early people survived cold weather in several ways." Then provide the transition words, e.g., *first, in addition, furthermore.*

A Frame using words from a mathematics text might be, "The Greeks demonstrated that no matter what the size and shape of a right triangle, certain relationships always held true. First, _____. From this concept, we find _____. Following this, we realize [discover, find out] _____."

When students then move from Frames to writing independently, they will have had intensive practice in fulfilling the basic rules of organization. Figures 7.11–7.14 show more detailed examples using starting or topic sentences in different content areas.

**Figure 7.11**    Fossils of Dinosaurs and Other Prehistoric Animals

How do we know so much about animals that roamed Earth millions of years ago?

Most of our knowledge comes from _____

_____

From this knowledge, we learn _____

_____

We also learn _____

_____

Finally, we learn _____

_____

Fossils are found in many places.

They may be _____

_____

Another place to _____

_____

Sometimes fossils are found _____

_____

Fossils are formed in several ways.

Sometimes _____

_____

A second way _____

Then there are fossils that _____

By studying fossils, we better understand _____

**Figure 7.12**    People and Weather

People in different parts of the world have to adapt to different kinds of weather. They wear different clothing, have different types of houses, and eat different types of food.

In cold climates, for example, _____

_____

_____

_____

However, in climates that are warm all year round,

_____

_____

_____

_____

People who live in places where the weather changes

_____

_____

_____

_____

Since I live in a place where the weather

_____,

I wear _____

I live _____

As for food, I am able to _____

_____

Because Earth has such varied climate, human beings have learned

_____

_____

_____

_____

**Figure 7.13**  Sculptures in Non-Western Cultures

There are many types of sculptures made by people in non-Western cultures.

Nomadic hunting groups, like the Inuit, have made

_____ ,

_____ , and _____

_____

_____

Each of these sculptures has a different purpose.

For example, _____

_____

Then there is the _____

_____

Traditional African sculpture is very diverse.

Among the Ashanti, _____

_____

In Nigeria, the Yoruba _____

_____

Further south, _____

_____

_____

In the Far East, the religious teachings of Buddha influenced much art. There are statues of

_____

that _____

Then there are buildings of worship in _____

_____

_____

Finally, there are representations of different individuals who

_____

_____

_____

**Figure 7.14**    How to Shoot a Free Throw in Basketball

First, stand behind the free-throw line with a basketball.

Second, _____

_____

_____

After that, _____

_____

_____

Then _____

_____

_____

Fourth, _____

_____

_____

Finally, _____

_____

_____

If you have followed these steps, you will _____

_____

_____

_____

# ABC STORIES—FRAMEWORK FOR INNOVATING ON LITERARY STRUCTURE

A frequent concern of teachers is that student writing lacks sentence variety. Teachers will exhort students to start their sentences with words other than *the, he,* or *and then* only to find their efforts are wasted, mainly because students can't think of other words. To help students realize the variety of words that they actually know and are capable of using, students can write ABC Stories—stories in which each sentence begins with a successive letter of the alphabet. We have placed this activity within Profiles and Frames, because in writing an ABC story, the student already has the framework of a previously created piece of writing for re-creating a new piece. By providing students the opportunity to innovate on literary structure, we offer them a roadmap for creative, interesting, and often humorous writing. This activity can be used from the primary grades through high school (and beyond). Figure 7.15 includes instructions for writing an ABC fairy tale plus a model for students to follow. Enjoy.

**Figure 7.15**    Writing an ABC Story

You can write a delightful, creative story by following these directions:

- First, think of a fairy tale that you know well. Some possibilities might be *Goldilocks and the Three Bears*, *The Three Little Pigs*, *Little Red Riding Hood*, *Cinderella*, or a similar type of story.
- Start the first sentence of your story with the letter A, the second sentence with the letter B, and so forth.
- Continue until you get to the end of the story. If you can, try to end with a sentence that starts with the letter Z.

Here is an example of an ABC story about the Three Little Pigs.

**A** long time ago, a Mother Pig told her three young pigs to build their own houses.

"**B**uild your houses of the best materials you can," she advised.

**C**arl, the youngest Pig, chose to make his house of straw.

**D**amien, the middle Pig, thought that sticks would make a strong house.

**E**dgar, the oldest and wisest of the Pigs, knew that a house of bricks might last forever.

**F**or a while, Carl was safe in his house of straw.

"**G**reat!" he thought.

"**H**aving a straw house is cheap and pleasant."

**I**magine his surprise when a Wolf came by one day and knocked on his door.

"**J**iggledy, jiggledy, jiggledy, jiggledy jin,

**K**eep out of my way as I blow your house in."

**L**ittle Carl's straw house was blown into hundreds of pieces and scattered everywhere.

"**M**aking a house of straw was not a good idea," thought Carl.

**N**ow Damien happened to meet a man selling sticks.

"**O**h goody!" thought Damien, "Sticks will make a perfect house."

**P**utting together a house with sticks was easy for Damien and in a few hours, he was nice and cozy.

"**Q**uaint ideas my brothers have," pondered Edgar.

**R**ealizing his brothers' mistakes, Edgar looked for a person selling bricks.

**S**oon, out of nowhere, a mason appeared with a wagon full of bricks.

*(Continued)*

**Figure 7.15** (Continued)

---

Taking the mason's whole stock, Edgar eventually had a strong, sturdy house.

Unfortunately, Mr. Wily Wolf had been watching this whole event with the three pigs.

Very quickly, he attacked each house, first huffing and puffing to blow down the straw house, then huffing and puffing to destroy the house of sticks.

Wily Wolf, however, would not be successful in blowing down Edgar's house of bricks.

eXpecting* the Wolf to be at his door after destroying his brothers' houses, Edgar placed a large fan at his door that would blow away Wily instead of Wily blowing away his house.

Yes, Edgar was indeed the wisest pig because the fan did just what he expected and the brick house remained strong and sturdy.

Zipping quickly over to his homeless brothers, Edgar invited them to stay until they too could build their own houses of bricks and live safely and independently without every again worrying about Wily Wolf and his huffing and puffing.

*A little trick for the lack of X words.

---

Obviously, with this activity, the student must use a variety of sentence starters—names, quotations, *-ing* verbs, exclamations, and whatever other forms come to mind. After re-creating several fairy tales, the students can write a variety of ABC pieces as in the examples below, an activity that will be enjoyable and will also develop sentence variety and expanded use of structure and vocabulary. Figure 7.16 is an example of a factual event using the ABC framework; Figures 7.17 and 7.18 use the acrostic framework, which uses the letters of a word as the basis for writing.

**Figure 7.16**    A Factual ABC Story

---

Almost four hundred years ago, people called Pilgrims were forced to leave England because of their religious beliefs.

But they were not sure of where to go.

Could they find a home outside of England, they wondered.

During their search for a place to live, they heard about Holland.

Every English Pilgrim who had visited Holland came back and spoke of the kindness of the Dutch people.

Freedom of religion was important to the Pilgrims, so they hired a ship and brought their families to Holland.

Giving up their English ways, however, was not easy.

Hearing their children speak Dutch and forgetting their English made the Pilgrims unhappy.

"It's time to sail to the New World," their leaders advised.

"Just as God brought us to Holland, so God will deliver us to America."

—Eighth Grade Student

**Figure 7.17** An Acrostic Story

In this assignment, students wrote a descriptive piece using an acrostic of a place they have visited.

Marco Island is my favorite place to visit in the winter.

At night we have the most beautiful sunsets.

Rising early is important if you want to watch the seagulls playing.

Children splash and swim in the warm Gulf waters.

Of all the places in the world, I love Marco Island best.

—Fifth Grade Student

**Figure 7.18** A Dialogue on Soccer

In a dialogue, students select a topic that interests them and create an acrostic using the letters of the topic to start each sentence. Following is an example of a student-created dialogue between two people talking about soccer.

| | |
|---|---|
| Person 1 | Some day I hope to be the soccer champion of the world. |
| Person 2 | Only people born with strong legs can be soccer champions. |
| Person 1 | Champions are made, not born. |
| Person 2 | Crazy ideas come into your head. |
| Person 1 | Everyone can dream, and playing soccer is my dream. |
| Person 2 | Remember that you will have to practice every day, seven days a week, and you can never give up. |

—Ninth Grade Students

# INTERNET LINKS

http://mendota.english.wisc.edu/~WAC/page.jsp?id=48&c_type=category&c_id=32

http://english.ttu.edu/kairos/3.1/news/paradigm/orgnfrms.htm

http://www.angelfire.com/wi/writingprocess/specificgos.html

Strategies, Genres,
Topics, and Tools

Words Are Free!

Have Words,
Can Write

Writing Is Thinking

Write to a Martian

Every Word
Has a Story

Organize
Your Writing

**Know Who You
Know and Know
Who You Are!**

Think in Threes

Everybody Has
to Be Someplace

Let's Make
a Movie!

Words Inspire

Know Thyself

Writers Are Editors

A Goal for
Every Student

# CHAPTER EIGHT

# *W*ho's Who

## Know Who You Know
## and Know Who You Are!

*The final mystery is oneself.*

~Oscar Wilde

## WHO'S WHO: THE HUMANITY IN WRITING

Who's Who is the strategy that combines Taxonomies, Profiles, Frames, and a variation of Defining Format (called Biographic Format) to guide students in writing three exciting genres: biography, autobiography, and memoirs. By creating Taxonomies of mathematicians, social activists, inventors, and so forth, students acquire a research bank to draw upon. The Profiles, Frames, and Biographic Format serve as the organizational formats for this form of nonfiction writing. These genres—biography, autobiography, and memoir—are linked by similarities and differences that make all of them valuable for learning and for having in one's files or folders throughout the school years.

Writing biographies and biographical sketches makes students focus on those persons who have contributed to a society's knowledge, values, and aspirations. Writing autobiographical pieces and memoirs gets students to reflect upon their own history and their future goals and hopes. These genres both bring us together and allow us to express our individual and cultural experiences, creating opportunities for identity development and making the curriculum relevant for all students (Hinton & Dickinson, 2005). In *Memoir Writing* (2003), Elizabeth Uhlig refers to memoir writing as "deliberate introspection." She points out that "in collecting family stories or simply writing their own, [students] must pass through the process of thinking about things in a different way . . . reaching deeper and deeper levels of self-knowledge" (p. 3).

Writers of all ages can write in these genres. Biographies are commonplace topics for all students, as they learn about or commemorate famous people or people of accomplishment. Today, fortunately, there is a greater interest in learning about people whose contributions to humankind have traditionally been deemphasized or overlooked. African Americans, American Indians, Hispanic people, and women are among those who now get named or listed in textbooks along with the explorers of North and South America, presidents, and world leaders of the past and present. For generations, students have written biographic reports as they have studied history and current events.

An aspect of biographical learning often missing in the classroom is the focus on persons of accomplishment who have added to humankind's knowledge in subject areas. For example, how many mathematicians, except for Archimedes, Euclid, and Pythagoras, do students study in relationship to mathematics, and then write about them? Do students become acquainted with the great health professionals who have discovered cures and medicines for the dread diseases of the world? Who have been the dispensers of knowledge in biology, botany, geography, and other disciplines? Many students study facts and concepts about transportation or physical science without learning how motivated, creative human beings gathered the knowledge that is in today's texts and literature. As advocates for teaching about persons of accomplishment in all fields, we have combined the previously described strategies with several new ones that we believe will inspire students to write about them in a variety of interesting ways and possibly to emulate their contributions and accomplishments.

# FOCUS FOR WRITING BIOGRAPHIES

The most important element in the biography of a person is her or his accomplishment or accomplishments. Yet, without guidance or strategies, many students write (or copy) a biography as a chronology—the person was born, went to school, got married, became a teacher of the deaf, and died. The purpose of writing a biography is to enable the students to understand why they are celebrating that person and what the events or driving force(s) were that compelled the person to do the extraordinary or unusual.

When they create Taxonomies of people of accomplishment, your students can have discussions prior to the writing that focus on questions such as, "What makes someone a great scientist?" or "Why were some women willing to give up personal and economic security to fight for the rights of other women?" What gave African American slaves the courage to lead others and face dangers and hardships? Following discussions of these questions, students research the names of persons of accomplishment, creating Taxonomies, Profiles, and Frames in preparations for writing.

## Setting Up Taxonomies for Biographical Writing

Early in the school year, you can plan with your students to maintain ongoing Taxonomies of people related to the curriculum or subject areas. The names of these persons may come from texts, newspaper articles, library and Internet research, or students' prior knowledge. The Taxonomies should be organized by related accomplishments, giving rise to titles such as "Women in the Arts," "Great American Indian Leaders," or "Hispanic People of Accomplishment." By having these Taxonomies posted and compiled in their Notebooks, students will become knowledgeable about the vast numbers of people who have affected their lives.

Below is a plan you can follow for having your students write a biography on a scientist of accomplishment. The plan includes a Taxonomy (Figure 8.1), a Profile (Figure 8.2) a Biographic Format (Figure 8.3, similar to a Defining Format), and a Frame (Figure 8.4). With the Who's Who Taxonomy serving as a data bank of names, students can select someone who interests them. Some students may read a full-length biography for information; others may use an article from an encyclopedia or the Internet. As they read or after they have read, the students need to extract the significant information that will allow them to write their pieces, focusing on accomplishments and reasons for these accomplishments. The Profiles, Frames, and Biographic Format are the guides for getting this information. By using all of these strategies, students develop a deepened understanding of the people they are studying and also have the skills and frameworks for writing about them.

These names were gathered from various websites on women, scientists, and African American scientists. See Internet Links for specific sites.

After completing a Profile, students can set up a Biographic Format, which is similar to Defining Format (Chapter 5) but is designed for writing about a person rather than an object or concept. The template requires the student to identify the person she or he will write about and to list that person's accomplishments. Notice the use of *who* as the connector.

## Using Frames for Biographical Writing

A Frame can be used as a tool to help students write a summary biographical sketch, either to keep track of people they are studying or as the outline of a fuller report. Using the Person of Accomplishment Frame (Figure 8.4), the student states the subject's identity (i.e., name), defines the subject's role (e.g., musician, mathematician, social activist), and describes the significant accomplishment(s) that mark that person's life.

**Figure 8.1**    Women Scientists of Accomplishment

| • TAXONOMY • | |
|---|---|
| A | Ayrton, Hertha Marks—British physicist and mathematician |
| B | Blackwell, Elizabeth—American physician |
| C | Curie, Marie—Polish and French physicist |
| D | Daly, Marie—African American biochemist |
| E | Elion, Gertrude Belle—American pharmacologist |
| F | Fossey, Dian—American primatologist |
| G | Goodall, Jane—British ethologist |
| H | Hypatia—Greek mathematician |
| I | |
| J | Jemison, Mae C.—African American astronaut |
| K | Kenny, Elizabeth—Australian nurse |
| L | Levi-Montacini, Rita—Italian American neurologist |
| M | Meitner, Lise—Austrian Swedish physicist and mathematician |
| N | Niebla, Elvia—American environmentalist |
| O | Ochoa, Ellen—American engineer and astronaut |
| P | Pickney, Eliza Lucas—American horticulturist |
| Q | |
| R | Ride, Sally K—American astrophysicist and astronaut |
| S | Sheehan, Bess—American preservationist and environmentalist |
| T | Tereshkova, Valentina—Russian astronaut |
| U | Uhlenbeck, Karen—American mathematical physicist |
| V | Velez, Argelia Velez—Cuban American mathematician |
| W | Walker, Madame C J.—African American inventor |
| X | |
| Y | Yalow, Roslyn Sussman, American medical physicist |
| Z | |

**Figure 8.2**   Scientist Profile

Directions: Select a scientist who interests you. Complete the Profile. When you have all the information, write a summary biography about that scientist.

Name of Scientist _____

Years of Scientist's Life _____

Scientist's Nationality _____

Major Fields of Study (e.g., chemistry, astronomy, technology, etc.) _____

_____

Major Contributions to Science and Humanity

_____

_____

_____

Publications

_____

_____

Special Recognition and Awards

_____

Other Information

_____

A completed Person of Accomplishment Frame might look like this:

Lise Meitner was an Austrian physicist and mathematician who was the first woman to earn a doctorate at the University of Vienna.

She often dreamed about working with the German Nobel Prize–winning physicist Otto Hahn and becoming a lecturer at the Institute of Theoretical Physics in Berlin.

To accomplish her goal, she agreed to allow her scientific works to be published under a male name. She also had to give up her hope of working in Berlin because of Hitler's persecution of the Jews.

As a result of her dedication to her dream, her writings, and her hard work, the Swedish government invited her to Sweden in 1938, and she became a full professor at the Nobel Institute.

Today, Lise Meitner is remembered for scientific work that eventually led to her papers being published in her own name and for winning the Enrico Fermi Prize for outstanding accomplishments in physics.

Figure 8.3    Who Was Lise Meitner—1878–1968

| • BIOGRAPHIC FORMAT • | | |
|---|---|---|
| Question | Identities | Accomplishments |
| Who was Lise Meitner? | | |
| Lise Meiter was a | physicist and mathematician who | 1. was one of the first women to earn a doctorate at the University of Vienna, Austria.<br><br>2. went on to become a physicist in Germany.<br><br>3. worked with the German Nobel Prize–winning physicist Otto Hahn.<br><br>4. became a lecturer at the Institute of Theoretical Physics in Berlin.<br><br>5. had to publish her scientific works under a male name to get them published.<br><br>6. moved to Sweden in 1938 because of Hitler's persecution of the Jews.<br><br>7. became a full-fledged professor at the Nobel Institute. |

This Frame gives students a simple way to keep track of and retain the essential information of well-known or accomplished people. Using these strategies, a sixth grade student wrote the following biography of Mary McLeod Bethune:

Mary McLeod Bethune was an African American educator who accomplished many things for African American girls. At the time she lived, African American girls could not go to school. In 1910, Mary moved from Chicago to Florida and decided to open up her own school for African American girls. She went everywhere asking people for money to help. A company named Proctor & Gamble and a very rich man named John D. Rockefeller thought she had a good idea and gave her the money for a high school. She named her school the Bethune School for Girls. By 1925, she had more than a hundred girls in her school and she decided that it would be a good idea to have boys too. So her school joined with Cookman Institute. A few years later the school added on a college and was named the Bethune-Cookman College. Mary McLeod Bethune realized her dream and became the college's first president.

## Expanding the Taxonomy for Elaboration and Details

As students prepare to write their biographies, they need to be aware of the identities (roles) of the persons about whom they are studying or writing. For example, Abraham Lincoln did not become a president until he had been a rail-splitter, a reader, a lawyer, and a debater. He also had geographic and family identities (Kentuckian,

**Figure 8.4** Person of Accomplishment Frame

Directions: Use this Frame to write a summary biographical statement about a person of accomplishment.

(Name) _____ was a _____ (identity of accomplishment) _____
who _____ (significant accomplishment) _____
_____
_____

She (He) believed (wanted, fought for, dreamed, hoped to)
_____

To accomplish her (his) goal(s) she (he)
_____

As a result of her (his) dedication (hard work, beliefs, sacrifices)
_____
_____

(Put in the person's accomplishment[s])
_____
_____

husband). To help students understand the journey taken by their biographic subjects, they should set up a Dual Taxonomy of identities. In this Taxonomy, students first list the significant geographic, family, and occupational identities. Since many students have difficulty evoking words to describe the characteristics or traits of persons, they can use the Dual Taxonomy to compile a list of descriptive words for adding details to their topic sentences. Next, students select appropriate adjectives that match the identities of the person they are writing about (e.g., *dynamic* speaker). This Dual Taxonomy can then be used in conjunction with Profiles, Frames, or Biographic Format. Figure 8.5 includes the instructions and an example of a Dual Taxonomy for Dr. Martin Luther King Jr. (enter in the Notebook as "Dual Taxonomy"). This is a model that you can use for any person of accomplishment your students are learning about.

**Figure 8.5** Dual Taxonomy—Person of Accomplishment

Directions for a Dual Taxonomy on Dr. Martin Luther King Jr.:

**Step 1.** Setting up the pages
- Open to a double-page spread in your Notebook.
- Fold both the even-numbered and odd-numbered pages in half.
- Write "Person of Accomplishment Taxonomy" across the top margin.
- On the first line, in the first column of the even-numbered page, write the word "Identity."
- Then write the letters *A* to *M*, skipping lines. Double up if you need to.
- In the second column, write the word "Characteristics."
- On the odd-numbered page, write the same words ("Identity" and "Characteristics").
- Write the letters *N* to *Z*. Skip lines, and put *X, Y,* and *Z* together.

**Figure 8.5** (Continued)

**Step 2.** Completing the Dual Taxonomy
- First, we are going to list all the identities of Dr. Martin Luther King Jr. For example, we can begin with Dr. King as a leader.* We will write *leader* next to the letter *L*. We can then add that Dr. King was a minister. From what we have read and what we know, we will write the many identities of Dr. King.
- Second, we will now think of all the characteristics of Dr. King that made him a person of accomplishment. We can do this by starting with "Dr. King was _____."** One characteristic would be *peaceful*. Another characteristic would be *courageous*. We will add as many characteristics as we can think of.

**Step 3.** Writing an Opening Sentence
- From the Dual Taxonomy, you can write an opening sentence that will help you write a biographic report about Dr. King.
- First, select an identity that you want to focus on or write about.
- Second, select a characteristic that you think matches that identity. An example would be *brilliant orator*.
- Third, write your opening sentence using this pattern: Dr. Martin Luther King Jr. was a brilliant orator who _____.
- Fourth, complete the sentence by adding information about Dr. King being a brilliant orator, as in this example: "Dr. Martin Luther King Jr. was a brilliant orator who convinced millions of people to fight for civil rights."
- Fifth, write a paragraph or more that supports your opening statement.

**• PERSON OF ACCOMPLISHMENT TAXONOMY* •**

| | Identity | Characteristics | | | Identity | Characteristics |
|---|---|---|---|---|---|---|
| A | African-American | activist | | N | Nobel Prize | noble winner |
| B | | brave | | O | orator | open-minded |
| C | civil rights activist | capable, caring | | P | peacemaker | peaceful |
| D | | determined | | Q | | |
| E | educator | energetic | | R | | reasonable |
| F | father | forceful | | S | Southerner | sympathetic |
| G | Georgian | generous | | T | teacher | thoughtful |
| H | humanitarian | humane | | U | unifier | understanding |
| I | | intelligent | | V | | valiant |
| J | | judicious | | W | writer | wise |
| K | | kind | | X, Y, Z | | zealous |
| L | leader | loyal | | | | |
| M | minister | magnificent | | | | |

*To form the sentence for the identity, have the students say, "Dr. King was a _____." When they use the word "a" (or "an"), the word that follows is a noun.

**To form the sentence for the characteristic, have the students say, "Dr. King was _____." When they omit the article, the word that follows is an adjective.

As the following writing samples show, the adjectives enhance the identity and provide the students with the words for creating a focused and detailed opening sentence.

---

Dr. Martin Luther King Jr. was a forceful civil rights activist who was determined to improve the lives of African Americans and other minority peoples.

or

Dr. Martin Luther King Jr. was a magnificent orator whose speeches moved people to take action against laws of segregation and inequality.

---

## USING WHO'S WHO TO WRITE AUTOBIOGRAPHIES AND MEMOIRS

An autobiography is a personalized biography, and therefore, many of the same strategies used for writing the biography can be used, with adaptations, for an autobiography. The autobiography has its own specific genre format, because the writer is working from a highly personal perspective. An autobiography, as distinguished from a memoir, generally has a chronological basis, whereas a memoir is more likely to focus on a selection of memories, with or without the chronology.

The students can begin by creating Taxonomies related to themselves, with topics such as "My Interests and Hobbies," "My Favorite Authors," and "Places I Would Like to Visit," among others. Again, the Taxonomy is the data bank that provides information for the personal Profiles that follow. From the Profiles, the students can move to a variety of Frames that are organized around personal themes or topics (e.g., memories, feelings, wishes).

Students generally enjoy writing about themselves, and students at all grade levels can write autobiographies or memoirs. One way to get started is to have students create a personal identity Taxonomy at the beginning of the school year, as described in Chapter 2, Figure 2.8. After the students have their individual personal identity Taxonomies, they complete the personal Profile (Figure 8.6). With these two preliminary items, they can create both short and long pieces about themselves, adding information each year and building an ongoing story of their lives. Students can use a personal Profile to help them create a valuable record of who they are and what they hope to become.

**Figure 8.6**    Personal Profile

Directions: Use this Profile to write information about yourself. When the Profile is completed, write a description of yourself, or use the Profile for information when you write your autobiography.

First Name _____ Middle Name _____

Last Name _____ Other Names _____

ADDRESS (for local and interplanetary use)*

House Number _____

Street (Avenue, Road, Lane, Circle, etc.) _____

Borough, Village, Town, or City _____

State _____ Zip Code _____ Country _____

Continent _____ Hemisphere _____

Planet _____

BIRTH INFORMATION

Date of Birth _____ Place of Birth _____

Present Age _____

PHYSICAL DESCRIPTION

Height _____ Weight _____ Color of Eyes _____

Color of Hair _____

Other physical characteristics (tall, curly hair) _____

PERSONAL INTERESTS

Sports I Enjoy _____

Favorite Television Programs _____

_____

Movies I've Enjoyed _____

_____

Music I Play and/or Music I Like _____

SCHOOL INFORMATION

School I'm Attending _____

Schools I've Attended _____

Best School Subjects _____

After-School Activities _____

Most Memorable Teachers _____

Other Information About Me _____

_____

*The interplanetary address will be discussed more fully in Chapter 10.

# FRAMES FOR AUTOBIOGRAPHIES AND MEMOIRS

An autobiography is not only a record of one's past but an ongoing endeavor that the writer uses to document events for future retrospection. The student who has been fortunate enough to have written anecdotes, feelings, beliefs, dreams, and other information about himself or herself has a personal gift for future sharing and the makings of a complete autobiography or memoir. Figures 8.7–8.14 illustrate Frames that can guide students at all levels in writing personal statements and full-length pieces. Use these Frames as models to meet the specific needs of your students.

**Figure 8.7**    Memories

I am now _____ years old, and I can remember many important events.

I remember the first time I _____

Then I remember when _____

When I was _____ years old, I _____

This year, when I started _____ grade, I _____

I know that next year _____

**Figure 8.8**    Memories Over Time

My life has had many events from the time I was born until now. Here are some highlights that I would like to share.

First, there were my early years, from my birth till I went to school. (Write several events.) _____

When I started school, there were many events and changes in my life.

_____

I also have memories of my family and my family life.

_____

I am now looking ahead and thinking of my future.

_____

**Figure 8.9**     Down Memory Lane

Directions: Think back to important events in your life and complete each sentence. Then add the details of that memory to the sentence.

One of my earliest memories is

_____

One of my happiest memories is

_____

One of my most exciting memories is

_____

In addition, I have other memories that I would like to share.

_____

**Figure 8.10**     My Accomplishments—From Then to Now

Although I am only _____ years old, I can look back on many accomplishments in my life.

When I was a preschooler, I already knew how to _____,

_____ , and _____

By the time I entered school, I could _____,

_____ , and _____

During my early school years, I _____,

_____ , and _____

At this time of my life, I can _____,

_____ , and _____

Having accomplished so much already, I know that I will be capable of _____,

_____ , and _____

**Figure 8.11**   Feelings

Like all people, I have many feelings, some pleasant and some unpleasant. Here are some of my feelings that I would like to share.

I laugh when

_____

I get angry when

_____

I feel great when

_____

I worry when

_____

I feel I have had a good day when

_____

**Figure 8.12**   If I . . . .

Directions: Complete these sentences. Then go back to each sentence and write three or four sentences telling more about what you would do to make what you could do happen.

If I could do one great act in my life, I _____

If I could honor a wonderful person, I _____

If I could travel to any place I wanted, I _____

If I could help people in need, I _____

If I could entertain one person of accomplishment, I _____

_____

**Figure 8.13**    I Have a Dream

Directions: Use the Frame to write your dream of the future. You probably have more than one dream, so use this Frame as often as you like to express your ideas. Your dream might be about your personal life or about how you might help others.

I have a dream that _____

In this dream, I see myself _____

To make this dream come true, I _____

_____

_____

**Figure 8.14**    Ten Years From Now

Directions: Imagine yourself 10 years from now, and complete this Frame. Then add details to each sentence.

Ten years from now, I will be _____ years old.

I expect to have _____

I might be living _____

Hopefully, I will be planning to _____

_____

As I look ahead to 10 years from now, I know that _____

_____

## ADDITIONAL WHO'S WHO PROFILES

Figures 8.15–8.18 show Profiles relating to people in different areas of accomplishment that you can use or modify for your own grade level or subject area.

**Figure 8.15**   Social Activist Profile

Directions: Select a social or civil rights activist who interests you. Complete the Profile. When you have all the information, write several paragraphs about that person.

Name of Activist _____

Years of Activist's Life _____

Nationality _____

Major or Significant Social Beliefs _____

_____

Accomplishments and Contributions to Humanity _____

_____

_____

_____

Publications _____

_____

Special Recognition and Awards _____

_____

Other Information _____

_____

**Figure 8.16**    Mathematician or Scientist Profile

Directions: Imagine that you are a scientist or mathematician making a presentation at a conference. Complete the following personal Profile as the basis for introducing yourself and your work to your colleagues.


My Name _____

_____


My Place of Birth and My Early Schooling _____

_____


My College and University Studies and Training (or other training)

_____


My work was mainly influenced by the previous studies of (add other names if appropriate)

_____

_____

_____


In my own work, I contributed the following information (ideas):

_____

**Figure 8.17**   Composer Profile

Directions: Select a composer who interests you. Then complete the Profile. Write a biographical sketch of this composer to present to your classmates. If possible, play a selection of the composer's music from a CD or tape when you do your presentation.

Name of Composer_____

Years of Person's Life _____

Birthplace (Nationality) _____

Category(ies) of Music (jazz, classical) _____

Musical Instruments Played or Composed for

_____

Famous Compositions_____

_____

Musical Influences in Composer's Life_____

_____

Challenges Faced and Overcome _____

_____

Special Recognition and Awards _____

_____

Other Information_____

Personal Reaction to this Composer's Music _____

_____

**Figure 8.18**   Explorer Profile

Directions: Select an explorer you are studying or interested in. Complete the Profile. Then write a biographical report about that explorer. Include pictures and maps if you can.

Name of Explorer _____

Nationality (Place of Birth) _____

Approximate Dates of Explorer's Life _____

Country Explorer Worked for _____

Reasons for the Exploration(s) _____

_____

_____

Major Places of Exploration _____

_____

Results of Exploration _____

_____

Places Named After Explorer _____

_____

Other Information _____

_____

## INTERNET LINKS

http://www.crystalinks.com/scientists.html

http://www.ziplink.net/~pik/Famous%20Scientists.html

http://chem.ch.huji.ac.il/~eugeniik/history/electrochemists.htm

http://www-groups.dcs.st-and.ac.uk/~history/BiogIndex.html

http://www.ncsu.edu/midlink/vy/vymath.htm

http://www.agnesscott.edu/lriddle/women/women.htm

http://www.millville.org/lakeside/afamsci/nickerson.html

http://www.libraries.psu.edu/gateway/referenceshelf/bio.htm

http://www.kidinfo.com/American_History/Famous_Historical_People.htm

http://www.ewebtribe.com/NACulture/famous.htm

http://www.personal.psu.edu/faculty/c/s/csr4/PSU3/Hispanic-Latino-Americans/
Hispanic-Latino-Americans.html

http://teacher.scholastic.com/activities/asian-american/notables.htm

http://www.edwardsly.com/biography.html

Strategies, Genres,
Topics, and Tools

Words Are Free!

Have Words,
Can Write

Writing Is Thinking

Write to a Martian

Every Word
Has a Story

Organize
Your Writing

Know Who You
Know and Know
Who You Are!

**Think in Threes**

Everybody Has
to Be Someplace

Let's Make
a Movie!

Words Inspire

Know Thyself

Writers Are Editors

A Goal for
Every Student

CHAPTER NINE

# Reasons, Causes, Results— The Basis of the Essay

## Think in Threes

*We usually say "reading and writing," so it sounds as though I'm putting the cart before the horse. But I call* writing *the horse. Nothing can be read unless it was first written.*

~Peter Elbow (2004)

"Write an essay of 250 words about. . . ." What high school or college student hasn't heard those words? And what student hasn't pondered over what, exactly, an essay is? The *Random House Webster's Unabridged Dictionary* (2003) defines *essay* as "a short literary composition on a particular theme or subject, usually in prose and generally analytic, speculative, or interpretative." Yet, even this definition doesn't necessarily help the student writer understand the required format or know quite what the teacher has in mind without being given a detailed explanation. One reason for the difficulty in writing an essay is that it is a form of "academic writing," and, as pointed out by Robinson, "is different from the kind of writing that one does naturally like writing letters to friends or [writing] entries in a journal" (1993, p. 205). However, once students have a clear definition of what an essay is, understand the different forms of essays, and have been *taught* a strategy or plan for writing in this genre, they begin to write clearly and pointedly.

To explain essays to your students, use the Defining Format template (Chapter 5), and have them enter the information in the Notebook. You might also want to post the templates for essays on the wall. In addition to providing a general definition of an essay, we have divided this genre into three formats based on the topics most teachers assign or the prompts students have to respond to on state tests. You will give your students a great gift—the skills they need for academic writing—by having them learn and practice these essay formats. Having learned the previously introduced strategies for fluency and organization, they are ready for *very good* essay writing.

Figures 9.1–9.4 illustrate the definitions of essays that your students need to understand and practice during much of their school lives.

**Figure 9.1**    What Is an Essay?

| Question | Category | Characteristics |
| --- | --- | --- |
| What is an essay? | | |
| An essay is a | writing genre that | 1. focuses on a particular theme or idea. 2. supports that idea with evidence or research. 3. can be written from a personal, persuasive, or explanatory point of view. 4. is short when compared to genres such as research reports or articles. |

**Figure 9.2**    What Is a Personal Essay?

| Question | Category | Characteristics |
| --- | --- | --- |
| What is a personal essay? | | |
| A personal essay is a | writing genre that | 1. is written from a first person perspective and generally includes the word "I." 2. states a theme, idea, or belief of the writer. 3. has supporting statements based on the writer's personal experiences or viewpoints. 4. can include supporting statements from others that relate to the writer's perspectives. |

**Figure 9.3**    What Is a Persuasive Essay?

| Question | Category | Characteristics |
|---|---|---|
| What is a persuasive essay? | | |
| A persuasive essay is a | writing genre that | 1. the writer uses to convince others of a specific belief or idea.<br>2. generally includes the words "we should," "we must," or "we need to."<br>3. has supporting statements based on the writer's perspective that these beliefs or ideas can benefit others or have merit or value.<br>4. indicates the writer's point of view or opinion. |

**Figure 9.4**    What Is an Explanatory Essay?

| Question | Category | Characteristics |
|---|---|---|
| What is an explanatory* essay? | | |
| An explanatory essay is a | writing genre that | 1. explains the why or how of a particular concept or idea.<br>2. contains factual information related to the concept.<br>3. includes research or evidence to support the concept.<br>4. is generally objectively stated, rather than an expression of an opinion. |

NOTE: *Schools often use the term *expository* to define an essay genre. We prefer the term *explanatory*, because the purpose of this essay is to *explain* rather than *exposit*. In addition, students are more like to understand the meaning of *explain* or *explanatory*.

# THINK IN THREES

In writing essays, students are likely to be told to have a beginning, middle, and end. To achieve this, we begin by telling them that they should think in threes and keep in mind the following sentence starters:

Three reasons

Three causes

Three ways

Three results

Three purposes

By understanding the differences in the three types of essays, and by using the phrases, "There are three reasons why . . ." or "Three ways to . . ." or "Three causes for . . .," students have a starting strategy for essay writing that can be expanded and elaborated upon. As students begin an essay, make sure they understand the specific essay genres, and recapitulate the descriptions in the summary of Three Genres of Essays (Figure 9.5).

**Figure 9.5**      Three Genres of Essays

In a **personal essay**, you are stating your own ideas, beliefs, interests, or opinions, and supporting those ideas from a personal point of view.

In a **persuasive essay**, you are expressing a belief or point of view that you want others to share with you. In this essay genre, you generally use the editorial *we* to suggest or imply that others share the same opinion. You then write three or several arguments to influence or win over others to your perspective.

In an **explanatory essay**, you objectively explain the why or how of a particular concept or event. You focus on factual information and support that information with facts and research with the goal of making your reader well informed.

# THE BASIC ESSAY FRAME

All three essay genres can have the same framework:

- Opening statement. Informs the reader of the theme, purpose, and genre of the essay. May have two or three detail sentences to clarify opening statement. Transition words then guide the reader.
- Statement of first reason, cause, result, or purpose. Add three to four detail sentences supporting first statement.
- Second reason, cause, result, or purpose with detail and supporting sentence. Transition words for second reason can be *furthermore* or *in addition.*
- Third reason, cause, result, or purpose with detail and supporting sentences. Transition can simply be *last* or *finally.*
- Concluding sentence that recapitulates the opening theme. May have one or two detail sentences.

## Personal Essays

After you have modeled the format of a basic essay, introduce the personal essay, which is one of the easier essays for students to write. It rarely requires research or background reading and can almost always be written in a short period of time. Teach or review the definition of the personal essay, and start with prompts that are likely to be of personal interest to the writer, similar to those below.

- Write about a person who has influenced your life. Include three reasons why or how this person influenced you.
- Tell about an exciting adventure you had on a trip with your family. Include at least three details, and tell how they made the trip an adventure.
- Think of a place you would like to visit, and tell why. Include three reasons.
- Write about three ways you use the computer for at school or at home. Include detail sentences for each way.

As usual, we recommend that the students begin their essay writing with draft copies and that they include their essay topics and related information in their Notebooks. To help students have a good opening sentence, have them create a Taxonomy (in their Notebooks) as shown in Figure 9.6.

Then have them organize their essays on a double-page spread, using a structure similar to that of the Metacognition Statements described in Chapter 4. They now have the outline for a summary essay. When you first use this strategy, students should write at least three summary essay statements in which they state major reasons, as illustrated in the following examples of student writing.

**Figure 9.6**   Verbs for Personal Essays

### • TAXONOMY •

Here are verbs you can use to start your personal essay, using a sentence such as, "There are three reasons why I admire (believe) (care about)...."

| | |
|---|---|
| A | admire |
| B | believe |
| C | care about |
| D | dream |
| E | enjoy |
| F | feel |
| G | |
| H | hope |
| I | intend |
| J | |
| K | |
| L | love, like |
| M | might |
| N | need |
| O | |
| P | plan, prefer |
| Q | |
| R | |
| S | |
| T | think |
| U | understand |
| V | |
| W | wish, want |
| X | |
| Y | yearn for |
| Z | |

---

There are three reasons why I admire Harriet Tubman.

First she helped her own people get free.

In addition, she came up with a good idea called the Underground Railroad.

Finally, she made sure that her son would never be a slave.

These are the reasons why I admire Harriet Tubman.

—Third Grade Student

> There are three reasons why I am planning for college now.
>
> First, I know that I must have good grades all through school so I can get into a good college like Duke or Michigan.
>
> In addition, I will need a lot of money for college, so I have to start saving money now.
>
> Finally, I want to get a basketball scholarship and to do that I must become the best player on my team.
>
> For these reasons I am planning for college now.
>
> —Sixth Grade Student

The personal essay below, written by a ninth grade student, is representative of a more advanced stage in writing. It begins with a personal opening statement and elaborates on the details of each reason:

> Every morning when I wake up and look at the housing project where I live, I dream of taking a bicycle trip to Utah. I have three good reasons for this dream. First, my friend told me that Utah has the most beautiful mountains in the United States and since I've never been to the mountains, this is where I want to go. In addition, my friend said that there are many bicycle paths that twist up and down and make riding lots of fun and exciting. Finally, I'm tired of riding my bicycle in traffic where there are always trucks and taxis and people in your way. I'm sure Utah is not like that at all. I think these are very good reasons for dreaming about a bicycle trip in Utah.

Once students have mastered this format, they have a template for all personal essays. The student who wrote the summary outline on Harriet Tubman went back and added details to each reason. For the first reason , she elaborated on how Tubman helped slaves reach freedom, using information from a book and class discussion:

> Harriet Tubman would secretly meet with other slaves in the woods. She would teach them songs that gave directions of where they should go. She also taught them how to make signals with their hands so that only slaves would know what the signals meant. Many slaves were scared about getting caught, but Harriet Tubman told them to be brave.

## Persuasive Essays

The personal essay is the springboard for the persuasive essay. In the persuasive essay, the writer may state her or his opinion or serve as the spokesperson for a group that wants to convince others to take action or take a specific position on a particular topic. The writer must clearly and positively state the position or point of view and then provide convincing arguments for that point of view. The conventional opening phrase for the persuasive essay is, "We should. . . ." In a persuasive essay, the writer uses *we,* rather than *I,* to make the audience believe that he or she represents a consensus. The word *should* is used to emphasize the significance of the belief or issue. Students can have the options of using *need to, must, have to,* or similar words that are meant to convince.

The format is similar to that of the personal essay, with the exception of the opening and concluding sentences. Since the persuasive essay advocates a cause or states a belief, it is a popular school genre and a necessary social genre. Following is a sampling of topics that lend themselves to persuasive writing. Of course, you will have your own topics, and students should search for ideas that allow them to express their beliefs.

### Prompts for Persuasive Writing

There are three reasons why we should

- Keep the environment free of pollution.
- Exercise every day.
- Eat an abundance of fruits and vegetables.
- Find homes for the homeless.
- Give to our favorite charity.
- Visit senior citizens who are homebound.
- Keep our bodies free of drugs and tobacco.

Following are three examples of persuasive writing from second, fourth, and eighth grade students, all on the same topic but with different levels of depth.

---

There are three reasons why we should eat lots of vegetables. First, vegetables have vitamins like vitamins A, B, C, and D. A second reason is that vegetables are good for your blood and your bones. A third reason is that you will feel strong and healthy. So even if you don't like how vegetables taste, you still should eat them for the reasons I said.

There are three reasons why we should all eat vegetables. First, vegetables have many vitamins and minerals that help you get strong bones and good teeth. In addition, vegetables help you have better digestion and you won't have so many stomachaches. Finally, vegetables can even taste good especially if you eat them in a salad with a good salad dressing and bread sticks. So listen to me and eat your vegetables.

Doctors, health teachers, and dietitians are all telling us that we should eat more vegetables and less meat. We should follow their advice. First, doctors say that many vegetables like broccoli and Brussels sprouts contain anti-oxidants that can help prevent cancer. Furthermore, there are vegetables such as kale and collard greens that give us calcium for strong bones and teeth. A third important reason is that vegetables provide our bodies with fiber to make our digestive system work better. If we want to have healthy lives we need to listen to doctors, health teachers, and dietitians who are telling us to eat more vegetables.

## Explanatory Essays

The writer of an explanatory essay generally takes a neutral position and provides the reader with factual information with little, if any, opinion. This type of essay almost always requires research and substantiation of information. It is the genre most frequently found in textbooks and academic writing. Explanatory essays are used to write about various topics; they lend themselves to all content areas. Following are suggested prompts for several different content areas that teachers can use as models to create their own prompts. Notice that in the explanatory essay, the writer begins with the words, "There are three reasons why," followed by the topic itself, as in "There are three reasons why the world is facing global warming."

There are three reasons why

- Dogs make great pets.
- The American colonists rebelled against King George.
- Cities often are built close to a river.
- Shakespeare's plays are still enjoyed today.
- The English Navy defeated the Spanish Armada.

Here is an example of a middle school student's writing about the Spanish Armada from material researched on the Internet. The first instruction by the teacher was for the student to write an introduction that gave the reader some background about the topic (e.g., Spain vs. England in 1588). After this introduction, the student was to think in threes as to Reasons, Causes, Results in relation to the introductory statement.

By providing the students with a guided system, the chances for clarity and organization are greatly enhanced. In this process, the student wrote the draft in the Notebook and received approval from the teacher, who read it solely to see that it was organized. She then asked the student to write it on the computer and to use the computer spelling and editing checks for making corrections. She reviewed it again (briefly) for its format and asked the student to read it aloud to a fellow student. With this arrangement, the eighth grade student created a well-written piece with barely any need for the teacher making corrections.

---

In 1588 Spain had the strongest navy in the world and was the world's most powerful country. King Philip II of Spain thought that if his navy could beat the English Navy, Spain would control all of North America as well as South America. He gathered 130 ships with 300,000 men that set sail for England. He put Alonso Perez Guzman, his best commander, in charge of the fleet and was sure that his ships would win against the English. But there were three major events that helped the English Navy defeat the Spanish Armada.

First, English spies found out about the plan and the English Navy attacked the Spanish Navy, damaging so many ships that the Spanish navy had to wait another year before it could set sail again. Then in July 1588, the Spanish Armada headed for England, but now the English navy was much stronger and they attacked again. They sank many Spanish ships and forced other ships to go back to a port in France. Third, there came an attack by the English led by Lord Howard. This time, the English sent out special fire ships that made the Spanish sailors panic and get separated from the other ships. The English navy was able to destroy fifty-four of the 130 ships.

Spain was too poor to build another navy, so England became ruler of the seas. Spain never again ruled the seas. These three significant naval events allowed the English to get control of North America and begin its settlements of the colonies and Canada.

# SUMMARIES OF THREE DIFFERENT ESSAY GENRES

An effective way to help students understand the distinction among essays is select one topic and model how it can be written in three different essay genres. Figure 9.7 shows an example of this, with the opening sentence and the first reason given for each of the three genres.

**Figure 9.7**    Australia as Discussed in Three Different Genres

| Personal Essay | Persuasive Essay | Explanatory Essay |
|---|---|---|
| There are three reasons why I want to visit Australia. | There are three reasons why we should visit Australia. | There are three reasons why Australia is popular with tourists. |
| First, I am eager to visit the Outback and see all the marsupials that inhabit Australia. | First, we can have a great time visiting Australian cities such as Sydney, Melbourne, and Perth. | First, Australia has many beautiful waterways and a mild, coastal climate almost all year round. |

# EXPANDING THE ESSAY

After students can comfortably write personal, persuasive, and explanatory essays, they can be shown how to use the same format for explaining causes and results. This extension into causes and results is valuable for writing in all the content areas.

In science, students might need to write an explanatory essay telling the results of an experiment or the causes of an earthquake. In mathematics, students can write an essay telling the results of a survey or a building project. Social studies teachers particularly focus on causes and results to understand the immediate and underlying causes of a war or the results of agreements and treaties.

Students learning about the American Revolution can create several Taxonomies: names of prominent American leaders, British opponents, American and British generals, battles and their locations, and perhaps others. The students can set up a chronology of events leading up to the war and another chronology of events leading to victory over the British. Students will use Defining Format and Biographic Format to answer questions such as "What is a revolution?" "What was the Declaration of Independence?" and "Who was John Adams?" On a regular basis, they should be writing brief Metacognition Statements that indicate growing knowledge and understanding of the war. With this continuous practice, students will be writing in greater depth, citing reasons, causes, and results. Below are examples of opening statements written by students at intermediate and secondary levels on the topic of the American Revolution.

There were three major underlying causes for the American Revolution. First, the colonists were angry at King George for making them pay taxes without their consent. Second, many colonists wanted to settle in lands west of the colonies and were stopped by British laws. Finally, American shipbuilders and traders did not want to be controlled by British ship owners and merchants.

There were three important results that came from the writing of the Declaration of Independence. For the first time, the thirteen colonies acted together and agreed upon separating from England. Then the writers of the Declaration wrote inspiring words that had not been said before like "All men are created equal," and all people are entitled to "life, liberty, and the pursuit of happiness." Most important, the Declaration of Independence made the colonists think of themselves as being Americans instead of British. These are the results that are most meaningful to me.

Even though George Washington and his men suffered from cold and hunger at Valley Forge, their suffering had good results for the American Revolution. One result was that the colonists admired George Washington for his courage and wanted him to win more than ever before. Another result was that the Continental Congress was able to raise more money from the colonists and then from France to help General Washington. The third result was that George Washington made sure that his men were better prepared with food and clothing for the next winter. So even though George Washington and his men had a terrible winter in Valley Forge, there were good results that came later.

The explanatory essay is also important in explaining and clarifying ideas and concepts in science, as illustrated in the following explanatory paragraph on genetics by a high school student.

There are three types of traits that humans inherit: physical, biochemical, and behavioral. The physical traits are those that relate to resemblance to parents such as height, weight, hair and eye color, body shapes, and so forth. The biochemical traits that humans inherit can be blood types, bone structure, and a tendency toward certain diseases or sicknesses. The behavioral traits, such as intelligence, aggression, or gentleness, can be either inherited or learned. For example, scientists are not always sure whether intelligence is a behavior that we inherit or we learn, or maybe it's both inherited and learned. I will now explain these three traits in detail.

In a high school mathematics class, a student explained the history of algebra by starting with an organizing sentence that stated how he would structure his paragraph.

> The history of algebra can be divided into three distinct periods. First algebra developed in the ancient civilizations of Egypt, Babylon, Greece, Persia, and Arab lands. The next stages of development took place during the Renaissance, mainly in Italy and France. The modern phase started late in the 18th century with discoveries and theorems of mathematicians from Germany, Great Britain, and the United States.

In Figure 9.8, we present a plan that uses a combination of strategies for studying the immediate and underlying causes related to historical actions or events as well as their results. The plan is called "How to Study a War," and it provides a framework for the essential information the students need to know to understand why wars begin, what happens during a war, and what results from a war. In this plan, the students continue to use all of the writing strategies they have learned.

The essay formats described here give students a simple structure for expressing complex ideas. The starting sentences also prepare the reader for what to expect and allow the writer to set up detailed, informative paragraphs. From these starters and thinking in threes, students can eventually graduate to the more complex forms of academic writing that will be required in the higher grades and beyond high school. Best of all, your students will have a way to start, a way to continue, and a way to conclude.

**Figure 9.8**     How to Study a War

In studying about a war, you will need to understand and write about the following aspects of this unfortunate human behavior. You will need to set up Taxonomies and write Metacognition Statements. Use Defining Format for all new terminology and Biographic Format for important leaders and heroes in the war. Write personal, persuasive, and explanatory essays relating to causes, outcomes, and results. Here are aspects of a war you need to study and write about:

- Combatants or opponents
- Underlying causes of the war
- Immediate causes
- "Players"—leaders, generals, heroes
- Significant battles and events
- Outcomes of the war
- Aftermath or results

# INTERNET LINKS

http://www.geocities.com/fifth_grade_tpes/persuasive.html

http://www.studygs.net/wrtstr4.htm

http://www.orangeusd.k12.ca.us/yorba/persuasive_writing1.htm

http://essayinfo.com/essays/personal_essay.php

http://www.jameslindlibrary.org/essays/fair_tests/introduction.html

Strategies, Genres,
Topics, and Tools

Words Are Free!

Have Words,
Can Write

Writing Is Thinking

Write to a Martian

Every Word
Has a Story

Organize
Your Writing

Know Who You
Know and Know
Who You Are!

Think in Threes

**Everybody Has
to Be Someplace**

Let's Make
a Movie!

Words Inspire

Know Thyself

Writers Are Editors

A Goal for
Every Student

**CHAPTER TEN**

# Where in the World

## Everybody Has to Be Someplace

*A client [of a travel agent] called inquiring about a travel package to Hawaii. After going over all the cost information, the client asked, "Would it be cheaper to fly to California and then take the train to Hawaii?"*

~www.jokes2go.com (April, 2006)

## GEOGRAPHY AS KNOWLEDGE AND VOCABULARY

Everybody and everything has to be someplace. This is an almost ridiculous statement, yet, with the exception of social studies, many school subjects are taught with very little reference to geography, a specific aspect of knowledge embedded in the term *social studies*. In fact, geography is rarely taught as a separate subject, and many students, even in middle school, are uncertain about the vocabulary of geography, including terms such as *city, state, province, colony, country,* and *continent.* In addition, many students reach middle and high school with only a vague knowledge of places that they are reading about in their texts. In the preface to *Cultural Literacy,* E. D. Hirsch Jr. refers to America's "lack of cultural literacy," a term that he uses to mean the "possession of the basic knowledge needed to thrive in the modern world" (1987, p. xiii). In his controversial lists of what he believes students need to know, Hirsch cites dozens of geographic references that he says most American high school students would be unable to locate either on a map or simply by telling where the places are. How many students, he asks, could readily locate the Alamo, Appomattox, Gettysburg, Seneca Falls, or Valley Forge?

Marzano, Pickering, and Pollock (2001) emphasize that knowledge of subject area vocabulary is critical to understanding, and one way to increase this vocabulary is through a combination of direct instruction (of vocabulary) intertwined with learning the content. This important statement means that students learn their vocabulary best when it is part of content material, as opposed to memorizing lists of words. They cite research that indicates that "student achievement will increase by 33 percentage points when vocabulary instruction focuses on specific words that are important to what students are learning" (p. 127). Our premise throughout this book is that the meaning of *instruction* must be extended to include enabling the student to become fluent in the *use* of vocabulary, which means communicating meaning through written expression. Jackson, in her extended work in urban schools with low-achieving students, points out that construction of meaning builds linguistic competence. Furthermore, "Culture molds language, and language is a way of thinking" (Jackson, 2005, p. 205). So, while all vocabularies are valuable, we believe that by knowing and using the vocabulary of geography, students acquire an expanded range of literacy—speaking, reading, writing, and culture.

## WHERE IN THE WORLD: A STRATEGY FOR LOCATION AND SETTING

The strategy Where in the World combines teaching the students an organizational system of geographic locations with Taxonomies; Composing With Keywords; Metacognition; Defining Format; Morphology and Etymology; Profiles and Frames; Reasons, Causes, Results; and Who's Who. The organizational system is based on the geopolitical concept that much of the world currently consists of political divisions (streets, cities, towns or villages, states, provinces, counties, and countries), which are entities created by humans; and natural divisions (continents, hemispheres, planets, and galaxies), entities resulting from forces of nature. These geopolitical or geographic terms often are difficult for students to understand, and many times textbooks use these terms without clear, or without any, definitions, assuming that students know exactly what a country or a city is. Yet, students need to grasp the distinction between political and natural divisions in order to know where they live or in order to understand the history of exploration, settlements, immigration, war, and their own families' lives.

## WHERE IN THE WORLD AND TEACHING WRITING

Many teachers today feel overwhelmed with the vast extent of material they are required to teach beyond subject areas—from drug abuse to computer literacy to conflict resolution. These extra teaching burdens leave the teacher with little time to stop and point out or explain geographic information. Often there is a lack of integration of geography or geographical terms and places into school subjects, so that the science teacher who mentions Gregor Mendel's experiments with pea plants in Austria may not mention or think about helping students locate Austria or any other place where scientific study has taken place. The mathematics teacher, having to cover so much material, has little time to stop and tell where Rome is when explaining Roman numerals or where the Arabs traveled when they discovered or invented Arabic numerals. The language arts teacher, too, may not want to stop to discuss the geography of Hannibal in *Tom Sawyer* or the Canadian North Woods in the story *Hatchet* with the pressure to get through the reading.

However, with the continuous implementation of the writing strategies previously introduced, students can develop an in-depth knowledge of where in the world they live and where in the world their knowledge comes from. We have set up this chapter by following the order of the strategies as they have been presented in this book and as they appear in the Planning Wheel (see Introduction). Adapt them to your students' needs, selecting vocabulary from your grade level for the Taxonomies and using the other strategies based on or related to that vocabulary. Figure 10.1 is a composite vocabulary that contains terms covering a wide range of geographic knowledge. Build other geography Taxonomies as appropriate. Figures 10.2–10.4 use Composing With Keywords and Metacognition to prepare students for writing about geography. Figure 10.4 illustrates a completed address and a Composing With Keywords letter to a Martian as a model for the students. Continue to use the Notebook with all these strategies.

**Figure 10.1**    Taxonomy of Geographic Terms (add others)

| • TAXONOMY • | |
|---|---|
| A | archipelago |
| B | beach |
| C | canal |
| D | desert |
| E | equator |
| F | France |
| G | glacier |
| H | hill |
| I | inlet |
| J | jungle |
| K | Kilimanjaro |
| L | longitude |
| M | mountain |
| N | Norway |
| O | Omaha |
| P | peninsula |
| Q | quadrant |
| R | radius |
| S | savanna |
| T | town |
| U | United States |
| V | valley |
| W | world |
| X | xeriscape |
| Y | Yorktown |
| Z | Zaire |

**Figure 10.2**    Composing With Keywords Using Geographic Terms

Directions: Now that you have a Taxonomy of geographic terms, you can write many sentences with these terms that show your knowledge. Here are three examples for you to follow.

1.  Words: Norway, beaches, mountains

    Sentence: Norway is a country that has many mountains and beaches.

2.  Words: desert, valley, peninsula

    Sentence: Deserts, valley, and peninsulas are all types of landforms, but each landform has its own features.

3.  Words: France, Zaire, Omaha

    Sentence: France and Zaire are both countries, but Omaha is a city.

**Figure 10.3** Metacognition: Thinking About Where I Live

Directions: Follow this plan and you will know your complete address for writing to a Martian.*

- Use a double-page spread in your Notebook.
- In the top margin write, "My Address to a Martian."
- On the even-numbered page, write the heading, "Political and Natural Divisions."
- On the odd-numbered page, write the heading, "Names of the Divisions."
- Number the lines in the margin of the even-numbered pages 1 to 10.
- On line one on the even-numbered page, write your house number and street name. Even if you live in a lane, or a circle, or an avenue, this is your street name.
- Opposite your street name, on the odd-numbered page, write, "This is my street."
- On line 2, write the name of your town or city. Opposite it, write, "This is my town (or city)."
- On line 3, write the name of your county. Opposite it, write, "This is my county."
- On line 4, write the name of your state. Opposite it, write, "This is my state."
- On line 5, write the name of your country. Opposite it, write, "This is my country."

Lines 1–5 show *political divisions*. Mark each one with the letter P.

- On line 6, write the name of your continent. Opposite it, write, "This is my continent."
- On line 8, write the name of your hemisphere. Opposite it, write, "This is my hemisphere."
- On line 9, write the name of your "system." Opposite it, write, "This is my planetary system."
- On line 10, write the name of your galaxy. Opposite it, write, "This is my galaxy."

Lines 6–10 are *natural divisions*. Mark each one with the letter N.

Memorize this address from line 1 through line 10 and from line 10 back to line 1. You will know your address forwards and backwards and really impress the Martian.

NOTE: *You may have to modify the political divisions at the city or town levels for different areas of the United States.

In preparation for using Defining Format as part of building a geographic vocabulary, have the students categorize political and natural divisions (Figure 10.5). Tell them briefly that a *political division* is marked by borders and boundaries that have been decided upon by humans. *Natural boundaries* were formed by nature, rather than by humans. As students begin to clarify the terms through Defining Format, they will get an in-depth understanding of the concept of geopolitical divisions. We suggest that if you teach social studies in any grade level, you teach students this basic categorization system, which will clarify the distinctions of geographic terms. (Add to the Notebook.)

A distinction that often confuses students is the difference between a continent and a country. Students can more readily understand these terms by using Defining Format, which defines continent as a *natural division* and country as a *political division,* as illustrated in Figures 10.6 and 10.7.

Some students have trouble understanding the distinction between their own country (the United States) and the state they live in (e.g., Iowa). Figure 10.8 compares this distinction by the characteristics. You may wish to add other characteristics.

Your students are now ready to compare states with cities and, when studying other countries, can understand how provinces can be similar to states. Furthermore, by using these content area Defining Formats, students can now develop paragraphs and full-length reports on these geopolitical entities by adding details to each characteristic.

**Figure 10.4**    An Address to a Martian

| 1.  4 Summit Drive | This is my street. P |
|---|---|
| 2.  Nyack | This is my town. P |
| 3.  Rockland | This is my county. P |
| 4.  New York | This is my state. P |
| 5.  United States of America | This is my country. P |
| 6.  North America | This is my continent. N |
| 7.  Western Hemisphere | This is my hemisphere. N |
| 8.  Earth | This is my planet. N |
| 9.  Solar System | This is my planetary system. N |
| 10.  Milky Way | This is my galaxy. N |

Here is an example of a letter written by an American Earthling to a Martian. Compose your letter that tells your information.

Dear Martian,

Here is my complete address. Many of us on Earth now use a complete address because of interplanetary travel.

My street is Summit Drive, which is in the town of Nyack. Nyack is part of Rockland County, which is in New York State. New York State is one of 50 states in my country, the United States of America. All of these political divisions are part of the continent of North America.

North America is a continent that is part of the Western Hemisphere. We are situated on Earth, your nearest neighbor in the Solar System. As you may be aware, we are in the same galaxy, which we call the Milky Way.

I look forward to receiving your address, so we can correspond through the new interplanetary service that our planets have established.

**Figure 10.5**    Categorizing Political and Natural Divisions

| **Political Divisions** | **Natural Divisions** |
|---|---|
| Countries (sometimes called nations, e.g., Germany, United States, and Brazil)<br>States* (divisions of countries such as the United States, Mexico, and Brazil)<br>Provinces (divisions of countries such as China, France, and Canada)<br>Counties (divisions within states, used mainly in the United States)<br>Cities, Towns, and Villages (in all countries)<br>Streets (lanes, boulevards, avenues—in all parts of the world) | Stars (Sun)<br>Planets<br>Continents<br>Landforms (e.g., islands, peninsulas, mountains, deserts)<br>Waterways (e.g., oceans, lakes, rivers) |

NOTE: *Occasionally, the word *state* will be used as a synonym for country as in "the state of Israel," just to add a bit of confusion to definitions.

Figure 10.6

| **What Is a Continent?** | | |
| --- | --- | --- |
| • DEFINING FORMAT • | | |
| Question | Category | Characteristics |
| What is a continent? | | |
| A continent is a | land division or landform that | 1. is naturally separated from other landforms by natural boundaries such as water and mountains.<br>2. was formed through geologic movements called plate tectonics.<br>3. is named Europe, Asia, Africa, Australia*, Antarctica**, North America, or South America.<br>4. has been divided (by humans) into countries in Europe, Asia, Africa, North America, and South America. |

NOTES: *Australia is a continent that "contains" one country, also named Australia.

**Antarctica remains undivided, probably because it is barely habitable for humans.

Figure 10.7

| **What Is a Country?** | | |
| --- | --- | --- |
| • DEFINING FORMAT • | | |
| Question | Category | Characteristics |
| What is a country? | | |
| A country is a | land division that | 1. is politically independent, sovereign, or self-governing.<br>2. has borders with other countries.<br>3. may be governed by a president, monarch, prime minister, chancellor, or dictator.<br>4. has its own army or defense system.<br>5. may issue its own currency.<br>6. has one or several main languages.<br>7. has shared customs and culture. |

Figure 10.8

| What Is a State (in the United States)? |
| :-- |

**• DEFINING FORMAT •**

| Question | Category | Characteristics |
| --- | --- | --- |
| What is a state? | | |
| A state is a | political division that | 1. is dependent upon the United States government. <br> 2. has borders with other states. <br> 3. is governed by a governor. <br> 4. does not have its own army or defense system, but may have a state militia. <br> 5. may not issue its own currency. <br> 6. has one government language, though other languages may be used by the population. <br> 7. may have shared customs and culture. |

# MORPHOLOGY, ETYMOLOGY, AND WHERE IN THE WORLD

How did America get its name? Where did the name *Europe* come from? What does *Antarctica* mean? What does *Los Angeles* mean and in what language?

What is the origin of the name *Tallahassee? Massachusetts? Utah?* Who gave us the names of dwellings such as *wigwam, tipi, chalet, chateau, hacienda,* or *bungalow?* The history of words, or *etymology,* is the story of human migration and conquest, a story that created the spread and interweaving of languages and exchange of cultures (Bryson, 1990; McArthur, 2003; McWhorter, 1998; Pinker, 1994, 2000).

Including the story of words through the strategy Morphology and Etymology offers students a gift of cultural and linguistic knowledge and is a natural addition to Where in the World as well as an extension of the activities in Chapter 6. Figures 10.9–10.11 are examples of three terms that students learn in social studies across the grades—*colony, slave,* and *revolution.* By expanding their meanings through use of the Morphology Template, the students not only gain a better understanding of the concepts but also acquire high-level words for writing.

# PROFILES AND FRAMES FOR WHERE IN THE WORLD

As indicated in Chapter 7, Profiles and Frames provide students with templates for focusing on information related to a specific topic or subject. The Profiles included here will help students write personal narratives and full-length pieces that encompass

**Figure 10.9**   Morphology Template for the Word *Colony*

| Noun | Verb | Adjective | Adverb |
|------|------|-----------|--------|
| colony<br>colonies<br>colonist<br>colonists<br>colonizer<br>colonizers<br>colonialism<br>colonization | colonize<br>colonizes<br>colonizing<br>colonized | colonial | |

**Figure 10.10**   Morphology Template for the Word *Slave*

| Noun | Verb | Adjective | Adverb |
|------|------|-----------|--------|
| slave<br>slaves<br>slavery<br>slaver<br>slavers<br>slaveholder<br>slaveholders<br>enslavement | enslave<br>enslaves<br>enslaving<br>enslaved | slavish | slavishly |

**Figure 10.11**   Morphology Template for the Word *Revolution*

| Noun | Verb | Adjective | Adverb |
|------|------|-----------|--------|
| revolution<br>revolutions<br>revolutionary**<br>revolutionaries<br>revolutionist<br>revolutionists<br>revolt<br>revolts<br>revolter<br>revolters | revolutionize<br>revolutionizes<br>revolutionizing<br>revolutionized<br>revolt<br>revolts<br>revolting<br>revolted<br>revolve***<br>revolves<br>revolving<br>revolved | revolutionary**<br>revolting* | revoltingly |

NOTES: *Adjectives that use -*ing* have generally been formed from the verb.

**Words, as you know, can shift their part of speech. The Revolutionary War was a war fought by revolutionaries who revolted against the king.

***Now the students can relate the word *revolution* (in the *revolution of the Earth*) to the verb *revolve*.

If possible, contrast *revolution* with *evolution* and have students compare the two words using Morphology and Etymology.

many aspects of social studies as well as other subject areas. If it is suitable for your class, begin with a personal geography Profile (Figure 10.12) that can lead to discussions about diversity in the classroom, map study of where students have come from and have lived, and places of general interest. From this Profile, students can write their own stories, or they can use the sentence Frames similar to those in Figure 10.13.

**Figure 10.12**   Personal Geography Profile

Directions: Set up your own personal geography page by filling in as many of these items as you can.

My Birthplace _____

My Mother's Birthplace _____

My Father's Birthplace _____

Birthplaces of My Grandparents

Maternal Grandmother _____

Grandfather _____

Paternal Grandmother _____

Grandfather _____

Places I Have Lived _____

_____

States I Have Visited

_____

Cities in the United States I Have Visited or Lived in

_____

Countries and Cities Outside of the United States I Have Visited or Lived in

_____

Places I Would Like to Visit

_____

**Figure 10.13**  From Personal Geography Profile to Writing About Yourself

Directions: Here are six sentence Frames. Select one of the sentence Frames to write about yourself. Then *think in threes** and add as many interesting details as you can. You might want to provide a map or pictures to go with your writing.

I was born in _____, which is a part of _____.

I have always wanted to visit my mother or father's birthplace in _____.

My grandmother (grandfather) has told me many interesting stories about growing up in

_____.

I have lived in many (just a few) places in my life such as _____

_____.

I have traveled to these different states (or countries) _____

_____.

The place I would like to visit most is _____

NOTE: *This activity can easily be related to Reasons, Causes, Results (Chapter 9).

Figures 10.14–10.18 include a Taxonomy of rivers and their cities and four Profiles—river, city, country, and continent. They can serve as the basis of numerous pieces of writing in different genres and of detailed research for your students. Use and adapt them as appropriate for your students.

# REASONS, CAUSES, RESULTS FOR WHERE IN THE WORLD

By combining the strategies described in this chapter, students have a repertoire for writing. Having created a Taxonomy and a Profile, they can now easily write a personal, persuasive, or explanatory essay. Figure 10.17 lists suggested writing topics around several organizational strategies that could follow as a result of studying rivers and cities. Figures 10.18 and 10.19 suggest writing topics for countries and continents and provide a structure to help students collect and organize information.

When teaching about continents, you may wish to divide your students into groups, and have each group research a particular aspect of the continent. Continents are both natural and political divisions, and in today's global culture, students from at least fourth grade through high school need to learn about these aspects of continents. Here are several suggested areas of study for creating Taxonomies, Metacognition Statements, and Explanatory Essays:

Rivers and other waterways

Mountains and other land divisions

Natural disasters (e.g., floods, hurricanes, earthquakes, volcanic eruptions)

Countries within the continent

Indigenous people and ethnic groups

Railroads and other transportation systems continentwide

Explorers, conquerors, and early settlers associated with the continent

Students also can design posters, create travel brochures, create various maps (physical, product, resource, language, climate), and write to the World Health Organization at the United Nations for information on health, population, and food consumption.

**Figure 10.14**   Rivers and Their Cities

### • TAXONOMY •

Directions: Many cities are built alongside rivers for many reasons that you might like to research. Create a brochure that tells about one of these cities (or any other), including the activities and sites that would make people want to visit that city.

| | |
|---|---|
| A | |
| B | Buenos Aires/La Plata, |
| | Baghdad/Tigris and Euphrates, |
| | Budapest/Danube |
| C | Cairo/Nile, Calcutta/Ganges, |
| | Cincinnati/Ohio, Cologne/Rhine |
| D | |
| E | Edinburgh/Clyde |
| F | |
| G | |
| H | Hamburg/Elbe |
| I | |
| J | |
| K | |
| L | London/Thames, Lyons/Rhone, |
| | Lagos/Niger |
| M | Montreal/St. Lawrence, |
| | Minneapolis/Mississippi |
| N | New York/Hudson, |
| | New Orleans/Mississippi |
| O | Omaha/Platte |
| P | Paris/Seine, Pittsburgh/Allegheny |
| Q | |
| R | Rome/Tiber |
| S | St. Louis/Mississippi, Stratford/Avon, |
| | Shanghai/Yangtze, |
| | St. Paul/Mississippi |
| T | |
| U | |
| V | Volgograd/Volga, Vienna/Danube |
| W | Warsaw/Vistula |
| X | |
| Y | |
| Z | |

**Figure 10.15**  River Profile

Directions: Select a city and its river that you would like to know more about. Draw a map showing the path or flow of the river and indicate where the cities are along that river. Then tell how the city you chose benefits from the river it is on.

Name of River _____

Country/Countries Where It Flows _____

_____

_____

Continent/Continents Where It Flows _____

_____

Length of River _____ miles

_____ kilometers

Source of River _____

Mouth of River _____

Special Features (e.g., waterfalls, rapids,reservoirs, dams) _____

_____

_____

Major Cities Along River _____

_____

Major Bridges That Cross River _____

_____

Other Information _____

_____

**Figure 10.16** City Profile

Directions: Select a city that interests you or you would like to visit and complete the Profile. Then create a project that would get other students interested in learning about this city.

Name of City _____

State (if in a country with states) or Province

(if in a country with provinces)

_____

Country in Which City Is Located _____

Area of City _____

Population _____

Waterways, Mountains, or Other Physical Features

_____

Major Attractions

1) _____

2 ) _____

3 ) _____

4 ) _____

5 ) _____

Major Industries

_____

City Motto (if any) _____

City Nickname (if any) _____

Description of City Flag _____

People of Accomplishment From This City

_____

Other Information _____

**Figure 10.17** Writing Topics for Cities and Rivers

Directions: Choose one of these sentences as an opening sentence for your essay.

There are three important reasons why many major cities of the world are located on rivers.

I would like to explore the _____ River for these three reasons.

We need to take care of our rivers for the following reasons.

There are many ways that people benefit from living near a river.

There are three reasons why I would enjoy visiting (city).

There are three reasons why the city of _____ is an important cultural or exciting _____ center in (country).

When cities build museums and other attractions, they can expect at least three important results.

There are at least three causes for the growth (or decline) of a city.

There are three historic places you should visit in (city). (Select from physical features, major attractions, and major industries.)

After you have finished writing, do one of the following activities:

Design a travel brochure.

Make a poster.

Create a street map.

Create a public transportation map.

Make an annotated list of major attractions: museums, parks, public buildings.

Make a Who's Who book of famous people from a particular city.

**Figure 10.18** Country Profile

Directions: Choose a country you would like to know about or visit. Complete the Profile. Then create a brochure that invites people to visit that country. Or write a persuasive essay giving three reasons why people should visit that country.

Name of Country _____

Continent Where Located _____

Bordering Countries and/or Waterways _____

_____

Area _____ Population _____

Capital City _____

Major Cities _____

Major Languages Spoken _____

Political Divisions Within Country (e.g., states, provinces) _____

Important or Major Attractions

_____

_____

_____

Major Industries _____

Description of Flag _____

Form of Government _____ Name of Main Currency _____

Three Significant Events Related to the Country

_____

_____

_____

Famous People Associated With Country _____

_____

Other Information _____

**Figure 10.19**  Continent Profile

Directions: Select a continent that you would like to know more about and complete the Profile. Create an interesting project and incorporate essential written information.

Name of Continent _____

Waterways Surrounding Continent _____

_____

Land Divisions Separating Continent From Other Continents

(e.g., mountains) _____

_____

Area of Continent _____

Population _____

Three to Five Countries on Continent (except for Australia)

_____

_____

Major River or Rivers _____

_____

Mountains or Mountain Chains _____

_____

_____

Three to Five Natural Resources _____

_____

Significant or Unusual Animal Life _____

_____

Other Information _____

_____

## COMBINING WHO'S WHO AND WHERE IN THE WORLD

The strategy Who's Who combines naturally with Where in the World. The study of explorers and explorations is one topic that brings both strategies together. In his delightful and informative books, *Don't Know Much About Geography* (1992) and *Don't Know Much About History* (1995), Kenneth C. Davis provides thumbnail sketches about explorers of the world that should fascinate students who are interested in adventure and discovery. We have created the Taxonomy of worldwide explorers (Figure 10.20) from these books and have added an explorer Profile (Figure 10.21) to guide students in their research of these people. By using the Dual Taxonomy and Profiles and Frames as described in Chapter 8, your students will continue on their path to fluency and organization.

## INTEGRATING WHERE IN THE WORLD ACROSS THE CURRICULUM

While social studies teachers include geography in their curriculum, teachers of other subjects, such as science, mathematics, and foreign languages, may not always see the connection or may feel they do not have the time to relate their subject to global issues or aspects. However, you can use a variety of Taxonomies and writing strategies that integrate geographical concepts with content area topics to show students the interrelationships of places with events, people, animals, and other subject matter.

Two useful Taxonomies are geographer's companions (Figure 10.22) and geographer's measurements (Figure 10.23). Geographer's companions lists the careers requiring knowledge of geography, and geographer's measurements connects geography to mathematics. By focusing on careers, students discover that studying geography opens the door to exciting careers and jobs that may not be discussed in classrooms or career guidance sessions and that geography and mathematics have a very close relationship.

Students can select those terms appropriate to their needs and set up Defining Formats to explain their meanings. They can use these Taxonomies to branch out into related topics. For example, students can do historical research on the origins of Greenwich mean time or the international date line, or they can research careers such as demographer, urban planner, cartographer, and navigator, among others.

**Figure 10.20** Worldwide Explorers

### • TAXONOMY •

Directions: Trace the voyages of any of the following explorers. Include the country the explorer sailed from and the places in the world he uncovered or touched upon. Use a map to show the routes.

| | |
|---|---|
| A | Amundsen |
| B | Balboa, Bellinghausen, Bering, Bingham, Bougainville, Bridger, Burton |
| C | Columbus, Cortes, Coronado, Cartier, Cook, Cabot, Champlain, Clark, Cousteau |
| D | da Gama, Drake, de Leon, Dias, Darwin |
| E | Eric the Red, Ericson |
| F | Frobisher, Fremont |
| G | Gray |
| H | Hawkins, Henson, Hillary |
| J | Joliet |
| L | LaSalle, Lewis, Livingston |
| M | Magellan, Mackenzie, Mallory |
| O | Orellana |
| P | Polo, Pissarro, Perry, Powell |
| R | Ricci, Raleigh, Ross |
| S | Selkirk, Scott, Speke, Stanley, Schliemann |
| V | Vespucci, Verrazano, Vancouver |

**Figure 10.21**   Explorer Profile

Directions: Select an explorer who interests you, and complete the following Profile. Then, use a map to trace the explorations of that explorer. Write a summary statement that tells of three to five contributions this explorer made to our geographic knowledge.

Name of Explorer _____

Years of Explorer's Life _____

_____

Nationality of Explorer _____

_____

Major Places of Exploration

_____

_____

Major Contributions to Geographic

Knowledge

_____

_____

_____

_____

_____

Other Information _____

_____

_____

_____

**Figure 10.22** Geographer's Companions

• TAXONOMY •

Directions: Below is a list of various occupations associated with geography. Select three or four of these occupations, and use Defining Format or Career Profile to describe them. Then try to locate a person in one of these occupations, and write a letter asking that person to tell you something about her or his work.

| | |
|---|---|
| A | archaeologist, astronomer, agriculturist, agronomist, anthropologist |
| B | botanist |
| C | cartographer, climatologist |
| D | demographer |
| E | economist, explorer, ecologist |
| F | financier |
| G | geologist |
| H | horticulturist |
| I | |
| J | journalist |
| K | |
| L | |
| M | meteorologist, mathematician, mountain climber |
| N | navigator |
| O | oceanographer |
| P | political scientist |
| Q | |
| R | |
| S | seismologist, sociologist |
| T | thermonuclear scientist |
| U | |
| V | |
| W | |
| X | |
| Y | |
| Z | zoologist |

**Figure 10.23** Geographer's Measurements

• TAXONOMY •

Directions. Find the terms in the Taxonomy that represent measurement. Then check in your mathematics book or another resource to find out what each measures (e.g., time, space) and to find definitions or equivalents for specific units of measurement.

| | |
|---|---|
| A | area, acre, arc, absolute zero |
| B | boundary |
| C | circumference, Celsius |
| D | degrees, density |
| E | equator, equinox, elevation |
| F | Fahrenheit |
| G | Greenwich mean time |
| H | hemisphere |
| I | international date line |
| J | |
| K | kilometer |
| L | longitude, latitude |
| M | meter, meridian, mile |
| N | nadir |
| O | orbit |
| P | population |
| Q | |
| R | radiant |
| S | solstice, scale, sphere, syzygy |
| T | temperature |
| U | |
| V | vector |
| W | |
| X | |
| Y | |
| Z | |

# THE ENGLISH LANGUAGE AND WHERE IN THE WORLD

The English language as it is used today is both a polyglot language and a global language. In the words of Ralph Waldo Emerson, "The English language is the sea which receives tributaries from every region under heaven" (as quoted in McCrum, Cran, & MacNeil, 1986, p. 11). English also is the language that sends American influence to every region of the world. Yet, this wonderfully rich and diverse composition of the English language, which has borrowed words from the world's languages and contributed its own words to other languages, is seldom discussed in the classroom and is almost never mentioned during traditional grammar lessons. Only in the occasional social studies classroom does the teacher mention the extensive migrations of the Aryan people of India, who gave the world the family of languages that later would be called Indo-European. And only a small number of students know the date 1066 and its significance in bringing into the English lexicon thousands of French words.

Figures 10.24–10.27 show several language-related Taxonomies and writing activities that will enhance students' understanding of the language they speak and its geographic connections.

**Figure 10.24**   Languages Around the World

### • TAXONOMY •

Directions: This Taxonomy is a sampling of the languages of the world. Choose one language from the Taxonomy. Then research information about that language on the Internet or in an encyclopedia or other reference book. Complete the Language Profile (Figure 10.25) and present the information to your classmates. (You can add other languages to this list.)

| | |
|---|---|
| A | Albanian, Amharic, Afrikaans, Arabic, Armenian |
| B | Bulgarian, Bengali, Burmese, Bantu |
| C | Czech, Chinese, Croatian |
| D | Dutch, Danish |
| E | English |
| F | Finnish, Farsi, French |
| G | German, Greek |
| H | Hungarian, Hebrew, Hindi |
| I | Icelandic, Italian |
| J | Japanese |
| K | Kirundi, Khmer, Korean |
| L | Lao |
| M | Malagasy, Mongolian |
| N | Norwegian, Nepali, Navajo |
| O | |
| P | Polish, Portuguese |
| Q | Quechan |
| R | Rumanian, Russian |
| S | Swedish, Serbian, Somali, Spanish, Swahili |
| T | Turkish, Thai, Tagalog |
| U | Urdu, Ukrainian |
| V | Vietnamese |
| W | |
| X | |
| Y | Yiddish |
| Z | Zuni |

**Figure 10.25** Language Profile

Directions: When you have completed this Profile, write a report about this language, and present the information to your classmates or family.

Name of Language

_____

Countries or Places Where Spoken

_____

Number of People Speaking This Language

_____

Family or Branch (e.g., Indo-European, Semitic, Native American)

_____

Writing System (e.g., Latin alphabet, Greek alphabet, Kanji characters)

_____

Numbers From One to Ten

_____

_____

Five Other Words and Their English Meanings

1. _____

2. _____

3. _____

4. _____

5. _____

Other Information _____

_____

**Figure 10.26**  Je Parle Français (I Speak French)

### • TAXONOMY •

In the year 1066, William of Normandy (a province that is now part of France) crossed the English Channel with his army and defeated Harold, the English ruler. England came under the rule of a French-speaking government and would remain under Norman (French) rule for 100 years. When the Normans were finally driven out of England, the English people were speaking a language that had added hundreds and hundreds of French words.

Directions: This Taxonomy contains words that are used in English but are of French origin. Find those that you don't know and look up their meanings in a college-level dictionary. Then write a story using as many French words as you can.

| A | adieu, au revoir |
|---|---|
| B | boutique, bonbon, bon voyage, bouquet, bourgeois, ballet |
| C | chauffeur, café, carte blanche, croissant, cachet, coup d'état |
| D | dejà-vu, dossier |
| E | esprit de corps, ennui |
| F | fête, fondue, fait accompli |
| G | gauche, genre, gratin |
| H | hospice, hors d'oeuvre |
| I | imprimatur, ingenue |
| J | joie de vivre |
| K | |
| L | lingerie, liqueur, legèrdemain |
| M | madame, maître d', mademoiselle, menu, massage |
| N | noblesse oblige, nouvelle cuisine |
| O | objet d'art, oblique |
| P | petite, panorama, parachute, parasol, partisan, pièce de resistance, premier, protégé, promenade, potpourri |
| Q | quiche, queue |
| R | raison d'être, rapport, regime, rendezvous, RSVP |
| S | savoir-faire, sauté, soirée, souvenir, suite |
| T | tête-à-tête, tour de force, tout de suite |
| U | unique |
| V | valet, vaudeville, vestibule, vogue |
| W | |
| X | |
| Y | |
| Z | zest |

**Figure 10.27**  Hablo Español

### • TAXONOMY •

The Spanish language, like English, is spoken in many parts of the world. You would speak Spanish in Spain, in most countries in South America, in Central America and Mexico, in Puerto Rico and the Dominican Republic, and in other places where Spanish-speaking people settled.

Directions: Look up the meanings of the words on the Taxonomy that you don't know. Then write a story using as many of these Spanish words as you can. You can add other Spanish words to this list.

| A | arroz, adobe, amigo |
|---|---|
| B | burrito |
| C | caballero, casa |
| D | dinero |
| E | enchilada |
| F | fiesta |
| G | gracias, gusto |
| H | hacienda, hasta la vista |
| I | |
| J | junta |
| K | |
| L | llama |
| M | muchacho, muchacha, mañana, mesa, mucho, momento, madre |
| N | |
| O | |
| P | patio, pollo, poncho, padre |
| Q | |
| R | ranchero, redondo |
| S | sombrero, serape, señorita, salsa |
| T | taco, tortilla, tío, tía |
| U | |
| V | |
| W | |
| X | |
| Y | |
| Z | zapatos |

# INTERNET LINKS

http://geography.about.com/
http://members.aol.com/bowermanb/101.html
http://www.nationalgeographic.com/maps/
http://www.lizardpoint.com/fun/geoquiz/
http://geography.usgs.gov/
http://www.ed.gov/pubs/parents/Geography/index.html
http://www.geography4kids.com/
http://www.aag.org/
http://www.loc.gov/rr/geogmap/

# CHAPTER ELEVEN

# Premises, Premises

## Let's Make a Movie!

*Life is a movie you see through your own eyes.*

~Denis Waitley
(http://en.thinkexist.com/search/search
quotation.asp?search=movies&page=2)—April, 2006

## FROM BOOK TO FILM

For some people, one of the greatest enticements to reading a book is to see the movie. For others, the pleasure is to read a book and imagine it as a movie. Either way, books and movies are now intertwined and provide us with the pleasure of both reading and entertainment. But in addition to having students read and watch, or watch and read, we can also combine the book and the film as an exciting way to develop a wide range of writing skills. Converting a book into a movie can be a total class activity in which all students, regardless of achievement levels, can participate while learning to write and writing to learn.*

In creating a movie from a book, the students will be involved in writing a genre that requires them to grasp the essence, also called the premise, of what the author is saying and to convey this essence to an audience who may not have read the book. In addition, a good movie must show the

---

*You can substitute writing a play for making a movie. But you will see that the movie genre has many aspects that allow fuller participation for all the students.

Strategies, Genres,
Topics, and Tools

Words Are Free!

Have Words,
Can Write

Writing Is Thinking

Write to a Martian

Every Word
Has a Story

Organize
Your Writing

Know Who You
Know and Know,
Who You Are!

Think in Threes

Everybody Has
to Be Someplace

**Let's Make
a Movie!**

Words Inspire

Know Thyself

Writers Are Editors

A Goal for
Every Student

interrelationship of the characters and depict or highlight each character's traits, longings or needs, and growth or changes. For example, by converting a biography into a film, the filmmaker highlights the beliefs, accomplishments, behavior, and growth or journey of the biographical subject. As students change a book into a movie, they learn new and specialized vocabulary, explore human emotions such as hope and fear, learn about new places, and practice the writing forms of the world of films and movies. They realize from this activity that a book made into a movie re-creates the joy and excitement that the book originally brought to the reader. Making a movie from a book brings about true differentiation in the classroom, giving every student an important and equal role in the process and product. Moreover, this creative activity can "build both the skill and desire to read [and write] increasingly complex material" by including reading materials that meet the needs of struggling readers, providing equal access to technology, and optimizing learning opportunities (Walker-Dalhouse, 2004, p. XV). We hope you can include Premises, Premises in your writing repertoire. A digital movie camera will be an asset, but even without one, your students can do a great simulation.

## STEPS IN PREMISES, PREMISES

Premises, Premises includes the following aspects of writing. Some will be new to the students, and others will draw from previously learned strategies:

- Listing the criteria for a book that will make a good movie
- Writing the Premise Statement, a succinct statement that tells what the book is about
- Building character Profiles for each character in the story
- Writing the *treatment*, a retelling of the story in a simple, sequential order
- Creating a storyboard or flow chart that highlights the main or essential scenes of the book for conversion into a film
- Writing the dialogue for the characters

In addition, students can be involved in set and costume design, writing the credits and publicity, and researching types of literary genres that make good movies. So let the cameras roll!

### Developing the Criteria for Book-to-Film

Early in the school year, tell your students that sometime later they will make a film from a favorite book or story. Suggest that as they read stories either in class or on their own, they should think about which of these stories would make a good movie. Then brainstorm with the students the criteria for going from book to film. Our own choice as a prototype for this strategy is *The Tale of Peter Rabbit* (1909) by Beatrix Potter based on the following criteria:

- The story is short and easy to follow and can be the first film at any grade level. Upper grade students can make films of young children's books (as occurs in the film industry) without feeling they are doing a baby activity.

- The five characters in the story are easy for students to play, and they represent different ages and behaviors.
- There are many opportunities for the nonacting students to be the filmmakers (producer, director, set and costume designers, scriptwriters, camera crew).
- This story can be the test film before moving to more advanced stories that require longer and more complex pieces of writing.

From the above criteria, we present the strategy Premises, Premises.

## Creating a Filmmaking Taxonomy

Have the students set up this Taxonomy in their Notebooks, and keep a master Taxonomy posted for ongoing entries related to the terms of filmmaking. Figure 11.1 contains many of the terms your students will enter as they work on this project. For example, the person who chooses the story from which the movie will be made and who pitches it to a producer is often called the *developer*—a term that should be included on the Taxonomy chart.

## Teaching the Premise Statement

The development or planning of a movie generally begins with a premise, or the Premise Statement, which succinctly states what the movie is about. Writing a Premise Statement requires the reader to have a clear understanding of the main or most significant character in the story, of how the character interacts with other characters, of how the character fits into the plot or action, and of how the character grows, changes, or develops. This statement fits a specific framework and is generally not more than three paragraphs long; often it is only one or two sentences. From the Premise Statement, the other aspects of the movie are developed: the treatment or fuller version of the story, the character Profiles that describe the characters in detail, the storyboards that show the main scenes or sequence of the story, and the characters' dialogue.

Figure 11.2 shows the framework of a Premise Statement. The first part is a statement about the main character; this is followed by the word *who* and a phrase that tells of the action or behavior of the main character that prompts the story or plot. The students now role-play being developers who write a Premise Statement for making this story into a film, and they pitch it to a producer.

**Figure 11.1** Filmmaking Taxonomy

| | • TAXONOMY • |
|---|---|
| A | audience, actors, artists, author |
| B | book |
| C | character, costumes, casting agent, camera technician, credits |
| D | dialogue, developer, director |
| E | editor |
| F | fadeout |
| G | grip |
| H | |
| I | |
| J | |
| K | |
| L | lighting |
| M | music, makeup |
| N | narrator, narration |
| O | outline |
| P | premise, problem, producer, production designer |
| Q | |
| R | |
| S | scenes, setting, storyboard, set designer, special effects, scriptwriter |
| T | treatment, titles |
| U | |
| V | voice-over |
| W | |
| X | |
| Y | |
| Z | |

**Figure 11.2**  Premise Statement Frame

The story _____ (name of story) by _____ (author) is
about _____ (name of main character) *who* _____
(action or behavior of character related to plot).

Writing the Premise Statement often requires several drafts, because of the need to fit more information into what is a summary format. In *The Tale of Peter Rabbit*, the first draft of the Premise Statement might be as follows:

The story *The Tale of Peter Rabbit* by Beatrix Potter is about a rabbit named Peter who steals vegetables from Mr. McGregor's garden and gets into trouble.

Now guide the students to revise and expand upon the Premise. Prompt the students to add details that a producer would need to know in considering the cast, the setting, and the plot of this story. Following are second and third drafts of a teacher-guided, revised, and expanded Premise Statement:

The story *The Tale of Peter Rabbit* by Beatrix Potter is about Peter, *the youngest of four rabbits,* living with his mother and siblings near *grouchy* Mr. McGregor's garden, who eats Mr. McGregor's vegetables and get into trouble.

The story *The Tale of Peter Rabbit* by Beatrix Potter is about Peter, the youngest of four rabbits, living with his *widowed* mother and siblings near grouchy Mr. McGregor's garden. Peter *does not pay attention to his mother's warning about danger* and goes into the garden to eat Mr. McGregor's *delicious* vegetables and *almost* gets into *serious* trouble.

The Premise Statement now has details about the number of children (rabbits), family, and location, followed by the word *who* and a statement that gives additional details about the action or behavior of the main character against an opposing character who prompts the story or plot. After students have practiced the format several times, they will be able to construct their own Premise Statements independently. This is a valuable skill for reading comprehension and summarizing (see Marzano, Pickering, & Pollock, 2001, pp. 32–34).

## Writing the Character Profiles

The next writing task is to guide the students in developing character Profiles. In *Playmaking*, Daniel Judah Sklar (1991) provides a step-by-step approach for students writing and performing their own plays or films. The class now assumes the role of casting agents. (Add *casting agent* to the Taxonomy.) Students can work in groups, with each group writing a character Profile for a different character.

Figure 11.3 is a character Profile template that can be used for characters in any book, movie, or play. Figures 11.4 and 11.5 are completed Profiles that represent the

**Figure 11.3**     Character Profile

Name of Character

_____

Age _____

Family

_____

_____

Habitat

_____

_____

Wishes

_____

_____

_____

Fears

_____

_____

_____

Character Traits

_____

_____

Other Information

_____

_____

_____

**Figure 11.4** Character Profile: Peter Rabbit

| | |
|---|---|
| Name of Character | Peter Rabbit. |
| Age | Four years old. |
| Family | Mother, Flopsy (five years old), Mopsy (six years old), Cotton-tail (seven years old). Father has died in an accident. |
| Habitat | A sandbank under the root of a very big fir tree. |
| Wishes | To eat Mr. McGregor's delicious vegetables<br>To do things by himself without his sisters and brother. |
| Fears | Getting caught by Mr. McGregor.<br>Being put into a pie by Mrs. McGregor.<br>Being punished by his mother. |
| Character Traits | Mischievous, disobedient. |
| Other Information | He cries when he gets caught. He doesn't like to take his medicine. Flopsy, Mopsy, and Cotton-tail listen to their Mother. |

**Figure 11.5** Character Profile: Mr. McGregor

| | |
|---|---|
| Name of Character | Mr. McGregor |
| Age | 38 |
| Family | His wife, Mrs. McGregor, and three children—Mary, age 10; Molly, age 12; Max, age 14 |
| Habitat | Small farmhouse with a vegetable garden for lettuce, French beans, radishes, cabbage, and parsley. |
| Wishes | To keep rabbits out of his garden so that his vegetables can grow to have enough food for his wife and children. |
| Fears | That his vegetables will be spoiled by rabbits. |
| Character Traits | Angry, sometimes mean to rabbits. Kind to his wife and children. |
| Other Information | |

two opposing characters in Beatrix Potter's story. Notice that the writers had to think deeply and inferentially to come up with information that is not stated in the story (another important learning skill). Students will need to infer certain information, such as the rabbits' ages, based on their "human" behavior.

From these two character Profiles, the students will be able to recognize points of view. They can see that Mr. McGregor is not totally mean or unreasonable in defending his garden. Peter, on the other hand, is mischievous and disobedient, but fortunately has a strict, caring mother. When the students are ready to write the script and playact the story, they will have a deeper understanding of all the characters.

## Writing the Treatment

The treatment is the complete story retold simply for the preparation of the storyboard and script. The treatment also provides the students with the opportunity to recapitulate the story, making sure that the necessary details are included. Because writing the treatment can be a lengthy process even for older students, the class can be divided into groups, with each group writing a portion of the story in sequence. In this way, all the students get the practice of both retelling and sequencing. Here is the continuation of the Peter Rabbit story from the Premise Statement as written collaboratively by fifth grade students:

> Mrs. Rabbit had to go shopping to buy a brown bread and five buns. She told her children to stay close to the house and not go to Mr. McGregor's garden. Flopsy, Mopsy, and Cotton-tail listened to her and only picked blackberries. But Peter didn't listen. He was a bad boy and sneaked into Mr. McGregor's garden. Then he ate so many vegetables that he got a stomachache. Suddenly Mr. McGregor jumped out and ran after Peter with a rake in his hand. "Stop thief," he yelled. Peter was so scared. He ran so fast that he lost both of his shoes. Then he got trapped by a net and tore his buttons off his jacket. He started to cry and cry and cry.

## Preparing the Storyboard

The storyboard is a sequence or flowchart of scenes that represent the entire story. In essence, it is like a series of snapshots that when appropriately arranged tell an entire story. From the treatment, the students, working in groups, either write out the story by scenes or illustrate the scenes of the story. Young students generally want to illustrate the story, but older students may prefer words to pictures or to use both. The storyboard for Peter Rabbit may look something like Figure 11.6, which contains lines that might be spoken by the characters and are the basis for developing the script.

## Writing the Script

Although some of the script may be started in the storyboard, there can be additional lines that include narration and conversations among the characters. Students now take on the role of scriptwriters and build in dialogues. For example, in the first

**Figure 11.6** Storyboard for *The Tale of Peter Rabbit* by Beatrix Potter

| Scene 1 | Scene 2 | Scene 3 |
|---|---|---|
| Mrs. Rabbit talks to her children.<br><br>"You may go into the fields or down the lane, but don't go into Mr. McGregor's garden. Your father had an accident there and was put into a pie by Mrs. McGregor. I am going out, so don't get into mischief." | Peter sneaks out of the house and runs to Mr. McGregor's garden.<br><br>"I just love eating these vegetables. Lettuce, French beans, radishes are so delicious. Oooh, I'm getting a stomachache. Maybe I should eat some parsley." | Peter meets Mr. McGregor at the cabbage patch.<br><br>"Get out of my garden you thief. If I catch you, I'll tell my wife to put you in a pie, just like we did to your father. Stop thief! Stop! Stop!" |
| **Scene 4** | **Scene 5** | **Scene 6** |
| Peter runs out of the garden.<br><br>"Oh, I'm lost. I can't find the gate out. Oh, I just lost my shoe. There goes my other shoe. More trouble. Now I'm caught in a net with my buttons. I'll never get out. Help! Help!" | Peter is rescued by friendly sparrows.<br><br>"Don't cry Peter. Just keep pushing till you get out of the net. We'll help pull you out." | Mr. McGregor catches up to Peter.<br><br>"I'll get you yet, you thief. I'll put this sieve over your head and you'll never get away now." |

storyboard frame, Mother says "I am going out, so don't get into mischief." Each of the "children" might answer her:

**Flopsy:**  We'll be careful, Momma.

**Mopsy:**  We know what we're supposed to do.

**Cotton-tail:**  We won't get into trouble.

**Peter:**  I'll be a good boy Momma.

Sometimes there is a narrator or narrators who connect the scenes and the story. A group of students can be the narration writers connecting the scenes from the storyboard. Scriptwriting is an activity that students often like to do. As a writing activity, it is challenging to come up with words that one has to imagine characters saying and, like character Profile, involves using inference and also empathy (Costa & Kallick, 2000). We can't imagine what a character might say, unless we can get into the mind of that character.

## Set Design

Designing the set is not only fun for the students but provides them with the opportunity to learn about interior and exterior places and the items and objects that are part of the story. When students design or build sets, they have to focus on details. Groups of students can work together as set designers. It will be their job to go through the book and list all the places and items either mentioned by the author or illustrated by the artist. After they have compiled the list, they present it to the class for preparation of the set. The set can be a simple mural or even a set of drawings that contain whatever objects can be gathered or even imagined. Most important is that the students are aware of the places and objects. For a Peter Rabbit production, the class set designers created the Taxonomy illustrated in Figure 11.7.

## Costume Design

Most students love to dress up in costumes. When acting out a story from an illustrated book, students can use the actual book to get ideas for costumes. Students or a student group can collect clothing items that can actually be used. But the learning aspect of this activity is getting the students to research what they need and to make a plan for getting the items. In the Peter Rabbit story, the class, as costume designers, will have to look at the pictures in the book carefully and name what each cast member needs. They can use an organizational chart like the one in Figure 11.8 to record information about the costumes.

**Figure 11.7** Set Design Places and Objects for *The Tale of Peter Rabbit*

**• TAXONOMY •**

| | |
|---|---|
| A | |
| B | bed, basket, bread, buns, blackberries, beans, bowl |
| C | currant bushes, cups, cover, cucumber frame, cabbage, chamomile tea |
| D | |
| E | |
| F | French beans, flowerpots |
| G | gate, garden |
| H | hoe |
| I | |
| J | |
| K | |
| L | lettuce, leaves |
| M | milk |
| N | netting |
| O | onions |
| P | pillow, parsley, potatoes, peas, pitcher |
| Q | |
| R | radishes, rake, rabbit hole |
| S | spoon, shovel, sieve |
| T | tree, tool shed, tablespoon |
| U | umbrella |
| V | watering can, wheelbarrow |
| W | |
| X | |
| Y | |
| Z | |

**Figure 11.8** Costumes for *The Tale of Peter Rabbit*

Mrs. Rabbit—
  Long blue dress with long sleeves
  White apron to cover most of dress
  Red cape and kerchief for head

Peter—
  Blue jacket with buttons
  Long nightgown
  White shoes

Flopsy, Mopsy, and Cotton-tail—
  Red capes
  White shoes

Mr. McGregor—
  Overalls
  Cap
  Make-believe beard

## The Program and the Credits

Designing and writing the program is both a small group and class activity that involves the students in the publishing aspect of writing. They have to decide on a name for the film or presentation and a name for the company that has made the film. They also have to decide who will be actors, who will be production crew members, and who will create the set, the costumes, and so forth.

You can bring in sample programs from plays, musicals, or other presentations to show students the elements to be included and the design and layout features. Students also can watch a movie on video or DVD and read the credits, noting who is listed, how names are presented, and other relevant information. People who love movies always watch the credits and realize how many professionals are involved in making a film. Figure 11.9 provides a template for the credits that can be used for any production.

**Figure 11.9**    Credits for Any Production

---

The _____ Production

Company of Class _____ Presents

Title _____

By (author) _____

Adapted for Filming by (students)

_____

Produced by

_____

Directed by

_____

Casting by

_____

Cast (list character actors)

_____

Scriptwriters

_____

Set Designers

_____

Costume Designers

_____.

**Figure 11.9** (Continued)

Artists

_____.

Lighting

_____.

Music

_____.

Special Effects

_____

Others _____

By the completion of the production, the students will have finished the Taxonomy on filmmaking. Depending on time and interest, teachers can ask students to write a one-sentence statement of what each term means. For example, a producer is the person who organizes and manages the entire production of a movie. The Taxonomy should have the terms listed in Figure 11.9 plus any others the students come up with during this activity.

## PREMISES, PREMISES IN THE INTERMEDIATE AND MIDDLE GRADES

### Historical Fiction

There are many book choices in the middle grades for Premises, Premises. An emotionally stirring story that works particularly well is _Number the Stars,_ a historical fiction story by Lois Lowry (1989). As soon as the students write the Premise Statement of this book, they will immediately perceive its potential as a movie.

_Number the Stars_ is about a 10-year-old Danish girl, Annemarie Johansen, living with her parents and younger sister Kirsti in Nazi-occupied Copenhagen (Denmark) during World War II (1940–1945), who has to help her family save her friend Ellen Rosen and Ellen's family from being deported by the Nazis to a concentration camp along with other Jewish families.

This story, written as historical fiction, lends itself to extensive research related to the true events that occurred in Denmark during World War II. For example, students reading *Number the Stars* can form research teams to

- Complete a country Profile on Denmark.
- Obtain information about the saving of the Danish Jews during World War II.
- Find out why Sweden was able and willing to admit Jews from Denmark.

By the intermediate and middle grades, students can work in teams as scriptwriters, focusing on the dialogues of the different characters. Writing dialogue from a novel can be tricky, because the students have to select or, at times, modify what the characters are saying in to order to keep the action moving. The students must also know that the screenwriter lets the words speak for themselves and gives very little, if any, narrative information. The example below was put together by two "screenwriters" in a fifth grade class reading *Number the Stars*.

---

**Scene:** The kitchen of the Johansen house. Family is eating dinner. Curtains are drawn and only candles are burning at the table to give the family light.

---

**Annemarie:** Is it true, Papa, that people say that all of Denmark is King Christian's bodyguard?

**Papa:** Yes. It is true. Any Danish citizen would die for King Christian, to protect him.

**Annemarie:** You too, Papa?

**Papa:** Yes.

**Annemarie:** And Mama?

**Papa:** Mama too.

**Annemarie:** Then I would too, Papa, if I had to.

*A brief silence as Mama takes away the dishes.*

**Annemarie:** Sometimes I wonder why the king wasn't able to protect us. Why didn't he fight the Nazis so that they wouldn't come into Denmark with their guns?

**Papa:** We are such a tiny country. And they are such an enormous enemy. Our king was very wise. He knew how few soldiers Denmark had. He knew that many, many Danish people would die if we fought.

## The Fairy Tale—A Book-to-Movie Activity for Intermediate and Middle School Students

The traditional fairy tales—meaning those recorded by Jacob and Wilhelm Grimm, Charles Perrault, and Joseph Jacobs—compose one of the most common genres taught to children. In his insightful work *The Uses of Enchantment*, psychologist Bruno Bettelheim points out that "the fairy tale simplifies all situations. Its figures are clearly drawn; and details, unless very important, are eliminated. All characters are typical rather than unique" (1975, p. 8).

Because of these characteristics, fairy tales

> came to convey . . . overt and covert meanings—came to speak simultane-
> ously to all levels of the human personality, communicating in a manner
> which reaches the uneducated mind of the child as well as that of the sophis-
> ticated adult. (p. 5)

From this point of view, Bettelheim promotes the absolute necessity of students
knowing fairy tales for their powerful message that shows

> a struggle against severe difficulties in life is unavoidable [and] is an
> intrinsic part of human existence—but that if one does not shy away, but
> steadfastly meets the unexpected and often unjust hardships, one masters
> all obstacles and at the end emerges victorious. (p. 8)

Bettelheim's description of fairy tales moves them beyond the realm of stories for
young children. When students in the intermediate and middle school grades are
reintroduced to fairy tales, they perceive (usually for the first time) the messages of
struggle, hardship, and the overcoming of obstacles that Bettelheim writes about.
Goldilocks, Little Red Riding Hood, Snow White, and Cinderella each represent a
different stage of growth or development, facing different situations that place them
in danger or difficulty. These characters have adversaries and make mistakes or face
challenges. These perspectives, detailed so brilliantly by Bettelheim, are captured in
the following activities, which lend themselves to dramatization, filmmaking, and
creative writing activities.

Begin by defining the elements of a fairy tale using Defining Format and entering the definition in the Notebook, as shown in Figure 11.10.

**Figure 11.10**

### What Is a Fairy Tale?

#### • DEFINING FORMAT •

| Question | Category | Characteristics |
|---|---|---|
| What is a fairy tale? | | |
| A fairy tale is a | story or literary genre that | 1. has a central character who usually (but not always) is female, not yet an adult, and is faced with a difficult problem or dilemma. <br> 2. has one or more characters who cause or add to the central character's problem. <br> 3. has one or more characters who come to the aid of the central character. <br> 4. has a resolution of the problem through help, resourcefulness, and a touch of magic. |

Figure 11.11 shows how the story of Snow White and the Seven Dwarfs exemplifies the characteristics of a fairy tale.

**Figure 11.11**    Example—Snow White

Central character—Snow White, about 14 years old, growing up in a castle with only her stepmother.

Problem or dilemma—Stepmother becomes jealous as Snow White becomes more beautiful, and she decides to have Snow White killed.

Additional characters who add to the problem—A hunter is ordered by the stepmother to kill Snow White in the forest and bring proof of her death.

Additional characters who help the central character—Animals in the forest help Snow White find shelter in the house of the Seven Dwarfs who, in turn, try to protect Snow White from the pursuit of the stepmother.

Resolution or solution to the problem—Stepmother tempts Snow White with a comb, a girdle, and finally a beautiful but poisoned apple that causes Snow White to appear dead. Dwarfs keep her in a glass coffin; prince arrives and through a kiss (the magic of love) revives Snow White.

## Writing a Treatment for Fairy Tales

After the teacher and students have discussed and defined the elements found in most fairy tales, students then select a fairy tale and write a treatment that covers the three aspects of the story: the characters, the problem or dilemma, and the solution. The students can also add a personal reaction. By using this format, students will have expanded the Premise Statement into an original retelling that is preparatory to developing a storyboard and dialogue for a book-to-movie presentation. Following is an example of a treatment related to the characters, the problem, the solution to the problem, and the personal reaction, all written by a seventh grade student. We have capitalized the word *WHO* in this statement to emphasize the major actions or roles of the characters; these indicate the essential aspects of the story.

### The Characters

*Beauty and the Beast* by Charles Perrault is about Beauty, an eighteen-year old young woman WHO asks her father to bring back just one rose from his trip to a faraway place. In addition, there are Beauty's two sisters WHO are greedy and want their father to bring back dresses and jewels and get angry at Beauty because they think she is just being too good by just asking for a rose. Then there is the father WHO wants to please all his daughters because he is a good father. After that comes a very important character, the Beast WHO once was a handsome prince but had a spell put on him by a wicked witch and is now very ugly.

### The Problem

The problem in this story is that the father gets caught in a storm and lands by mistake at the Beast's house. The Beast gives the father food and a place to sleep, but in the morning the father steals a rose from the Beast's garden to bring back to Beauty. Now the Beast is very angry and tells the father that the only way he can go home to his family is if he sends his daughter Beauty to take his place. The father promises to do this, although he thinks that once he escapes he will not send Beauty. But when he gets home and gives Beauty the rose and tells her what happened, she says she must keep the promise her father made. So Beauty magically gets to the Beast's castle, but even though the Beast is kind to her, she is afraid of him because he is really very, very ugly. Beauty is now sad, but she doesn't know what to do to solve her problem. Beauty gets so sad that the Beast feels sorry for her and tells her that she can go home for a short while to visit her father and her sisters. But he makes her promise that she will return in a few days. Beauty thanks the Beast for being so kind and magically gets home. Her father is very happy to see her, but her sisters still think she is acting too good and won't talk to her. Beauty doesn't want to leave her father, but then she has a dream that the Beast is dying because she didn't go back as she promised.

### Solution to the Problem

The problem begins to be solved when Beauty tells her father that she has to go back to the Beast or else he will die. She magically gets back, but it is almost too late. The Beast is lying on the ground and can hardly breathe. When Beauty sees him she realizes that he has been very good to her and loves her. She also now loves him even though he is very ugly. But she doesn't care that he is ugly so she begs him to live and says, "I love you because you have been so good to me." When the Beast hears these words, he sits up and suddenly his ugly looks begin to change, first his hair, then his eyes, then his skin. Beauty is amazed. The Beast has suddenly become handsome. He then tells her, "A wicked witch turned me into a Beast and said only if someone really, truly loved me could I be changed back to a Prince." So Beauty and the Beast who was now a Prince got married and lived happily ever after.

### My Reaction to the Story

As a result of reading Charles Perrault's story *Beauty and the Beast,* I now realize that we should love someone because they are good and kind, not just because they are handsome. I would recommend this story to everyone who believes this idea and needs to learn about this idea. This is truly my favorite fairy tale.

## INNOVATING ON FAIRY TALES FOR DRAMATIC OR FILMED PERFORMANCES: *PLAINTIFF V. DEFENDANT*

By using selected fairy tales, students in the upper grades, including high school, can write from the point of view, or perspective, of one of the characters as if the characters were going to address the problem in a court of law. One character is the plaintiff and the other is the defendant. Students write from the perspective of one character and tell the story from that character's point of view. Each student also can write as an attorney for the defendant, an attorney for the plaintiff, a witness for either side, or the judge.

Students can work in cooperative groups, each student writing from a different point of view, so that all of the characters are represented. When the writing is finished, the group can conduct a trial, and the rest of the class can serve as the jury.

Following are familiar fairy tales and the problems in each that could be used in a *Plaintiff v. Defendant* assignment:

Goldilocks: Mrs. Bear sues Goldilocks's mother for the crime of irresponsibility and negligence in letting her daughter break in and enter the Bears' house.

Little Red Riding Hood: Grandmother charges the wolf with physical harassment and intent to kill.

Cinderella: Cinderella charges her stepmother with abuse and negligence for making her work long hours at hard labor.

Jack and the Beanstalk: Giant sues Jack for break-in and theft, demanding recovery of stolen items.

Before the students begin work on the trial, they will need to work as a group to complete character Profiles of the characters they are writing about. Provide each group with a character Profile (Figure 11.3), and explain each section as outlined below.

*Age of Character:* In many stories, the age of the character is unspecified, and the reader has to infer the age from the behavior. For example, the reader might infer that Little Red Riding Hood is about six or seven years old. This could be why she is unable to recognize that the wolf is the stranger her mother has warned her about. She naively tells the wolf where she is going. She is easily fooled by outward appearances when the wolf is dressed as her grandmother, and she is dependent upon being rescued by an adult (the woodcutter).

*Family:* Here, too, there is inference. Again, in Little Red Riding Hood, no family members other than the mother and the grandmother are stated. However, the reader of the story might wonder if there are younger children in the household that necessitate the mother to send the oldest child on an errand alone. Students might wonder if the father is away or at work. Therefore, in completing this line, students might add other family members.

*Habitat:* The habitat should be described with as many details as possible. For example, Little Red Riding Hood lives in a three-room cottage at the northern end of a huge pine tree forest.

*Wishes and Fears:* Through discussion, the students begin to expand their ideas of the character's wishes and fears. Little Red Riding Hood is likely to wish that her grandmother gets well, she recognizes a stranger, she doesn't have to go alone through the forest, her mother would go instead, and so on. Similarly, the students have to consider all the fears of a young child making this trip alone.

*Character Traits:* The students need to be able to distinguish between behavioral traits and appearance traits. Bravery is a character trait, whereas beauty is an appearance trait. In addition, the students have to consider both positive and negative traits (e.g., generous versus selfish).

## Using a Profile Template

After completing the character Profiles, students can use a Profile template, illustrated in Figures 11.12 and 11.13, if they are creating a scene in which there is a trial.

**Figure 11.12**  Preparation for Trial

Directions: Your group will be preparing a trial for one of the characters in a fairy tale that your group has selected. Complete the following information before the trial begins.

Name of Case _____

Plaintiff _____

Defendant _____

Attorney for the Plaintiff

_____

Attorney for the Defendant

_____

Witness(es) for the Plaintiff

_____

Witness(es) for the Defendant

_____

Plea of Defendant (Guilty or Not Guilty)

_____

Date of Trial _____

Location of Trial _____

Presiding Judge _____

Other Information

_____

_____

_____

**Figure 11.13**   Presenting Your Case

Directions: Choose who you will be in the trial: the plaintiff, the defendant, the attorney for the plaintiff, the attorney for the defendant, or a witness. Before you make your choice, read what role each of these people plays in a trial.

Your Name  _____

Role in this Case  _____

_____

_____

Write your presentation, giving your side of the story with as much detail and credibility as possible.

- If you are the plaintiff, give specific accusations, citing at least three details that support your argument.

- If you are the defendant, give strong reasons why the charges against you are wrong or improbable.

- If you are the attorney for the plaintiff, you must make the strongest possible case against the defendant, providing numerous details of wrongdoing.

- If you are the attorney for the defendant, you must convince the jury that under no circumstances could your client have done the crime she or he is accused of.

- If you are a witness, you must establish that you are truthful, careful in what you say, and perfectly clear about what you have witnessed.

In your writing, first identify who you are: For example, "My name is Cunning B. Fox, and I am a witness for Hermit T. Wolf."

_____

_____

Explain your position by giving three significant arguments for or against the accusation. Give times and dates and very specific reasons for your actions or beliefs; e.g., "I married Cinderella's father ten years ago when the little girl was barely five years old. I have always loved Cinderella and treated her as my own daughter."

_____

_____

Use positive words to describe yourself or your client; e.g., "I'm a gentle giant, living my life on a mountaintop, bothering no one, caring for my lovely wife. All I have are a few simple possessions."

_____

_____

Below is a sampling of writing from sixth graders in a rural Tennessee school who wrote and videotaped the complete trial of *Sarah Hood v. Harry T. Wolf.*

---

### Sarah Hood v. Harry T. Wolf

*Opening Argument Presented by*
*T. J. Nakita, Attorney for Harry T. Wolf, Defendant*

Ladies and gentlemen of the jury. I will prove that my client is in no way guilty of the alleged crime. First off, he is a Buddhist, and therefore a vegetarian. He respects and loves all living creatures and would die at the thought of eating any sort of meat. He wouldn't hurt a fly on the basis of his beliefs. He also has very bad stomach problems. You might call it an ulcer, so there is no way he could have eaten an entire woman and/or her granddaughter. I submit two pieces of evidence for the record, #310, his birth certificate, and #311, his doctor's statement.

*Mr. Harry T. Wolf is indeed Buddhist as stated on his birth certificate and signed below by a Buddhist monk.*

—Tibetan Monk

*Mr. Harry T. Wolf does indeed have an ulcer. Medical records of this condition are at the Central City Hospital.*

—Chief of Stomach Problems

---

### Testimony of the Defendant Harry T. Wolf

**Nakita:** Mr. Wolf, please share your side of the story.

**Mr. Wolf:** I was sitting behind a tree eating a very full dinner, when I heard footsteps. I looked around and saw Little Red Riding Hood coming my way. I asked her where she was going and she said to her grandmother's house. I decided to be a nice gentleman by offering a short cut. After a while, I decided to see if she had made it there safely. She wasn't there yet and so I decided to wait for her inside. I was very tired from the walk and I saw some nightclothes. I decided to put them on and take a nap. I heard a scream from the kitchen. It was Grandmother Hood, so I put her in the closet just to get her quiet. Little Red then came in and so as not to scare her, I pretended to be Grandmother Hood. She gave me the goodies, and we talked for a while. When she left, I went to the closet to get the old Mrs. Hood. She was asleep, so I put her on the bed and left.

---

## BOOK-TO-MOVIE IN THE HIGH SCHOOL

In the high school, where short class modules and departmental schedules curtail dramatization of a book, students can use a modified version of the book-to-movie procedures but still keep the elements of dramatization.

First, have the students write a Premise Statement so they have a statement of what the book is about. Often, the Premise Statement can lead to a discussion as to why the book might or might not be a good movie. Who would be the audience for a movie with this premise? Would it have enough action or emotion? Have there been other successful movies with similar premises? The teacher might want to have a class work in groups, with each group writing one treatment on a book the group has selected.

Another aspect of the writing should be a character Profile for understanding of the characters. Students reading *The Pigman* by Paul Zindel (1968) can work in groups of four or five, with each group responsible for completing a character Profile of a different character. Then, the students in each group work together to keep a journal of the ongoing events in their character's life. After the journals have been completed, actors from each group play characters by taking turns reading from their journals so that the audience hears the different voice and point of view of each character.

Figure 11.14 shows a journal assignment based on *The Pigman* with sample entries written from the point of view of Mr. Pignati.

**Figure 11.14**  Keeping a Journal on a Book in Preparation for a Film

---

Directions: Imagine that you are one of the three main characters in *The Pigman*—John, Lorraine, or Mr. Pignati. Keep a journal of your interactions with the other two characters who affect your life. Write the journal from your point of view. Focus on your feelings and the changes that are taking place in your life. Use the outline of the story as a guide for your journal.

**Example of Journal Entry by Angelo Pignati**

Chapter 4—The first contact by telephone between Mr. Pignati and Lorraine and John.

This afternoon I got a call from a delightful young woman calling on behalf of a charity called the L & J Fund. Her name was Ms. Truman. She was not only friendly but full of good jokes. I couldn't help laughing and then I told her about how my wife always laughs at my jokes. I told her the joke about the best get-well cards—four aces—and she laughed. Of course, I said I would make a contribution to her cause. Such a nice young woman. She just brightened up my day.

**Subjects of Subsequent Journal Entries**

Chapter 5—The first meeting of Mr. Pignati with Lorraine and John. Include the contribution and the pigs.

Chapter 6—The visit to the zoo.

Chapter 7—Mr. Pignati's wife.

Chapter 8—The visit to Beekman's Department Store.

Chapter 10—Visiting Mr. Pignati, confessions and games.

Chapter 11—Heart attack.

Chapter 13—The party.

Chapter 14—Apologies and death, final entries and reflections.

---

# INTERNET LINKS

http://www.lessonplanspage.com/LAOMakeBookIntoMovieProjectIdeaHS.htm

http://www.emints.org/ethemes/resources/S00000449.shtml

http://www.eduction-world.com/a_curr/curr295.shtml

**CHAPTER TWELVE**

# Quotable Quotes

## Words Inspire

Words Are Free!

Have Words,
Can Write

Writing Is Thinking

Write to a Martian

Every Word
Has a Story

Organize
Your Writing

Know Who You
Know and Know
Who You Are!

Think in Threes

Everybody Has
to Be Someplace

Let's Make
a Movie!

**Words Inspire**

Know Thyself

Writers Are Editors

A Goal for
Every Student

*Piglet sidled up to Pooh from behind. "Pooh," he whispered.*

*"Yes, Piglet."*

*"Nothing," said Piglet, taking Pooh's paw, "I just wanted to be sure of you."*

~A. A. Milne (1957, p. 41)

## QUOTABLE QUOTES FOR REMEMBRANCE, INSPIRATION, AND RESPONSE

Quotable Quotes is the strategy that asks or inspires students to respond to specific quotations from literary characters or people of note or accomplishment. Students that have been given an opportunity to read and ponder the words of others can respond with their own ideas and perhaps even with their own newly minted personal sayings, quotations, and maxims. Responding to the words of others is a metacognitive activity that requires thought, reflection, and empathy. Quotable Quotes combines naturally with Who's Who and Reasons, Causes, Results and provides students with an effective strategy package for writing.

## USING QUOTABLE QUOTES

*If there is no struggle, there is no progress.*

~Frederick Douglass

The purpose of Quotable Quotes is to have students establish an imaginary dialogue with the characters or people who have made noteworthy statements. In this dialogue, students express their own opinions or beliefs in relationship to the quoted statement, or Quotable Quote. They are also encouraged to seek out quotations that they can include in their own writing, especially those that relate to the ideas and beliefs they are expressing.

Quotable Quotes can come from nursery rhymes, children's literature, and novels as well as the words of presidents, social activists, scientists, writers, and anyone else who has uttered words worth remembering. The Internet is now an easy source for quotes, and we have included several sites for quotations in Internet Links.

# QUOTABLE QUOTES FROM THE WORLD OF MOTHER GOOSE AND OTHER CHILDREN'S RHYMES

*Just leave them alone and they will come home . . .*

Many children's rhymes are pithy stories written in rhyme that teach lessons, give information, or tell of human behaviors both positive and negative. Because of their brevity, many of these rhymes are easily quotable. They tell of kindness, loyalty, hospitality, and industriousness; others tell of lateness, disobedience, or indifference to others. This wide range of behaviors, stated in charming, easy-to-memorize rhymes, can be the basis of class discussion, which can be followed by having students write their own ideas and beliefs. The writing can be in the form of letters to the characters expressing opinions or giving advice. Or students can respond in personal essays (three reasons why . . .) or in journal entries in which they imagine themselves as a nursery rhyme character, such as Little Bo-Peep, going through the pain of losing their sheep or other pets.

Since many rhymes relate to values of kindness and gentleness, particularly to animals, they can serve as the stimulus for students to express their own feelings and values about similar topics. Following are examples of selected rhymes with suggestions for writing. Additional examples can be found in other poems and children's stories.

## Kindness to Animals

The rhymes in Figures 12.1–12.4 can build empathy for animals. After students hear these rhymes and discuss their meanings, use the prompts that follow, which relate to the ideas in the rhymes. Add other rhymes and poems from material in your own classroom, and continue to use the Notebook for the draft copy and the strategy formats you have already introduced. Then have the students "publish" their writings with illustrations related to the rhyme. You can have a beautiful display on Kindness to Animals.

**Figure 12.1**     My Kitty

I like little kitty, her coat is so warm,

And if I don't hurt her she'll do me no harm;

So I'll not pull her tail, nor drive her away,

But kitty and I very gently will play.

**Prompts:**

Write three ways that you can be kind to a cat (or other pet).

Write three reasons why a cat can be a good pet.

**Figure 12.2**     The Robin

The little robin grieves

When the snow is on the ground.

For the trees have no leaves,

And no berries can be found.

The air is cold, the worms are hid:

For robin here what can be done?

Let's strew around some crumbs of bread,

And then he'll live till snow is gone.

The north wind does blow

And we shall have snow,

And what will poor Robin do then?

Poor thing!

He'll sit in a barn

And keep himself warm,

And hide his head under his wing,

Poor thing!

**Prompts:**

Write three ways that tell how winter makes life hard for Robin.

Write an imaginary letter to Robin telling him several ways that you will help him get through the cold winter.

Write three ways that spring and warm weather will make Robin feel better.

**Figure 12.3** The Turtle

A turtle is a reptile.

Its home is on its back.

It never has to worry,

If someone will attack.

When it spies an enemy,

What does it do so well?

It simply takes its head and feet,

And tucks inside its shell.

**Prompts:**

Write a letter to a Martian or someone who has never seen a turtle. Describe the turtle, telling three characteristics that make it different from any other animal.

Write a letter to the turtle telling three reasons why you admire it.

**Figure 12.4** What Is a Whale?

A whale is not as small as us.

Most whales are bigger than a bus!

A whale is not like a fish in the sea.

A whale breathes air like you and me.

A whale can't walk upon the ground.

A whale must swim to get around.

A whale is a mammal just like me.

But its home is in the deep blue sea.

**Prompts:**

Write a Defining Format for the question, what is a whale? Use some of the information from the poem and get other information from a book or article on whales.

Write a Metacognition Statement telling three important facts you know about whales.

Write an essay that tells three reasons why we should protect whales.

## Quotable Quotes From Children's Literature

The world of children's literature is filled with wise sayings, opinions, and beliefs expressed through human, animal, and other imagined characters. In the story *The Way Mothers Are* (Schlein, 1993), a kitten worries if her mother still loves her, even though she does "naughty things." The kitten gets various assurances from her mother, but is not satisfied until her mother says, "So you think I love you just when you're good and stop loving you when you are naughty, do you? I love you all of the time, because you are mine." A quotation such as this can serve as the stimulus for writing about many subjects; for example, titles could include "Why I Love My [Mother, Father, Grandmother, etc.]," "How I Know My Mother Loves Me," and "Why a Mother Animal Loves Its Baby."

In using children's literature, you can involve your students in Quotable Quotes by posting Quotable Quotes on word walls and bulletin boards. Have your students select their favorite Quotable Quotes and write them in their Notebooks. Use them as motivators and springboards not only to help students read and write, but also to help them interact with the literary characters.

Among the many examples of children's stories with Quotable Quotes are A. A. Milne's classic stories of Winnie the Pooh and his friends, who reflect the concerns and thoughts of young children everywhere. Figure 12.5 shows two quotes from Winnie the Pooh for discussion and writing.

For students in the intermediate and middle grades, there are humorous and thought-provoking Quotable Quotes from *The Phantom Tollbooth* by Norton Juster (1989), which is an excellent book to read aloud and use for postreading and post-writing activities. This novel tells the story of Milo, a spoiled boy of about 10 or 11 who is totally bored by his abundance of toys and gadgets, including his own car. Then one day he gets a tollbooth as a gift from his uncle, and taking his car through the tollbooth, he enters a land "beyond expectations." Milo's life will never be the same, and Milo's adventures and new understandings can be vicariously shared by students. Figure 12.6 shows quotes from *The Phantom Tollbooth* that can be used to inspire reflection and discussion as well as serve as prompts for writing.

**Figure 12.5**     From the Wisdom of Pooh Himself

*For I am a Bear of Very Little Brain, and long words Bother me.*

—A. A. Milne (1957, p. 50)

**Question:** How do you feel about long words?

**Activity:** Make a Taxonomy of your favorite long words.

**Prompt:** Write several sentences or a story using as many of your favorite long words as you can.

*My spelling is Wobbly. It's good spelling, but it Wobbles, and the letters get in the wrong places.*

— A. A. Milne (1957, p. 78)

**Question:** Why do you think the letters get in the wrong places?

**Activity:** Collect words that your classmates have trouble spelling correctly, and arrange them in a Taxonomy with their correct spellings.

**Prompt:** Write a letter to Pooh giving him three pieces of advice to help him improve his spelling.

**Figure 12.6** Quotable Quotes—*The Phantom Tollbooth*

*Expectations is the place you must always go to before you get where you're going.*

—the Whether Man (p. 19).

**Activity:** Interview three or four classmates or adults and ask them what possible events in their lives would be "beyond expectations."

**Prompt:** Write a letter to your teacher or another adult telling her or him about three of your expectations.

*Then one day I realized that I'd never amount to anything without an education and, being naturally adept at spelling, I decided that. . . .*

—the Spelling Bee (p. 52)

**Prompt:** You probably guessed that the Spelling Bee decided to become a champion speller. Write three good reasons for knowing how to spell correctly.

**Activity:** Collect 10 words from your classmates or friends that they think would be very challenging to spell. Then see if you can meet the challenge by spelling the words correctly.

*Words and numbers are of equal value, for, in the cloak of knowledge, one is warp and the other woof.*

—Rhyme and Reason (p. 77)

**Explanation:** On a loom, the lengthwise threads are called the *warp* and the threads that are interwoven are the *woof.*

**Prompt:** Write a three-paragraph essay explaining how our lives would be different if suddenly numbers were to disappear.

## Quotable Quotes From Aesop

Aesop, the moralist of antiquity, has given the world the pithy statements that come in handy when one wants to prove a point. No one knows whether or not he wrote the stories for these numerous aphorisms, but when people think of fables, they most likely think of Aesop. Another fable writer was Jean de la Fontaine, the French fabulist of the seventeenth century, who is probably best known for his story, "The Fox and the Crow." Students generally enjoy writing fables, because they have a direct plot, contain characters that are simply drawn, and end with a moral or lesson.

Students may, at some time in their school years, be asked to write a new fable to fit the moral. A variant on such a writing exercise is to ask students to write about the consequences of ignoring the moral or lesson or to think about the contradiction in the lesson. Figure 12.7 shows several Quotable Quotes from Aesop with an added statement. Ask students to select two or three of these statements, and write what happens or what a person should do when the moral or lesson is ignored.

**Figure 12.7**   Quotable Quotes—Aesop

Select two or three of these statements and follow the prompt given in the text.

If too many cooks spoil the soup, describe the soup that too many cooks spoiled.

If in unity there is strength, tell what happens when groups split apart.

If slow and steady wins the race, tell what happens to those who speed and then dawdle.

If we should make hay while the sun shines, what should we do on a rainy day?

If silence is golden, why do we speak?

If haste makes waste, when should we work slowly?

# HISTORICAL QUOTABLE QUOTES

To many students, the study of history seems to be about dates and battles or the rise and fall of civilizations. Yet, history is about humans, many of whom are simply caught up in the march of events, while others seem to make history happen. Most of the people who make history happen have made statements that get quoted, and often these people are remembered not only for what they did but for what they said. The following Quotable Quotes are from American presidents, fighters for freedom and equal rights, and women who have spoken out specifically for women's issues. An excellent classroom activity is to have students collect their own quotes for discussion and respond to them in their own writings.

## Quotable Quotes of American Presidents

All through the study of American history, students hear the words of many of the American presidents and may discuss their meaning or importance in social studies classrooms. Figure 12.8 shows prompts for responding to the selection of Quotable Quotes of several American presidents. Students can use them as starters for writing about their own ideas and opinions on the issue stated in the quote.

## Quotable Quotes in the
## Fight for Freedom and Equal Rights

From the very beginning of American history, words have played a role in shaping individuals' ideas and actions. Throughout most people's schooling, they

**Figure 12.8**   Quotable Quotes—American Presidents

The quotations below came from speeches of American presidents and have become an important part of ideas that have shaped American history. Write your own response to these quotations. Use the prompt to get started.

*I believe this country cannot endure permanently half slave and half free.*

—Abraham Lincoln

**Prompt:** Imagine that you are Abraham Lincoln and are writing a persuasive essay convincing your audience about your belief. Write three reasons why you hold to this idea.

*Walk softly and carry a big stick.*

—Theodore Roosevelt

**Prompt:** Write a letter to Theodore Roosevelt. Tell him why you agree or disagree with his statement. Write three convincing arguments for either position.

*The only thing we have to fear is fear itself—nameless, unreasoning, unjustified terror which paralyzes needed efforts to convert retreat into advance.*

—Franklin D. Roosevelt

**Prompt:** Imagine that you have been asked to speak to your fellow students about overcoming fear. Start your writing with a definition of fear, and then write three ways that fear can be overcome.

*Ask not what your country can do for you, but what you can do for your country.*

—John F. Kennedy

**Prompt:** Write three slogans that offer ideas about what you can do for your country. Put these slogans on posters and illustrate them.

*The Great Society is a place where every child can find knowledge to enrich his mind and to enlarge his talents.*

—Lyndon B. Johnson

**Prompt:** Write a personal essay in which you state three ways that you can enrich your own knowledge or develop your talents.

hear (if they are listening) the words of Patrick Henry, Benjamin Franklin, and Thomas Paine. As they move through the years, they consider the calls or messages of Davy Crockett, Chief Joseph, Earl Warren, and Dr. Martin Luther King Jr. Figure 12.9 shows several of these truly Quotable Quotes with suggestions for student reactions and responses. Add your own favorites as well as those offered by your students.

**Figure 12.9**   Quotable Questions—Freedom and Equal Rights

---

*I know not what course others may take, but as for me, give me liberty or give me death.*

—Patrick Henry to the
Virginia House of Burgesses on March 20, 1755

**Prompt:** Write your own definition of liberty. Then tell why liberty, as you defined it, is important to you.

*These are the times that try men's souls.*

—Thomas Paine in his pamphlet
*Common Sense,* written around 1775

**Prompt:** Every period in history has its difficult times. Imagine that you are writing a letter to Thomas Paine and are using his quote to tell him of one problem today that is "trying our souls." In your letter, tell Thomas Paine why we are struggling and how we might overcome this problem.

*We conclude that in the field of public education the doctrine of "separate but equal" has no place.*

—Chief Justice Earl Warren in
*Brown v. Board of Education,* May 17, 1954

**Prompt:** After you have studied this significant Supreme Court decision outlawing separate educational facilities for African American people, write a personal essay stating your own three reasons why "separate but equal" has no place in American schools.

*I have a dream that my four little children will one day live in a nation where they will not be judged by the color of their skin but by the content of their character.*

—Spoken by Dr. Martin Luther King Jr. in his
"I Have a Dream Speech" in Washington, DC, August 28, 1963

**Prompt:** Write your own "I Have a Dream" speech in which you state three to five dreams you have that will make America an even better place to live than it is now.

---

## Quotable Quotes From Women in History

Until recent times, the words of women were rarely quoted except within the circles of the women who stated them. Yet, women, like men, also spoke out for freedom and liberty, both for themselves and for others. Figure 12.10 shows a sampling of women's words with suggestions for written responses.

# OTHER QUOTABLE QUOTES

Figure 12.11 shows Quotable Quotes that can be presented to students whenever they seem appropriate to a specific lesson. Students can respond to these statements

**Figure 12.10**  Quotable Quotes—Women In History

---

*In the new code of laws which I suppose it will be necessary for you to make, I desire you would remember the ladies and be more generous and favorable to them than your ancestors. Do not put such unlimited power into the hands of the husbands. Remember men would be tyrants if they could.*

—Abigail Adams in a letter to her husband,
John, a delegate at that time to the
Continental Congress, March 31, 1776

**Prompt:** Imagine that you are Abigail Adams speaking before the Continental Congress. Explain what you mean by being "more generous and favorable" and why you worry that "men would be tyrants."


*It is not easy to be a pioneer—but oh, it is fascinating! I would not trade one moment, even the worst, for all the riches in the world.*

—Elizabeth Blackwell, who after many years of
being rejected because she was a woman, was finally
admitted to the Philadelphia Medical School in 1850

**Prompt:** Write a letter to Elizabeth Blackwell, congratulating her on getting into medical school. Then tell her three reasons why you admire her pioneering spirit.


*Men their rights and nothing more; women their rights and nothing less.*

—Susan B. Anthony, the women's rights activist,
in her paper *The Revolution* (1868)

**Prompt:** Write a list of rights that you believe belong to both women and men. If you think that there are different rights for women and men, write a separate list. Make a poster of your list with a slogan and illustrations.


*Science may have found a cure for most evils; but it has found no remedy for the worst of them all—the apathy of human beings.*

—Helen Keller, speaker, educator,
and writer, in her book *My Religion* (1963)

**Prompt:** *Apathy* means indifference to what happens to others. Imagine that you are a scientist or social scientist working on a "cure" for apathy. Write a report telling of three ways that you can make people more concerned with the welfare of others.

---

in a variety of ways. They may have had a personal experience they can relate to the quote, or the quote may evoke a personal reaction. They may want to collect their own Quotable Quotes to use as introductions to their writings as is often customary with published works. Quotable Quotes can serve as the focus or theme for bulletin boards and are great discussion starters.

**Figure 12.11**   Quotable Quotes—Collections for Your Writings

*I never worry about action, only inaction.*

—Winston Churchill

**Prompt:** Winston Churchill was the prime minister of Great Britain during World War II and an extraordinary person of action. Research three actions of Winston Churchill, and write a statement about what might have happened if Churchill had not taken these actions.

*If anything can go wrong, it will.*

*If an experiment works, something has gone wrong.*

*No matter how long or how hard you shop for an item, after you've bought it, it will be on sale somewhere else.*

—selected from *Murphy's Law and Other Reasons Why Things Go Wrong* (Block, 1980)

**Prompt:** Pick one of the above quotes. Tell a story from your personal life that illustrates the quote.

*Good fences make good neighbors.*

—Robert Frost in "Mending Wall"

**Prompt:** In this, the last line of the poem "Mending Wall," Robert Frost quotes his neighbor. Decide if you agree or disagree with this quote, and then write three reasons for your opinion.

# INTERNET LINKS

http://www.quotationspage.com/

http://www.famous-quotations.com/asp/categories.asp

http://www.quoteworld.org/

http://www.brainyquote.com

# CHAPTER THIRTEEN

# Personifications and Interactions

## Know Thyself

Strategies, Genres,
Topics, and Tools

Words Are Free!

Have Words,
Can Write

Writing Is Thinking

Write to a Martian

Every Word
Has a Story

Organize
Your Writing

Know Who You
Know and Know
Who You Are!

Think in Threes

Everybody Has
to Be Someplace

Let's Make
a Movie!

Words Inspire

**Know Thyself**

Writers Are Editors

A Goal for
Every Student

*It's all in how you look at things.*

~Alec in *The Phantom
Tollbooth* (Juster, 1961, p. 102)

## PERSONIFICATIONS AND INTERACTIONS: ANOTHER POINT OF VIEW

Alec, the character in *The Phantom Tollbooth* who grows down (rather than up),
teaches the young character Milo the importance of point of view. Pointing to
a bucket of water, he tells Milo that

> from an ant's point of view it's a vast ocean, from an elephant's just
> a cool drink, and to a fish, of course, its home. So, you see, the way
> you see things depends a great deal on where you look at them from.
> (Juster, 1989, p. 108)

The writing strategy Personifications and Interactions shows students
how to write from another person's point of view or an object's point of view
by assuming the persona of that person or object.

A student is often asked to write in her or his own voice. One of the challenges to that direction is that students often do not understand the concept of

voice. In addition, each of us uses different voices for difference circumstances. By learning how to write from different points of view, the students develop a clearer understanding of the concept of voice, along with literary skills to express different voices.

This is a form of writing that allows the writer to think flexibly and with empathy. Costa and Kallick (2000) state that "flexible thinkers are able to shift through multiple positions at will" (p. 25). In addition, they can perceive "another person's orientation," allowing for empathizing with someone else's feelings and perspectives (p. 25). Through Personifications and Interactions, a student writer can assume the role of an historic person writing to another historic person across time, such as Betty Friedan writing to Susan B. Anthony, or as one literary character writing to another literary character, for example, Portia (from *The Merchant of Venice*) writing to Katherine (of *Taming of the Shrew*). Or Portia could write to Susan B. Anthony across a broad era of time but with a similar perspective. An object can write to another object, as when a triangle describes itself to a square, gold describes itself to iron, and the digestive system exchanges information with the nervous system.

In this broadly encompassing strategy, the writer thinks of herself or himself as an historic person or person of note, a literary character, an animal, or an inanimate object. In the guise of a new persona, the writer writes to another writer (classmate) who has assumed a similar historic, literary, animal, or inanimate persona, creating writing interactions. When students engage in Personifications and Interactions, they must know who or what they are to take the point of view of that persona. Through Personifications and Interactions, students are involved in the subject area and the creative processes, valuable tasks for developing "attention to detail, precision, and orderly progression" (Costa & Kallick, 2000, p. 26).

## PERSONIFICATIONS AND INTERACTIONS ACROSS THE CURRICULUM

We recommend teaching this strategy from the primary grades through high school as a way of imparting information, opinions, beliefs, and narrative events. Through Personifications and Interactions, students get the opportunity to get out of themselves, be animate or human or inanimate, and write seriously or humorously. By assuming a new persona, writers operate under the concept of "know thyself" in order to present or state their point of view to someone or something else. In addition, the strategy Personifications and Interactions lends itself particularly to the genre of letter writing while including many of the previously introduced strategies.

## PERSONIFICATIONS AND INTERACTIONS IN THE PRIMARY GRADES

For young students, assuming another identity is natural and easy. A student can be a storybook character, a flower talking to an animal, or a teacher speaking to her class. Because of the ease that many students have with role-playing, they can write fluently and creatively from another point of view. A simple way to begin is with letter writing, in which one student chooses to be a storybook character writing to another student role-playing a different storybook character. In using letter writing, the students create an address and follow the conventions of friendly correspondence as illustrated in the letter in Figure 13.1, in which Boy Blue writes to Bo Peep. A second example using personified numbers is illustrated in Figure 13.2.

**Figure 13.1**    Letters Between Boy Blue and Bo Peep

---

Directions: Here is a make-believe letter written by Little Boy Blue to Bo Peep. Notice how their addresses come from information from the nursery rhymes that tell about them. After you have read these letters, choose two other nursery rhymes (or other poems) with characters. Team up with a classmate, and each take a character. Then write to each other about an event in your life that is described in the rhyme or poem.

Boy Blue
4 Meadow Lane
Corn Row, Iowa 54321

writes to

Bo Peep
6 Shepherd Drive
Sheeptown, Oklahoma 87654

Dear Bo,

I just heard from Jack and Jill that you lost your sheep. I am so sorry. I know how you must feel, because I once lost my cows. I fell asleep, and when I woke up, the cows were gone. But my friend Jack Horner told me to not worry. Cows always come home, he said. So I think you shouldn't worry either. Your sheep will come home, and they will be so happy to see you that they will be wagging their tails and making happy sounds like baaaa. Write to me as soon as you find your sheep, and tell me what happened.

Your friend,

Boy Blue

Bo Peep writes to Boy Blue (include addresses)

Dear Boy Blue,

Thanks so much for your good advice. I left them alone, and guess what? They did come home, and they were so happy. Every one of the sheep was wagging its tale, and I gave every sheep a hug. I hope you don't lose any of your cows.

Your friend,

Bo (Peep)

**Figure 13.2**    Letters Between an Odd Number and an Even Number

Directions: Here is an example of an odd number writing to an even number. After you have read these letters, team up with a classmate. Choose your own number up to 100. Then write a letter to your classmate's number telling as much as you can about yourself. Include addresses.

I. M. Odd
135 Uneven Road
Numbertown, New Jersey 97531

writes to

U. R. Even
44 22nd Street
Double Village, Arkansas 86422

Dear Ms. Even,

I am very happy that you are moving next door to me. For a long time I have only lived with odd numbers such as 11, 13, 15, and 17. Whenever we wanted to split up, there was always one number left over. No one was happy. But now that you are here, we won't have that problem. Your numbers will easily fit in between us, so 2 can be between 1 and 3, and 6 can be between 5 and 7, and 9 can be between 8 and 10. We will all have fun together, especially when we play our favorite games—adding and subtracting. Please write soon, and tell me as much about yourself as you can.

Very sincerely,

I. M. Odd

The strategy Personifications and Interactions is a lively and creative way to help students learn and define words, keep journals, create an animal in the form of a human, compare concepts and terms in subjects areas, understand behaviors of fictional and nonfictional characters, and have the joy of sharing their writing with their classmates and others. Below are examples of ways to use this strategy across the curriculum.

## Deepening Word Knowledge

The Paired Taxonomy (Figure 13.3) is an example of two items or concepts that share a category (as in Defining Format, Chapter 5) but have different character-istics. These paired items can be the topics for two students writing to each other, in which they describe themselves as these objects. You may wish to use the Paired Taxonomy as illustrated, or have your students create their own Paired Taxonomy related to terms in a subject area (e.g., amphibian/mammal in science, novel/poem in language arts). Suggested directions are in Figure 13.3.

**Figure 13.3** Paired Taxonomy for Personifications and Interactions

Directions: Imagine that you are one of the items in this Taxonomy. Write a letter to the adjoining item telling as much as you can about yourself. Be sure to include your address and the address to which you are writing, as in this example.

Granny Smith
14 Orchard Lane
Macintosh, Washington 65432

writes to

Clementine O. Range
12 Grove Circle
Citrus, Florida 12345

• TAXONOMY •

| A | apple/orange |
| B | ball/bat |
| C | centimeter/inch |
| D | dime/nickel |
| E | |
| F | foot/hand |
| G | |
| H | hot/cold |
| I | inch/foot |
| J | |
| K | kitten/puppy |
| L | light bulb/candle |
| M | microscope/telescope |
| N | number/letter |
| O | ocean/river |
| P | pencil/pen |
| Q | quilt/blanket |
| R | rain/snow |
| S | shoe/sock |
| T | tent/cabin |
| U | |
| V | violin/clarinet |
| W | water/sand |
| X | |
| Y | |
| Z | zither/mandolin |

## Keeping a Journal

Another effective way to use Personification as a springboard for writing is to assume the identity of one of the characters of a story, and write a journal in the voice of that character. (Journal entries can be kept in the Notebook.) Figures 13.4 and 13.5 show two examples: one using a Frame for the story *The Ugly Duckling* (1993) by Hans Christian Andersen, and the other using a Frame for the story *Math Curse* (1995) by Jon Scieszka and Lane Smith.

**Figure 13.4**  Keeping a Journal—My Life as an Ugly Duckling

---

Directions: Read the story *The Ugly Duckling*. Imagine that you are the ugly duckling. Use this Frame as a journal that tells about your sad and difficult days. Use the starters below to help you write your journal. Write two or three sentences after each starter.

Today was the first day of my life and nothing went right.

_____

This morning a hunter's dog almost attacked me.

_____

My brothers and sisters were mean to me all day.

_____

Since everyone thinks I'm so ugly, I will run away and go out into the wide world.

_____

Today was worse than ever when hunters started shooting at me.

_____

Winter has come and I'm shivering in the icy water.

_____

The weather is warm and I hear the sounds of birds.

_____

I am looking at the most beautiful white birds in the world.

_____

What do I see in this reflection?

_____

I'm not a duck at all.

_____

**Figure 13.5**     Keeping a Journal—*Math Curse*

Directions: Read the book *Math Curse* (or any book that tells events in order). Use the Frame to tell the story as if you are the character in the book. .

On Monday, my teacher told us _____

All morning I worried _____

By lunch, I _____

Then, in the afternoon, _____

We were just about to go home when _____

By dinnertime, I was _____

That night I dreamed _____

By the next morning, _____

## Animal Job Application—An Anthropomorphic Point of View

All through literature, animals are *anthropomorphic* or cast as humans. Begin with Figure 13.6 in creating a Taxonomy of animals who would be good to hire for specific jobs. Figure 13.7 illustrates an animal job application (as a Profile) in which a lion is applying for a job as a security guard. Students will not only enjoy the fun of this activity but will learn about animals and their characteristics while also having practice in filling out a job application and writing a letter of reference. Figure 13.8 is a Frame for a letter of reference.

## Comparing Concepts and Terms

Comparing and contrasting is a significant way of learning and is used in just about every subject. Marzano, Pickering, and Pollock (2001) devote a whole chapter to this aspect of learning, stating that "there is a strong research base supporting the effectiveness of having students identify similarities and differences" (p.15). Furthermore, they point out that using graphic and symbolic representations of similarities and differences enhances students' understanding of content.

**Figure 13.6** Animals for Hire

**Figure 13.7** Animal Job Application

### • TAXONOMY •

Directions: This Taxonomy gives a sampling of animals who are applying for a job to help with household tasks. Add your own animals. Next to each animal, write the name of a job this animal could do around the house. There are some examples to get you started.

| | Animal | Animal Job |
|---|---|---|
| A | | |
| B | | |
| C | cheetah | messenger |
| D | dolphin | lifeguard |
| E | eagle | security guard |
| F | | |
| G | giraffe | window cleaner in tall houses |
| H | | |
| I | | |
| J | | |
| K | | |
| L | | |
| M | mole | gardener's assistant |
| N | | |
| O | owl | night watchman |
| P | parrot | telephone answering service |
| Q | | |
| R | | |
| S | | |
| T | | |
| U | | |
| V | vulture | garbage collector |
| W | | |
| X | | |
| Y | | |
| Z | | |

Directions: Imagine that you are an animal applying for a job. Complete the follow job application. There is a model for you to follow after the application.

### Animal Job Application

1. Full Name
2. Social Security Marking
3. Address (Habitat, Region)
4. Position Wanted
5. Phone Number
6. Education and/or Experience
7. Qualifications (List skills or experiences that you believe qualify you for this job.)
8. References (List people or animals we can contact, other than family.)
9. Availability (List starting date and scheduling preferences.)

### Model of Completed Application

1. Full Name: *Leo panthera*, aka Lion
2. Social Security Marking: Paw
3. Address: 40 High Plain Road, P.O. Den 312, Central Africa
4. Position Wanted: Security guard for home, bank, office, or school
5. Phone Number: 1-800-3JUNGLE
6. Education and/or Experience: Cub Scout, Big Cat High School, Lion University, apprentice to chief of pride
7. Qualifications: Superb roaring ability, sharp tearing teeth, ferocious physical appearance, great stamina
8. References: Clyde Beatty, supervisor of lion tamers, Barnum & Bailey Circus, Sarasota, Florida
9. Availability: Immediately after spring mating season, prefer daytime hours

**Figure 13.8** Frame for a Letter of Reference

Directions: Ask one of your classmates to complete the Frame for this Letter of Reference. Make sure that the classmate is an animal that admires you as an animal. For example, a chimpanzee may admire an eagle for its vision and flying abilities.

[Put your animal address here]

[Put the address of the human who wants to hire you here]

[Put the date you are writing the letter here]

[Write the salutation] Dear Ms. (Mr., Dr.) _____,

[Follow this outline:]

I am delighted to recommend _____ for the position of _____.

I have known _____ since _____ when we

_____

You will find that [name you are recommending] has excellent qualifications for _____

He he/she can _____.

In addition, he/she _____.

Above all, he/she _____.

By hiring _____, you will have _____.

Very sincerely,

[Put your animal name here]

The strategy Defining Format (Chapter 5) is one effective way to teach comparing. You can strengthen this skill for your students by setting up a Profile template as illustrated in Figure 13.9, comparing a sheep with a goat, followed by a letter using Personifications (Figure 13.10).

**Figure 13.9** Separating the Sheep From the Goats

Directions: The template below shows how to compare one animal with another. You will notice that sheep and goats have both similarities and differences. Use this template as a model to compare two other animals that in some ways are similar and in other ways are different. For example, cheetahs and lions are both felines; they have some similar and some different characteristics.)

| Sheep (only) | Goat (only) | Similar Characteristics (Both) |
|---|---|---|
| No beards | Males have beard | Bovines |
| Merino wool, lambs wool | Angora wool, mohair wool | Short tail |
| Spiral horns | Long, hollow horns | Cloven hoofs |
| Can't leap | Makes flying leaps | Eat grass |
| Babies are called lambs | Babies are called kids | Good runner |
| Female is called a ewe | Female is called a nanny | Climb hills and mountains |
| Male is called a ram | Male is called a buck | Produce wool |
| | | Produce milk (used by humans) |
| | | Produce meat (used by humans) |
| | | Can adapt to different climates |
| | | Can pull lightweight carts |
| | | Can be kept as pets |

**Figure 13.10**   Sharing and Comparing

Directions: Here is a Frame for a letter that B. B. Black Sheep is using to write to its cousin Nanny B. Goat telling how much they have in common and yet are also different. After you have made your own template comparing two animals that are similar, team up with a classmate and write your own Personification letters to each other using this Frame as a model for getting started.

B.B. Black Sheep
12 Wide Ranch Lane
Adelaide, Australia

writes to

Ms. Nanny B. Goat
14 Mountainside Drive
Rocky Hill, Montana 83864

Dear Cousin Nanny,

I was so happy to get your picture and the information telling how similar we are, although we also have out differences.

First, _____

Then, _____

Furthermore, _____

Most interesting, _____

On the other hand, I _____

while you _____

Another difference is that _____

A most noticeable difference is _____

_____

Please write back and tell me _____

_____

I hope that _____

and look forward to _____

Sincerely,

_____

# UNDERSTANDING BEHAVIORS OF LITERARY CHARACTERS

Jabari Mahiri, in his book *Shooting for Excellence* (1998), writes of literary events as the "involvement of one or more persons" in which "production and comprehension of print play a role" (p. 27). He then elaborates on the idea of a literary event as one that combines literacy skills with literate behaviors. By using Personifications and Interactions, you can effectively and delightfully merge student skills with student behaviors. In this strategy, students read both to themselves and to each other (skills and interaction), assume a literary persona for deep understanding (literary behavior), and write to a known audience (literacy skill and literary behavior).

The following activity, based on Greek mythology, is one of our favorite examples of Personifications and Interactions and can be used from about fifth grade on up. The students read the story of the competition between the goddess Athena and the mortal Arachne, discuss its characteristics as a myth, and then team up for interactive letter writing. Figure 13.11 shows the procedures for the students.

**Figure 13.11**   Arachne and Athena

---

The story of Arachne and Athena is a Greek myth. A myth is a story that explains a scientific or social idea in a nonscientific way. This myth "explains" why spiders are also called arachnids.

Directions: First, team up with a classmate. Divide up the story, and read it to each other. Choose who will be Arachne and who will be Athena. Then follow the letter writing directions that come after the story.

### Arachne's Plea

The Greek goddess Athena was famous for her skill in weaving, and she allowed no mortal to surpass her in this skill. However, a young mortal woman named Arachne, also skillful in weaving, challenged Athena, saying, "I am equal, if not better than you, in weaving garments of great beauty."

Now, no goddess ever accepted a challenge from a mortal, and certainly not Athena, who prided herself on her great skill. "This arrogance will not go unpunished," Athena vowed. Nevertheless, the goddess pretended to accept the contest with Arachne. They each began weaving, working tirelessly for days.

Arachne was sure her work would be far superior to Athena's and eagerly presented her magnificent garment to the goddess. Athena instantly recognized the mortal woman's ability. "Indeed, Arachne," you are a woman of great talent. I am sure all the other gods and goddesses in Olympus would choose your weaving over mine."

Arachne could hardly believe what she heard. The goddess had said her work was equal to, in fact better than, that of Athena. She was about to leave, thrilled with winning the challenge, when she heard Athena's words echoing across the landscape. "For your skill in weaving you shall weave forever and ever, not as a mortal, but as...."

Arachne waited for the magic words. Would Athena declare her a goddess? Or was she at least equal to a goddess? Athena's voice boomed, "not as a mortal, but as a spider. For the rest of your days, you will spin eternally, taking the threads from your own body and never again challenging me as a weaver."

---

*(Continued)*

**Figure 13.11** (Continued)

---

**Personification Writing**

Decide who is Arachne and who is Athena. If you are Arachne, write a letter to Athena asking her forgiveness and begging her to return you to human form. In your letter, do all of the following:

- Praise and compliment Athena for her skill and her positive characteristics as a goddess.
- Tell Athena of your mistake in challenging a goddess of such esteem.
- Make Athena offers of loyalty, gifts, devotion, obedience, or whatever else you think would placate her and make her forgive you.

If you are Athena, write a letter to Arachne either holding firm to your punishment or else forgiving her:

- If you continue your punishment, give her three reasons for your decision.
- If you choose to forgive her, demand that she complete three tasks, and describe these tasks in detail.

---

# UNDERSTANDING HISTORIC FIGURES

The ability to role-play brings about the ability to understand what it is like, as stated succinctly in American Indian folklore, to "walk the path in someone else's moccasins." As your students study persons of accomplishment (see Chapter 8), they can further develop an understanding of motivation and dedication by interactive writing, a process of making the person that one is studying come alive. In the activity in Figure 13.12, the student reads a touching excerpt written by Frederick Douglass (1845/2003) and then writes to Douglass in the role of friend, comforter, or admirer.

**Figure 13.12** Writing to Frederick Douglass

---

Introduction: Frederick Douglass was born a slave in 1818 in the state of Maryland but was able to escape from slavery in 1838 and get to New York City. He became an active abolitionist, fighting against the evils of slavery, and over time wrote the story of his life. This excerpt is from his story *Narrative of the Life of Frederick Douglass, an American Slave.* Read the excerpt to yourself or to a friend. Then follow the guidelines for writing a letter to Frederick Douglass.

**Reading**

My mother was named Harriet Bailey. She was the daughter of Isaac and Betsey Bailey, both colored and quite dark. My mother was of darker complexion than either my grandmother or grandfather.

My father was a white man. He was admitted to be such by all I ever heard speak of my parentage. . . . My mother and I were separated when I was but an infant—before I knew her as my mother. It is a common custom, in the part of Maryland from which I ran away, to part children from their mothers at a very early age. Frequently, before the child has reached its twelfth month, its mother

**Figure 13.12** (Continued)

> is taken from it, and hired out on some farm a considerable distance off, and the child is placed under the care of an old woman, too old for field labor. For what this separation is done, I do not know, unless it is to hinder the development of the child's natural affection to its mother, and to blunt and destroy the natural affection of the mother for the child. This is the inevitable result.
>
> Directions: Write to Frederick Douglass as if you were living in the same time period and were about the same age he is. Use your actual age now, so that if you are 12 years old, that is, the age of Frederick. In your letter, include the following ideas:
>
> - How you feel about Frederick's early life
> - How your life is different or similar
> - Why you would like to know more about Frederick
> - What you wish for Frederick now and in his future

## USING PERSONIFICATION AND INTERACTIONS IN CONTENT AREAS

The Personifications and Interactions strategy lends itself well to content areas, such as social studies. In the activity shown in Figure 13.13, students complete a Profile of a colony, and imagine they are one of the colonists writing to another such person in a different colony. (See Rothstein, Rothstein, & Lauber, 2006, for using this strategy in your mathematics class and adapting it to other content areas).

**Figure 13.13**  Colonist Writes to Colonist

> Directions: Imagine that you are a colonist in one of the 13 American colonies. Write to a friend who lives in another colony. Tell about your life in the colony. Use your colony Profile for facts and information.
>
> **Profile of a Colony**
>
> Name of Colony _____
>
> Location _____
>
> First Settlers _____
>
> Reasons for Settlements _____
>
> Leaders Associated With Colony _____
>
> Major Products or Industries _____
>
> Types of Governance _____
>
> Attitudes Toward Outsiders _____

*(Continued)*

**Figure 13.13** (Continued)

Major Occupations or Work of Males _____

Major Occupations or Work of Females _____

**Letter to a Colonist**

Now, write your letter using the following format:

Your Colonial Name
Address in Your Colony
Name of Your Colony

Your Friend's Colonial Name
Address of Your Friend
Name of Your Friend's Colony

Dear _____,

Tell why you are writing (e.g., "So much has happened since I last wrote to you. . . .")

Give news about your family and what each family member is doing to help each other in a new settlement.

Tell about important happenings in the colony—decisions of leaders, conflicts with Indians or other peoples, issues related to slavery, new arrivals, or other newsworthy events.

Ask your friend questions about her or his life in a different colony.

Invite your friend to visit. Give suggestions about how to travel and how to get to your house.

Sign off with a friendly greeting.

# INTERNET LINKS

http://www.tnellen.com/cybereng/lit_terms/personification.html

http://www.imschools.org/cms/Units/Poetry/personif.htm

http://www.americanrhetoric.com/figures/personification.htm

http://www.abcteach.com/Writing/personification.htm

http://library.thinkquest.org/J0112392/personification.html

http://www.english.emory.edu/classes/Handbook/personification.html

# CHAPTER FOURTEEN

# Writing as Editing

## Writers Are Editors

Strategies, Genres,
Topics, and Tools

Words Are Free!

Have Words,
Can Write

Writing Is Thinking

Write to a Martian

Every Word
Has a Story

Organize
Your Writing

Know Who You
Know and Know
Who You Are!

Think in Threes

Everybody Has
to Be Someplace

Let's Make
a Movie!

Words Inspire

Know Thyself

Writers Are Editors

A Goal for
Every Student

*For every writer . . . there are always elements that need changing.*

~Donald H. Graves (1983, p. 57)

## THE RED PEN

For persons schooled before the advent of teaching writing as a process, the red pen was the symbol of the English teacher. Students handed in papers in black and blue ink and got them back marked in red, often with coded abbreviations such as *punc., inc., org,* or *sp* that informed them that their writing needed work (or *n.w.*). The teacher was often the editor and the sole determiner of what was good writing and what needed serious rewriting. Students were likely to receive two grades—one for content (having something worthwhile to say) and the other for grammar (split infinitives, verb disagreements, faulty plurals, lack of parallel construction, speech forms such as "me and my friend," and other serious faults)! Very good writers got *A/A,* mediocre writers got *B/B,* and some writers (such as one of the authors of this book) got *D/A—D* meant there was nothing worthwhile in the content, but *A* meant the work was written with perfect grammar and impeccable spelling.

## WRITERS ARE EDITORS

Most students, as fledgling writers, are puzzled about the need to "write it over again" and then after "writing it again" find they are disappointed when they fail to get the grade they think they deserve. Worse yet, for students, is to get back a paper "edited" by the teacher in red (or any other color). On the other hand, getting back a paper with few comments, even with a satisfactory grade, leaves students feeling empty. They often feel that they have put in a lot of work for what appears to be very little reward. Either way, too much teacher editing or too little is likely to leave both the *student writer* and the *teacher editor* dissatisfied with the process. Yet, all writers need to revisit their writing, which means rereading, restating, rereading again, and rewriting again. What strategies and procedures work for both students and teachers and for both the skilled and less skilled writer?

# TEACHING EDITING

Just as we teach writing, so too we need to teach editing so that teaching the whole process of writing includes planning, brainstorming, practicing strategies, drafting, reading aloud, peer editing, matching writing to rubrics, revising and editing, and publishing. Obviously, all of these steps are lengthy, time-consuming procedures that leave little time for everything else you have to teach. Nevertheless, the rewards of helping your students become writers are great, and we present the following editing strategies and activities to bring about these rewards.

## The Draft Copy

As we began in Chapter 1, students must think of *all* of their writing as starting with a draft copy (see Figure 1.13). If they are writing by hand, they need to head their papers *Draft Copy* and *leave room for editing,* which means skipping lines or double-spacing. They need to know in advance that their first writing on a topic is a work in progress that may reach final or published copy. However, some pieces of student writing may only remain as drafts for various reasons: practice of a new genre or strategy, entry in a personal journal, not enough time for revision, or perhaps the need to move on to other strategies. As students receive instruction in editing, combined with writing strategies, they will create more first drafts that are worthy of revision and "publishing."

## The Editing Taxonomy

Because they have kept Notebooks, your students will be able to review strategies, have a personal thesaurus in the form of Taxonomies, and have models of writing as resources for further writing. As editors, they need to understand the components of editing and, once again, they need to set up a Taxonomy chart for keeping track of terms that relate to editing. In addition, post this Taxonomy within clear view of the students, and expand upon those aspects of editing that require extended instruction. Figure 14.1 illustrates an example of an editing Taxonomy.

**Figure 14.1**  Taxonomy for Editors and Editing

| • TAXONOMY • | | |
|---|---|---|
| A | audience, accuracy of information, | |
| | add | |
| B | | |
| C | capitalization, | |
| | character development, | |
| | consistent point of view, | |
| | closing statement, conclusion | |
| D | delete, details | |
| E | expanding ideas | |
| F | format | |
| G | | |
| H | | |
| I | indent, introduction | |
| J | | |
| K | | |
| L | length | |
| M | move | |
| N | | |
| O | opening statement | |
| P | period, proofreading, paragraph, | |
| | punctuation, peer editing, publishing | |
| Q | question mark | |
| R | revising, rubrics | |
| S | substituting, spelling, | |
| | support statements, | |
| | sentence structure, self-editing | |
| T | transitions, theme, thesis, | |
| | topic sentence | |
| U | usage, unity of ideas | |
| V | voice, verb agreement | |
| W | word choice, word variety | |
| V | voice | |
| W | | |
| X | | |
| Y | | |
| Z | | |

## The Four Improvers of Writing

One of the benefits of using a computer for writing is the opportunity for making changes. Unlike writing by hand (or, in the olden days, on a typewriter), writing using a computer enables the writer to add, delete, substitute, and move or rearrange. These four options on the computer are basically the four ways to edit writing, which include

1. Adding significant information or ideas.

2. Deleting redundant or insignificant information.

3. Substituting better words for weak or repetitive words.

4. Moving or rearranging misplaced or poorly sequenced phrases or sentences.

Figure 14.2 is a summary chart of how these improvers work. Review them with your students, and then have them practice and apply them in improving their draft copies.

**Figure 14.2**  The Four Improvers of Writing

Here are four ways you can revise or edit your draft copy to improve your writing. Practice these improvers to become a top quality writer. You can

**1. Add** information.

Draft: The student got high marks.

Revised: The student got high marks in all subjects, including mathematics, chemistry, and social studies.

**2. Delete** or take away extra or redundant words.

Draft: Seven days a week from Sunday to Saturday, Mark struggled and struggled to make a living.

Revised: Seven days a week Mark struggled to make a living.

**3. Substitute** words.

Draft: Maria *got up* very early and *made* breakfast for *everyone.*

Revised: Maria *awoke* at 6:00 AM and *prepared* breakfast for her parents and two sisters.

**4. Move or rearrange words, sentences, or paragraphs.**

Draft: The teachers at the beginning of the school year passed out the textbooks.

Revised: At the beginning of the school year, the teachers passed out the textbooks.

These writing improvers provide a teaching methodology for helping students learn to edit in contrast to depending upon the teacher as the corrector of all that was wrong. First, you can provide students with writing activities in which they add, delete, substitute, and move information. Next, you can clue students as to how they could improve their draft copies with questions relating to each improver:

- What words can you add to make your writing more interesting, vivid, or exciting?
- What information can you add to help your audience know more about what you want to say?
- What punctuation do you need to add to avoid writing two sentences as one sentence?
- Are there commas or question marks or other punctuation marks you need to add?
- What words or statements have you repeated that you can delete or take out of your writing?
- Have you used *and then* more than once or used too many *ands?* Which of these repeated words can you delete?
- Do you need to delete punctuation marks that make your sentences incomplete or unfinished?
- What vivid, meaningful words can you substitute for plain, boring, unexciting adjectives that you have used?
- What transition words can you use to substitute for *first, second,* or *finally,* or for *and then?*
- What verbs can you substitute for verbs such as *go, get, run, walk, say,* and others to make your audience want to read more of your writing?
- What lowercase letters need to be replaced with capital letters?
- What periods need to be replaced with question marks? What commas need to be replaced with periods?
- What words, phrases, or sentences do you need to move to make your writing more understandable to your audience?
- Can you move any *-ly* adverbs to the beginnings of your sentences or before the verbs for sentence variety?
- Have you told your story in the right sequence, or do you need to move any events from one part of the story to another?

If students have systematically developed Taxonomies and have used Defining Format, Frames, Profiles, and Three Reasons Why for organizing their writing, they will easily recognize their editing needs and understand how to apply the improvers when they are ready to edit. Posting charts that give a quick overview of writing tips or ways to refine writing provides a guide to students for their own writing and for serving as peer editors to their classmates.

## Using Transitions

Organizational formats and transitions are essential tools that give the audience the road map to the writer's paths. So, again, you need to provide your students with a Taxonomy of transition words that prompt and remind the students of their importance in writing (see Figure 14.3). Post this Taxonomy, and also have the students enter it into the Notebook. After they have built their transition Taxonomies, have the students read a story with transition words and do their own Composing With Keywords, as illustrated in Figure 14.4.

**Figure 14.3**  Transition Words for Guiding Your Audience

### • TAXONOMY •

Directions: Use these words when you need to guide your audience through your writing. For practice, revise one of your previous writings, and add any of these words that will make your writing clearer to your readers. Then continue to use these words in your new writings.

| | |
|---|---|
| A | as soon as, although, above all |
| B | by and by |
| C | consequently |
| D | during, despite |
| E | eventually |
| F | frequently, furthermore, first, finally, following that |
| G | generally |
| H | however |
| I | immediately, in addition |
| J | just then |
| K | |
| L | lately, last |
| M | meanwhile, moreover, most important |
| N | nevertheless, naturally |
| O | often, occasionally, otherwise |
| P | perhaps |
| Q | quickly, quietly |
| R | rarely |
| S | suddenly, since, scarcely, similarly, second |
| T | therefore, though |
| U | usually |
| W | while |
| Y | yet |
| Z | |

**Figure 14.4**  Writing Sample Using Transition Words

Directions: In the following writing sample, the writer used the strategy Composing With Keywords to show the use of transition words. After you have read this sample, write your own story using as many transition words as you can. Refer to your Taxonomy for these words.

Polly Parrot was hungry and very upset with Ms. M. for not feeding her. **However,** Polly loved Ms. M. and **naturally** hoped that her owner was not ill. **From time to time**, Polly tried to call out to Ms. M., but with no success. **Suddenly**, Polly had an idea. "**Although** she's the one who should feed me, perhaps I should be the one to prepare dinner. **Moreover**, Ms. M. may have missed her train. **In the meantime**, I'll set the table. Since we usually eat at six o'clock, I'll start cooking shortly."

**Scarcely** had this thought crossed Polly's mind, when Ms. M. burst into the kitchen full of apologies. "My darling Polly," she pleaded. "Please forgive me. **Despite** what you may have been thinking, I have not forgotten you. **Generally** I leave you something to eat, but today I decided to walk home and I forgot the time."

**Rarely** was Polly upset with Ms. M., but this indeed was a weak excuse. **Nevertheless,** Polly accepted the apologies. **Otherwise,** she would have to face a sullen owner and an angry mealtime. "I forgive you Ms. M. Hopefully, we can enjoy the meal I've prepared for you." **Fortunately**, Ms. M. remained in good spirits. **As soon as** dinner was ready, Polly Parrot and Ms. M. quietly sat down at the table and ate their meal. **Eventually,** each one forgot any bad feelings and enjoyed the rest of the evening.

# PEER EDITING
# BY READING ALOUD

Every writer must learn to self-edit. Yet, at the same time, the writer needs a peer, a person willing to read or listen to the writing and address the writer's concerns. The peer editor must also respond gently, with just enough judgment or ideas to encourage the writer to continue writing and make the necessary changes. These are mature behaviors that can be taught and learned.

For the first step of peer editing, pair any two students together, regardless of their writing ability. Each student serves as the listener to the other and gets to read his or her writing to the peer. Instruct the listener, at first, to listen to the whole piece of writing and suggest one word, phrase, or idea to be added. The suggestion can be as simple as, "I would like you to add your friend's name in the first sentence." Or, "I think you should add the color of the shoes the elf wore." Tell the students they will add their words by inserting a caret mark (^) and then writing the word or words. They are not to erase any of the original words but should *cross out* words if they are making a change. Erasing obliterates any possibility of returning to the original, which writers often want to do or consider. Erasing also is a terrible time waster for students and makes them forget what they wanted to change to. Encourage each student to add at least one item to the writing.

Continue this process of peer reading, taking the students through each improver. After practicing *adding*, for example, the students then listen for words that their peers have repeated or overused. With their writing implement, they cross out the overused or excessive words. Again, with the class, discuss words that were deleted. Move through the steps of substituting better words using posted Taxonomies and published thesauruses. Repeat the steps of adding, deleting, and substituting several times before explaining moving, since this last improver is generally more difficult for inexperienced writers or editors.

# PEER REVIEW

Many teachers report that they have asked students to read other students' writing with very poor results. The student readers often can't find anything wrong with the writing except an occasional spelling or punctuation mistake. This isn't surprising, because without direct instruction in peer review, students generally don't know what the reviewer is supposed to look for.

In peer review, the peers read classmates' papers to themselves. They use stick-on notes to write suggestions or comments, and post them on the paper. Neither a peer editor nor any other editor should write directly on a writer's paper. This is a serious breach of editorial ethics. Tell the students that they are moving from being listening editors to being peer (equal) reading editors. They should carefully read their partners' writing; write their suggestions for adding, deleting, substituting, or moving on stick-on notes; and put the notes along the edge of the paper near the words that need changing or fixing. Teaching students to be peer reviewers helps them develop their own editing skills as well as serve as editing buddies to their classmates. Suggestions for peer editing and review are in Figure 14.5.

**Figure 14.5**  Peer Review

Directions: You have been asked to read a classmate's paper to help your classmate submit an improved piece of writing. Read the paper carefully, and write each suggestion on a separate stick-on note. Be as specific as you can and use the words of the writing improvers as often as you can. Here are examples for you to follow:

**Add** the word *into.*
**Delete** the words *and then.*
**Substitute** the word *magnificent for nice.*
**Move** the words *last night* to the front of the sentence.

**Add** more about how you felt.
**Substitute** a lowercase for a capital letter.

**Add** a question mark
**Delete** the extra *p* from the word *hopping* to make *it hoping.*
**Substitute** a word like *cheerful* for *happy.*
**Move** the fifth sentence to the end of the paragraph.
**Combine** these two sentences
**Separate** into two sentences.

**Add** to these words so you have a completed sentence.

# TEACHER EDITING

When students learn how to edit their own work and use peer editing and review to improve their writing, you can become more of an adviser on aspects of editing that are not yet within the maturity of your students. For example, you may need to explain formal versus informal word usage. Students who begin sentences with "Me and my friend" need to know that written language requires "My friend and I." Mistakes in agreement—"She don't need so much"—generally come from the student's natural speech dialect and can be discussed in lessons on dialects or in a private conference with the individual student. From the Taxonomy for editors and editing (Figure 14.1), the following suggestions are offered, which will hopefully make the task of editing easier for the teacher and more beneficial for students.

Audience—Before your students start to write, ask them to imagine who they are writing to and to write who their audience is in the top margin of their draft copy (e.g., my classmates).

Consistent Point of View—Either with a small conference group or with the whole class, point out to the students that the audience must know where the writer stands on an issue or idea. Is the writer for or against? Does the writer like or dislike? Does the writer want or not want? If the writer wants to show the other side, does she or he clue the audience?

Length—Writing has length. Short stories are shorter than novels. Haikus are shorter than epics. A research paper is longer than an abstract, but rarely longer than a short book. The length of a writing assignment is important because of the relationship of length to genre. Students are generally graded on appropriate length and, therefore, they need to know length requirements before they can begin to plan their writing.

Theme—The theme is the unifying or dominant idea of a piece of writing, and the reader should easily recognize the theme and be able to state it in his or her own words. Students can check if they have written a clear theme by asking three or four of their peers to write their understanding of the theme in one sentence. Be sure to give examples of themes from both literature and factual writing. For example, many books have themes of friendship, cooperation, and caring among humans and animals. Students who have had consistent practice in writing Premises will be able to state themes and more easily develop their own themes.

Thesis—This is a proposition stated or put forward for consideration that has to be proved or defended by the writer.

Voice—The "sound" of the writer—friendly, formal, advisory, admonishing, angry, mature, young, and so forth. The writer must take on a persona—I am writing as your friend. I am writing as your parent. I am writing as your mentor or teacher. Voice is related to audience. Therefore, the student writer must match her or his voice to the intended audience, much like giving a talk or speech.

# RUBRICS

Many local and state assessment requirements use rubrics for writing. The *Random House Webster's Unabridged Dictionary* (2003) defines a rubric as "any established conduct or procedure." As applied to the assessment of writing, rubrics can be used to reflect the basic benchmarks or established rules of writing as contrasted to speech or conversation. Figure 14.6 provides your students with generic standards for all written communication that need to be reviewed during every aspect of writing instruction. These basic rubrics, which don't come easily to many students, are the standards for all writing, excepting possibly personal journals and now the new genre of e-mail and text messaging.

**Figure 14.6**    Rubrics for Top Quality Writing

Your writing will be **very good** or **excellent** if you

- Keep to the topic throughout the whole piece of writing and don't slip or slide (as in conversation) to another topic.
- Organize the ideas in some sequence that the reader can follow or recognize.
- Provide the reader with details or information that makes the reader satisfied and not filled with puzzlement or too many questions.
- Use the written conventions of capitalization, punctuation, and spelling.
- For academic writing, use the grammar of standard written English in contrast to the informal grammar of speech.

Figures 14.7–14.9 show checklists that you can use to guide students in following the rules or conventions of writing. Modify or adapt them to your own students' needs, and align them if you need to with your state's standards. (There is a *Not Applicable* column for rubrics that may not apply developmentally for some students.)

**Figure 14.7**     Rubrics for Teacher Evaluation of Student Writing—Primary Grades

Scores 4, 3, 2, 1 (high to low)

Name of Student _____

Title of Writing _____

Genre (narrative, biography, persuasive, etc.) _____

Date _____

|  | 4 | 3 | 2 | 1 | NA |
|---|---|---|---|---|---|
| Wrote on the topic |  |  |  |  |  |
| Organized logically or sequentially |  |  |  |  |  |
| Had consistent point of view |  |  |  |  |  |
| Indicated sense of audience |  |  |  |  |  |
| Used topic sentence(s) |  |  |  |  |  |
| Added support sentences |  |  |  |  |  |
| Included significant details |  |  |  |  |  |
| Used varied sentence structure |  |  |  |  |  |
| Had a variety of words or terms |  |  |  |  |  |
| Used pronouns appropriately |  |  |  |  |  |
| Used capital letters appropriately |  |  |  |  |  |
| Put in end punctuation |  |  |  |  |  |
| Spelled conventionally |  |  |  |  |  |
| Potential for excellent revision |  |  |  |  |  |
| Comments |  |  |  |  |  |

**Figure 14.8** Rubrics for Teacher Evaluation of Student Writing—Intermediate Grades and Above

Scores 4, 3, 2, 1 ( high to low)

Name of Student _____

Title of Writing _____

Genre (narrative, biography, persuasive, etc. ) _____

Date _____

|  | 4 | 3 | 2 | 1 | NA |
|---|---|---|---|---|---|
| Followed the genre format |  |  |  |  |  |
| Kept to the topic, theme, or thesis |  |  |  |  |  |
| Organized logically or sequentially |  |  |  |  |  |
| Had consistent point of view |  |  |  |  |  |
| Indicated sense of audience |  |  |  |  |  |
| Used topic sentence(s) |  |  |  |  |  |
| Added support sentences |  |  |  |  |  |
| Included significant details |  |  |  |  |  |
| Used varied sentence structure |  |  |  |  |  |
| Had a variety of words or terms |  |  |  |  |  |
| Used pronouns appropriately |  |  |  |  |  |
| Used necessary transitional words |  |  |  |  |  |
| Had appropriate length for assignment |  |  |  |  |  |
| Used capital letters appropriately |  |  |  |  |  |
| Put in end punctuation |  |  |  |  |  |
| Used appropriate internal punctuation |  |  |  |  |  |
| Spelled conventionally |  |  |  |  |  |
| Potential for excellent revision |  |  |  |  |  |
| Comments |  |  |  |  |  |

**Figure 14.9**  Student Checklist of Improvements

This checklist is for student use for self-editing or for use after peer review.

Name _____

Title of My Writing _____

Date _____

I revised and edited my paper and made the following improvements:

| | Yes | Not Needed | Need Help |
|---|---|---|---|
| Added descriptive and other important words | | | |
| Substituted (replaced) weak vocabulary | | | |
| Combined short, choppy sentences | | | |
| Deleted unnecessary or repetitive words | | | |
| Shifted or moved words as necessary | | | |
| Shifted or moved sentences to make my writing easier to follow | | | |
| Added missing transitions | | | |
| Added missing or significant details or information | | | |
| Corrected errors in punctuation, grammar, and spelling | | | |
| Other (please list) | | | |

# INTERNET LINKS

http://www.studygs.net/revising.htm

http://www.geocities.com/fifth_grade_tpes/edit.html

http://www.webgrammar.com/

http://www.powa.org/edit/index.html

http://rubistar.4teachers.org/index.php

Strategies, Genres,
Topics, and Tools

Words Are Free!

Have Words,
Can Write

Writing Is Thinking

Write to a Martian

Every Word
Has a Story

Organize
Your Writing

Know Who You
Know and Know
Who You Are!

Think in Threes

Everybody Has
to Be Someplace

Let's Make
a Movie!

Words Inspire

Know Thyself

Writers Are Editors

# Writing—A Curriculum Unifier

## A Goal for Every Student

*All students have profoundly fertile literacy abilities.*

~Jeannie Oakes and Martin Lipton (1999, p. 153)

## INTEGRATING WRITING ACROSS THE CURRICULUM

I know about butterflies. A butterfly has six legs and twelve eyes. First the butterfly lays about a hundred eggs and then dies. Then the eggs lay in a warm place for 14 days till they hatch into larvae. They now eat a lot of food and move on to being a caterpillar. When they get bigger, they turn into a chrysalis. In the chrysalis they turn into a butterfly and when they come out of the chrysalis they are so pretty. That's how much I know about butterflies.

~Third Grade Student

I am a light bulb. I have many pleasures being one. First, I can light up soccer fields at night. While the humans watch, I can watch too. Last week I was astounded when one of the teams made five goals in a row. In addition, I can light up a whole city. I love making night into day. Best of all, I get to help people read. Not only am I doing a great service, but I get to catch up on some great books. Now you too might want to be an electric light bulb like me.

~Sixth Grade Student

What short answer or worksheet response could match the learning and creativity that are represented in these charming and informative voices? It is predominantly through writing that the student becomes an active learner—not easily at first, but eventually.

This chapter presents a model for integrating the 12 writing strategies with the teaching of earth science. You can substitute your own subject areas—social studies, mathematics, language arts, health, biology—and include all the strategies. Your students will become fluent, organized, and much better writers.

**Figure 15.1**    Earth Science and the Strategies

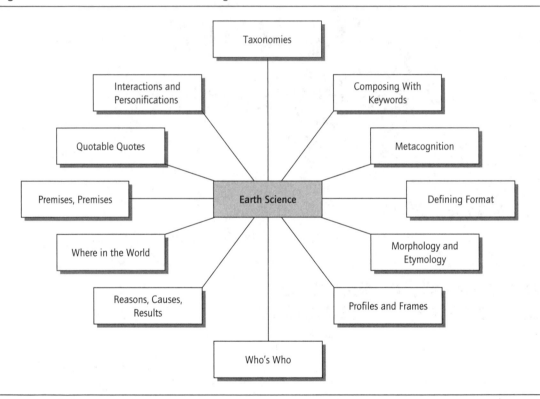

**Figure 15.2**    Earth Scientists Are Writers

Scientists keep notebooks and notes.

They have a specialized vocabulary for their subject.

They keep notes on what they are learning.

They share their knowledge with others.

They study the work of other scientists.

They quote the work of other scientists.

They explore the world near and far.

They are always learning.

Students need to recognize the connection between what they have to learn and how they can learn. As we have indicated in Personifications and Interactions (Chapter 13), a good learner is often a role-player. In mathematics, the learner becomes a mathematician and a trapezoid. In literature, the learner is Shakespeare and Juliet. In science, the learner is an inventor and a presenter at an international conference of scientists. By assuming these roles or personae, students become what they learn. In Figures 15.2–15.14, we present a summary of the 12 strategies that can help all students learn more through writing as well as learn the principles of writing across the curriculum.

**Figure 15.3**    Taxonomy of Earth Science Terms

| | • TAXONOMY • |
|---|---|
| A | avalanche |
| B | bays, debris |
| C | cliffs |
| D | deltas |
| E | estuaries |
| F | faults |
| G | glaciers, geology |
| H | headlands |
| I | ice age |
| J | |
| L | lava |
| M | magma, molten rock, moraine |
| N | nunatak |
| O | oxbow lakes, ocean |
| P | Pinatubo mountain |
| Q | quagmire |
| R | rivers |
| S | sandstorms, sea level, surface |
| T | tectonic plates |
| U | |
| V | volcano |
| W | weathering, wave action, wave-cut platforms |
| X | |
| Y | |
| Z | |

**Figure 15.4**    Composing With Key Words in Earth Science

Directions: Use the words from your earth science Taxonomy to compose scientific statements that show your knowledge of this subject. Here are some examples:

The *wave action* of the *ocean* at *sea level* causes *wave-cut* platforms.

*Molten rock* pouring out of the earth forms hot *rivers* of *lava*.

*Avalanches* bring *debris* to the *glacier* surfaces.

**Figure 15.5**    Metacognition in Earth Science

---

Directions: Write a Metacognition Statement about three ideas you have thought about in your study of earth science. Here is a model for you to follow:

We have been studying earth science for two weeks and I have been thinking about three important topics on this subject: glaciers, erosion, and volcanoes.

First, I know that glaciers are formed when enormous piles of snow freeze into solid ice. What I have been wondering about is why glaciers once covered half of the earth.

In addition, I have been thinking about erosion. I know that erosion takes place when water removes tops of mountains or sand from the beaches. I have been wondering why some beaches have so much erosion and are disappearing, but other beaches seem to stay year after year.

Finally, I have learned that volcanoes are caused by heat building up in the earth below a mountain which then makes the rocks and soil erupt. I have been thinking about the mountains near my house and wondering why they never erupt and hoping that they never will.

This is some of the information I have on glaciers, erosion, and volcanoes. I now hope to find more answers about these earth science topics.

---

**Figure 15.6**    Defining Format: What Is a Delta?

---

Directions: The template below is a model for you to follow when you are defining terms from earth science. Select one of the landform terms from your Taxonomy and write your own Defining Format.

**What Is a Delta?**

### • DEFINING FORMAT •

| Question | Category | Characteristics |
|---|---|---|
| What is a delta? | | |
| A delta is a | type of landform that | 1. is formed at the mouth of a river where the water creates channels.<br>2. contains sandbanks and small islands called levees built up by deposits from the river.<br>3. is often, but not always, triangular in shape.<br>4. is flat.<br>5. gets its name from the Greek letter *delta*, which looks like this: $\Delta$.<br>6. is part of the mouth of the Mississippi River. |

**Figure 15.7**    The Morphology and Etymology of the Word *Geology*

Introduction: *Geology* is another term for the study of earth science. This word comes from the Greek language and contains two forms—*geo*, which means earth or land, and *logo*, which means *word* and has come to mean "the study of."

Here is a Morphology Chart that shows the many combinations of *geo*, all of which have to do with the earth or land.

## MORPHOLOGY CHART

| Noun | Verb | Adjective | Adverb |
|---|---|---|---|
| geology | N.A. | geological | geologically |
| geologist | | geographical | geographically |
| geologists | | geothermal | |
| geography | | geocentric | |
| geographer | | geodesic | |
| geographers | | | |
| geometry | | | |
| geometer | | | |
| geometers | | | |

Directions: Research the etymology (origin) of the words *collide, erupt,* and *erode* (or others that teacher or students choose), and write a short story about them. Then set up a Morphology Chart that shows their different forms. Complete the chart using an unabridged dictionary to help you. Present this information to your family or friends who are not in your class.

**Figure 15.8    Profiles and Frames: Report on a River**

---

Directions: Research a river that interests you, and complete the Profile. Then use the Frame that follows to write a report that would be included in a book about rivers. Find or draw a map that shows the route of the river.

**Profile of a River**

Name of River _____

Country/Countries Where Located _____

Continent(s) Where Located _____

Length of River _____ Miles _____ Kilometers

Source of River _____

Mouth of River _____

Special Features (Waterfalls, Rapids, Reservoirs, Dams) _____

_____

Major Cities Along River _____

Bridges Along River _____

Other Information _____

_____

**Frame for Report on a River**

Get ready for an adventure along the _____River.

This river is located _____

in the continent of _____.

If you travel the full length of this river, you will cover _____miles

or _____ kilometers. You will start your journey in _____,

at the river's source, and end in _____, its mouth.

Along the way, you will see many sites, such as _____,

_____, and _____.

Most interesting will be some of the cities that are along this river, such as _____

_____, _____, and _____.

If you get to stop and go on land, you can cross the _____Bridge and get a

view of _____.

Here are three other interesting pieces of important information you might like to know about the

_____ River.

First, _____

Furthermore, _____

Most memorable, _____

**Figure 15.9**    Who's Who in Earth Science

**Taxonomy of People of Accomplishment in Earth Science**

Directions: Here are the names of some of the people who have contributed to the scientific knowledge of our planet Earth. Select at least one of them, and use the person of accomplishment Profile to write about this person.

**Person of Accomplishment Profile**

Directions: Research the life and accomplishment about a person in the field of earth science or geology. Then complete the Profile and present this information to a classmate, friend, or family member.

Name of Person _____

_____

_____

Years of Person's Life _____

_____

_____

Birthplace _____

_____

_____

Dreams and Goals _____

_____

_____

Challenges Faced and Overcome _____

_____

_____

Accomplishments and Contributions to Humanity _____

Special Recognition and Rewards _____

Other Information _____

_____

**• TAXONOMY •**

| A | Anning, Mary |
|---|---|
| B | Bascom, Florence |
| C | Cotton, Charles |
| D | Darwin, Charles |
| E | Ebert, Heinz |
| F | Ferrier, Walter Frederick |
| G | Grove, Karl Gilbert |
| H | Hutton, James |
| I | |
| J | |
| K | Kraft, Katia |
| L | Leakey, Mary |
| M | Mohs, Frederich |
| N | Nedland, Dan |
| O | |
| P | Pitcher, Wallace |
| Q | |
| R | Richter, Charles |
| S | Smith, William |
| T | Tharp, Marie |
| U | |
| V | |
| W | Woodward, Harry M. |
| V | |
| X | |
| Y | |
| Z | |

**Figure 15.10**    Reasons, Causes, Results in Earth Science

While learning about earth science, you can write different types of essays to show and share your knowledge. Here are three starters, one for a personal essay, one for a persuasive essay, and for an explanatory essay. Follow the essay format of thinking in threes.

There are three reasons why I would like to explore (add your own place or landform)

_____

There are three steps we must take to prevent (put in your own topic related to earth science)

_____

Because of changes in the earth's climate, scientists have observed three significant differences in

(put in your own topic). _____


**Figure 15.11**    Geology is Geography and Geography is Geology

One of the great benefits about learning geology or earth science is that you get to know geography, or where places are. For example, in learning geology you learn about tectonics or the movement of continents. Here is a Profile for writing geologic information about a continent. When you have finished, create a geologic travel brochure of this continent.

Name of Continent _____

Waterways Surrounding the Continent _____

Waterways Within the Continent _____

Mountains _____

Other Landforms (islands, peninsulas) _____

Mineral Resources _____

Climate _____

Other Geologic Information _____

**Figure 15.12**     Premises, Premises in Earth Science

Directions: Create a documentary film or PowerPoint presentation about a topic in earth science. Focus on both a scientific idea and a person or persons involved in developing this idea. If possible, work with a team of three to five classmates.

The model below shows some of the steps for creating a visual presentation based on the book *The Map That Changed the World* by Simon Winchester (2001), a biographic story of William Smith, the founder of modern geology, who lived in England in the 1800s.

### The Premise Statement Based on the Book

*The Map That Changed the World* (2001) by Simon Winchester is about "the work of one man," William Smith, who "was bent on the all-encompassing mission of making a geological map of England and Wales" (p. 192). William Smith's hobby and passion was collecting unusual rocks and making maps of the places where he found the rocks. From this passion, he "soon picked up a nickname—Strata Smith" (p. 193) and began his life's work of "making a proper geological map of England" (p. 195).

### The Treatment for the Documentary Film on William Smith

Directions: Plan for your presentation to run about 10 to 15 minutes with a focus on William Smith's creation of the map. Write a one- or two-page summary of what this presentation will
be showing. If you were actually using this story, you would include an illustration of the geologic map that William Smith created (p. 141) and a short flashback about Smith's interest in geology and maps:

- The Great Map conceived (Chapter 10)
- The creation of the map—"The Map That Changed the World" (Chapter 12)
- The contribution of William Smith and the map to the founding and history of the study of geology
- Geology—the lost and found man (Chapter 16)
- Related illustrations from the book and possibly from Internet sites

**Figure 15.13**  Quotable Quotes in Earth Science

Directions: Earth scientists, like many other people engaged in the search for knowledge, have made notable statements that give us food for thought. Here are eight quotes from people from different fields of study who have made statements about the earth and earth science. Write your own response to these quotes. Then create your own Quotable Quote and share it with your classmates.

*The world is round so that friendship may encircle it.*

—Teilhard de Chardin

*We learn geology the morning after the earthquake.*

—Ralph Waldo Emerson

*The fifth revolution will come when we have spent the stores of coal and oil that have been accumulating in the earth during hundreds of millions of years. . . . It is to be hoped that before then other sources of energy will have been developed. . . .*

—Charles Galton Darwin

*The environment, after all, is where we all meet, where we all have a mutual interest. It is one thing that all of us share. It is not only a mirror of ourselves, but a focusing lens on what we can become.*

—Claudia Alta Johnson
(Lady Bird Johnson) (nee Taylor)

*The earth we abuse and the living things we kill will, in the end, take their revenge; for in exploiting their presence we are diminishing our future.*

—Marya Mannes

*We won't have a society if we destroy the environment.*

—Margaret Mead

*The earth is given as a common stock for man to labor and live on.*

—Thomas Jefferson

*One does not sell the earth upon which the people walk.*

—Crazy Horse

**Figure 15.14**  Personifications and Interactions: Earthlings Write to Earthlings

Directions: All of us share our planet Earth, whether we are earth scientists or just Earthlings—dwellers on this planet. All of us benefit from a healthy Earth, and all of us can contribute to its well-being. Below are suggested topics for letter writing related to earth science. Select one (or more) that interest you. Then team up with a classmate and write to each other about that topic or idea.

A tree in an endangered forest writes to a human asking for help. The human responds.

A river that is becoming polluted writes to a resident living on its banks and makes suggestions for stopping the pollution. The resident responds as to ways to help.

A polar bear is losing its home because the glaciers are melting. It writes to a seal asking to have a meeting about the problem to discuss what solutions they can agree on. The seal responds.

An oil well is about to run dry. It wants to save its neighboring oil wells from this problem. It writes to the owner of the wells, telling of its worries. The owner responds.

# References

Allen, J. (2005). Knowing a word or defining a word—it's a world of difference. *Voices from the Middle, 13*(1), 54–55.

Alvermann, D. E. (2005). Literacy on the edge: How close are we to closing the achievement gap? *Voices from the Middle, 13*(1), 8–14.

Andersen, H. C. (1993). *The complete Hans Christian Andersen fairy tales* (L. Owens, Ed.). New York: Gramercy.

Aton, J. (1990). *Dictionary of word origins.* New York: Little, Brown.

Atwell, N. (1998). *In the middle: New understandings about writing, reading, and learning* (2nd ed.). New York: Greenwood-Heinemann.

Bereiter, C., & Scardamalia, M. (1985). Cognitive coping strategies and the problem of inert knowledge. In S. C. Chipman, J. W. Segal, & R. Glazers (Eds.), *Thinking and learning skills: Vol. 2. Current research and open questions* (pp. 77–85). Hillsdale, NJ: Erlbaum.

Bettelheim, B. (1975). *The uses of enchantment.* New York: Random House.

Block, A. (1980). *Murphy's law and other reasons why things go wrong.* Los Angeles: Price/Stern/Sloane.

Brenner, B. (1993). *Wagon wheels.* New York: HarperCollins.

Brown, A. L., Bransford, J. D., Ferrara, R. A., & Campione, J. C. (1983). Learning, remembering and understanding. In J. H. Flavell & E. M. Markman (Eds.), *Handbook of child psychology: Vol. 3. Cognitive development* (pp. 177–266). New York: Wiley.

Bryson, B. (1990). *The mother tongue: English and how it got that way.* New York: William Morrow.

Caine, R. N., & Caine, G. (1991). *Teaching and the human brain.* Alexandria, VA: Association for Supervision and Curriculum Development.

Carroll, L. (1965). *Through the looking-glass.* New York: Random House. (Original work published 1871)

Christelow, E. (1998). *Five little monkeys jumping on the bed.* New York: Clarion Books.

Claiborne, R. (1983). *Our marvelous English tongue: The life and times of the English language.* New York: Times Books.

Cooper, E. J. (2004). The pursuit of equity and excellence in educational opportunity. In D. Lapp, C. C. Block, E. J. Cooper, J. Flood, N. Roser, & J. Villamil Tinajero (Eds.), *Teaching all the children* (pp. 12–30). New York: Guilford.

Cooper, E. J. (2005). It begins with belief: Social demography is not destiny. *Voices from the Middle, 13*(1), 25–34.

Costa, A. L. (1991). *The school as a home for the mind.* Thousand Oaks, CA: Corwin Press.

Costa, A. L. (2000). *Discovering and exploring habits of mind.* Alexandria, VA: Association for Supervision and Curriculum Development.

Costa, A. L., & Kallick, B. (Eds.). (2000). *Activating and engaging habits of mind.* Alexandria, VA.: Association for Supervision and Curriculum Development.

Culham, R. (2003). *6 + 1 traits of writing: The complete guide grades 3 and up.* New York: Scholastic.

Davis, K. C. (1992). *Don't know much about geography.* New York: HarperCollins.

Davis, K. C. (1995). *Don't know much about history.* New York: HarperCollins.

Davis, K. C. (2001). *Don't know much about the universe.* New York: HarperCollins.

Delpit, L. (1995). *Other people's children.* New York: New York Press.

Dixon, D. (1993). *The changing earth.* New York: Thomson Learning.

Douglass, F. (2003). *Narrative of the life of Frederick Douglass, an American slave.* New York: Barnes & Noble Classics. (Original work published 1845)

Editors of the American Heritage Dictionaries. (1980). *Roget's II—The new thesaurus.* Boston: Houghton Mifflin.

Editors of the American Heritage Dictionaries. (1986). *Word mysteries and histories.* Boston: Houghton Mifflin.

Einstein, A. (1954). *Ideas and opinions.* New York: Bonanza Books.

Elbow, P. (2004). Writing first. *Educational Leadership, 62*(2), 9–13.

Ertmer, P. A., & Newby, T. J. (1996). The expert learner: Strategic, self-regulated, and reflective. *Instructional Science, 24,* 1–24. Dordrecht, Netherlands: Kluwer.

Feuerstein, Reuven., Feuerstein, Rafi, & Schur, Y. (1997). Process as content in education of exceptional children. In A. Kozulin (Ed.), *The ontogeny of cognitive modifiability: Applied aspects of mediated learning experience and instrumental enrichment* (pp. 1–24). Jerusalem: ICELP & HWCRI.

Fry, E. B., Kress, J. E., & Fountoukdis, D. L. (2000). *The teacher's book of lists* (4th ed.). Paramus, NJ: Prentice Hall.

Gardner, H. (1983). *Frames of mind.* New York: Basic Books.

Gardner, H. (1993). *Multiple intelligences.* New York: Basic Books.

Gomez, K., & Madda, C. (2005). Vocabulary instruction for ELL Latino students in the middle school science classroom. *Voices from the Middle, 13*(1), 42–47.

Grabinger, R. S. (1996). Rich environments for active learning. In D. H. Jonassen (Ed.), *Handbook of research for educational communications and technology* (pp. 665–692). New York: Simon & Schuster.

Graves, D. H. (1983). *Writing: Teachers and children at work.* Exeter, NH: Heinemann.

Hinton, K., & Dickinson, G. K. (2005). Narrowing the gap between readers and books. *Voices from the Middle, 13*(1), 15–20.

Hirsch, E. D. Jr. (1987). *Cultural literacy: What every American needs to know.* Boston: Houghton Mifflin.

Hyerle, D. (1995). *Thinking maps: Tools for learning.* Cary, NC: Innovative Sciences.

Jackson, Y. (2005). Unlocking the potential of African American students: Keys to reversing underachievement. *Theory Into Practice, 44*(3) 203–210.

Jensen, E. (1998). *Teaching with the brain in mind.* Alexandria, VA: Association for Supervision and Curriculum Development.

Johnson, D. W., & Johnson, R. T. (1999). *Learning together and alone.* Boston: Allyn & Bacon.

Juster, N. (1989). *The phantom tollbooth.* New York: Random House.

Kennedy, C. (1996). Teaching discourse through writing. In J. VanTassel-Baska (Ed.), *Developing verbal talent* (pp. 133–148). Boston: Allyn & Bacon.

Langer, J. (2000). Excellence in English in the middle and high school: How teachers' professional lives support student achievement. *American Educational Research Journal, 37*(2), 397–439.

Langer, J., & Applebee, A. (1987). *How writing shapes thinking: A study of teaching and learning.* Urbana, IL: National Council of Teachers of English.

Lapp, D., Block, C. C., Cooper, E. J., Flood, J., Roser, N., & Villamil Tinajero, J. (Eds.). (2004). *Teaching all the children.* New York: Guilford.

Lederer, R. (1990). *The play of words.* New York: Simon & Schuster.

Lederer, R. (1994). *Adventures of a verbivore.* New York: Simon & Schuster.

Lederer, R. (1998). *Crazy English.* New York: Simon & Schuster.

Livingston, J. (1997). *Metacognition: An overview.* Retrieved July 9, 2006, from http://www.gse.buffalo.edu/fas/shuell/CEP564/Metacog.htm

Lowry, L. (1989). *Number the stars.* New York: Dell.

Mahiri, J. (1998). *Shooting for excellence.* Urbana, IL: National Council of Teachers of English.

Mahiri, J. (2004). *What they don't learn in school.* New York: Lang.

Martin, B. (1991). *Brown bear, brown bear, what do you see?* New York: Holt, Rinehart, & Winston.

Marzano, R. J. (2004). *Building background knowledge for academic achievement.* Alexandria, VA: Association for Supervision and Curriculum Development.

Marzano, R. J., Pickering, D. J., & Pollock, J. E. (2001). *Classroom instruction that works.* Alexandria, VA: Association for Supervision and Curriculum Development.

Maxwell, R. (1996). *Writing across the curriculum in middle and high schools.* Boston, MA: Allyn & Bacon.

McArthur, T. ( 2003). *The Oxford guide to world English.* New York: Oxford University Press.

McCrum, R., Cran, W., & MacNeil, R. (1986). *The story of English.* New York: Viking.

McWhorter, J. (1998). *Word on the street.* Cambridge, MA: Perseus.

Milne, A. A. (1957). *The complete collection of Winnie the Pooh.* New York: Penguin.

National Council of Teachers of English. (1996). *Standards for the English language arts.* Newark, DE: International Reading Association.

Oakes, J. & Lipton, M. (1999). *Teaching to change the world.* Boston: McGraw-Hill.

Ogle, D. (1986). K-W-L: A teaching model that develops active reading of expository text. *The Reading Teacher, 39,* 564 571.

*Oxford Dictionary of Quotations* (3rd ed.). (1980). New York: Oxford University Press.

Paola, T. (1992). *Strega Nona.* New York: Simon & Schuster.

Paulsen, G. (1987). *Hatchet.* New York: Simon & Schuster.

Perkins, D. (1992). *Smart schools.* New York: Free Press.

Pinker, S. (1994). *The language instinct.* New York: HarperCollins.

Pinker, S. (2000). *Words and rules.* New York: HarperCollins.

Potter, B. (1909). *The tale of Peter Rabbit.* New York: Frederick Warne.

Public Schools of North Carolina. (n.d.). *Writing across the curriculum: High school teacher handbook.* Retrieved July 9, 2006, from http://www.ncpublicschools.org/docs/curriculum/languagearts/secondary/writinghandbook.pdf

*Webster's Random House Unabridged Dictionary.* (2003). New York: Random House Reference.

Reeves, D. R. (2002). *Reason to write.* New York: Kaplan.

Ridley, D. S., Schultz, P. A., Glanz, R. S., & Weinstein, C. E. (1992). Self-regulated learning: The interactive influence of metacognitive awareness and goal-setting. *Journal of Experimental Education, 60*(4), 293–306.

Robinson, A. (1993). *What smart students know.* New York: Three Rivers Press.

Rothstein, A., Rothstein, E., & Lauber, G. (2006). *Write for mathematics.* Thousand Oaks, CA: Corwin Press.

Scarborough, H. A. (Ed.). (2001). *Writing across the curriculum in secondary classrooms: Teaching from a diverse perspective.* Upper Saddle River, NJ: Merrill.

Schlein, M. (1993). *The way mothers are.* Chicago: Albert Whitman.

Scieszka, J., & Smith, Lane. (1995). *Math curse.* New York: Viking Press.

Scott, J. A. (2004). Scaffolding vocabulary learning. In D. Lapp, C. C. Block, E. J. Cooper, J. Flood, N. Roser, & J. Villamil Tinajero (Eds.), *Teaching all the children* (pp. 275–293). New York: Guilford.

Simmons, J. S., & Baines, L. (Eds.). (1998). *Language study in middle school, high school, and beyond.* Newark, DE: International Reading Association.

Sklar, D. J. (1991). *Playmaking: Children writing and performing their own plays.* New York: Teachers & Writers Collaborative.

Smith, F. (1982). *Writing and the writer.* New York: Holt, Rinehart, and Winston.

Spivey, N. N. (1996). Reading, writing, and the construction of meaning. In J. VanTassel-Baska, D. T. Johnson, & L. N. Boyce (Eds.), *Developing verbal talent* (pp. 34–55). Boston: Allyn & Bacon.

Stahl, S. A., & Fairbanks, M. M. (1986). The effects of vocabulary instruction: A model-based meta-analysis. *Review of Educational Research, 56*(1), 72–110.

Steckler, A. (1979). *101 words and how they began.* Garden City, NY: Doubleday.

Steinbeck, John. (1990). *The pearl.* New York: Penguin Books. (Original work published 1947)

Strong, R. W., Silver, H. F., & Perini, M. (2001). *Teaching what matters most.* Alexandria, VA: Association for Supervision and Curriculum Development.

Tomlinson, C. A. (1999). *The differentiated classroom.* Alexandria, VA: Association for Supervision and Curriculum Development.

Uhlig, E. G. (2003). *Memoir writing and illustrating for children.* New York: Marble House Editions.

VanTassel-Baska, J. (1996). *Developing verbal talent.* Boston: Allyn & Bacon.

Vygotsky, L. (1962). *Thought and language.* Cambridge: MIT Press.

Walker-Dalhouse, D. (2004). Preface. In D. Lapp, C. C. Block, E. J. Cooper, J. Flood, N. Roser, & J. Villamil Tinajero (Eds.), *Teaching all the children* (pp. xvii–xxi). New York: Guilford.

Weaver, C. (1996). Teaching grammar in the context of writing. *English Journal, 85*(7), 15–24.

Weaver, C. (Ed.). (1998). *Lessons to share on teaching grammar in context.* Portsmouth, NH: Boynton/Cook-Heinemann.

Williams, B. (Ed.). (1996). *Closing the achievement gap.* Alexandria, VA: Association for Supervision and Curriculum Development.

Winchester, S. (2001). *The map that changed the world.* New York: HarperCollins.

Winn, W., & Snyder, D. (1996). Cognitive perspectives in psychology. In D.H. Jonassen (Ed.), *Handbook of research for educational communications and technology* (pp. 665–692). New York: Simon & Schuster.

Wooten, D. E. A., & Cullinan, B. E. (2004). Metacognition through writing and sharing connections. In D. Lapp, C. C. Block, E. J. Cooper, J. Flood, N. Roser, & J. Villamil Tinajero (Eds.), *Teaching all the children* (294–305). New York: Guilford.

Zindel, P. (1968). *The pigman.* New York: Harper & Row.

Zinsser, W. (1980). *On writing well* (2nd ed.). New York: Harper & Row.

# Index

ABC stories, 106–108
Adjectives, 77–80, 84, 88–89
Adverbs, 81, 85, 88, 148, 212, 225
Aesop's fables, 188–189
Alphabetical lists. *See* Taxonomies
American English, 91–92
Andersen, H. C., 199
Animals, 62, 94–96, 103, 202 203
Art, 94, 97
Atwell, N., 10
Audience, 38, 58, 68, 182, 212, 215
Autobiographies, 111, 118–123

Background knowledge, 26–27
"Be" verb, 86–88
*Beauty and the Beast* (Perrault), 176–177
Bereiter, C., 36
Bettelheim, B., 174–175
Biographies, 111–118. *See also*
    Autobiographies, Who's
    Who strategy
Book-to-film conversion, 163–164, 181–182.
    *See also* Filmmaking
British English, 91–92
Bryson, B., 70
*Building Background Knowledge for
    Academic Achievement* (Marzano), 26
Bulletin boards, 15

Careers, 62, 97–98, 157, 159
Categories:
    adjective, 77–80, 84
    defining, 58–66
    geographic, 146–147, 224
    noun, 72–75, 83
    personal identity, 31–32
    taxonomy of, 61
    verb, 75–77, 84
    vocabulary, 24
    writing genre, 130–131
    *See also* Taxonomies

Categorization, 24, 30, 32, 60, 144, 145.
    *See also* Taxonomies
Characters:
    film 165–169, 175–177, 182
    literary, 205–206
Children's literature, 187. *See also* Nursery
    rhymes, Fairy tales
Claiborne, R., 75–76
Classification. *See* Categorization,
    Taxonomies
Cognition. *See* Metacognition
Comparison, 59, 62, 66, 77–78, 201–204
Competence, 57–58
Composing with Keywords strategy,
    5, 35–44, 223
Computer links, 34, 44, 55, 68, 92, 109,
    128, 139, 162, 183, 193, 208, 219, 208
Computers, 21, 136, 211
Cooper, E., 24
Cooperative learning, 26–27
Costa, A. L., 45
*Cultural Literacy* (Hirsch), 141

Davis, K.C., 157
de la Fontaine, J., 188
Defining Format strategy, 5, 57–60, 63–68,
    83–84, 146–147, 224
Definition. *See* Defining Format strategy
Dictionaries, 89
Differentiated classroom, 43
*Don't Know Much About
    Geography* (Davis), 157
*Don't Know Much About History* (Davis), 157
Double bubble maps, 66–67
Douglass, F., 206
Drafts, 19–20, 42, 210

Earth science, 222–230
Editing, 19–21, 210 212, 214–217, 219
Emerson, R. W., 160
Empathy, 196

English language:
  British and American, 91–92
  grammar, 69–70, 72, 75–76, 78, 83–84
  morphology and etymology, 85–91 160
Essays:
  definition of, 129–130
  explanatory, 131, 136–137
  genres of, 12–14, 130–132, 137
  length of, 216
  personal, 132–133
  persuasive, 134–135
Etymology, 70, 89, 147
Evaluation, 216–218
Existing knowledge, 45–46, 49. *See also*
    Metacognition
Explanatory essay, 131, 136–137

Fairy tales, 39–41, 107–108, 174–178
Fiction, 12–13
Filmmaking, 163–172, 229. *See also* Book-to-film
    conversion
Fluency, 2, 4, 10
Format, 6, 12, *See also* Organization
Frames, 100–103, 113, 120

Gardner, H., 3
Genres, 12–14, 130–132, 137
Geography, 141–143, 149, 157–159, 228. *See also*
    Where in the World strategy
Geology, 225, 228–229. *See also* Earth science
Geometry, 67–68
Grading, 209. *See also* Rubrics
Grammar, 70–73, 75, 83
Greek mythology, 205–206

High school, 16, 33, 46, 50, 97, 102, 138, 181
Hirsch, E.D., Jr., 26, 30, 141
History, 50, 137–139, 189–192, 206–208
Hyerle, D., 66

Improvement, 211-212, 219. *See also* Editing
Instruction. *See* Writing instruction
Interactions. *See* Personifications and
    Interactions strategy
Intermediate grades, 25, 62, 173–174. *See also*
    Middle School
Internet. *See* Computers

Jackson, Y., 57
Journals, 182, 199–200

Knowledge. *See* Metacognition
KWL, 46

Langer, J., 36
Language, English. *See* English language
Languages, world, 160–162
Length, 216

Letters, 91, 145, 197–198, 203–204, 208
Linguistics, 3
Lists. *See* Taxonomies
Literary characters, 205–206
Literature, 52–53
Lowry, L., 173–174

Mahiri, J., 205
Martian, writing to a, 57–58
Marzano, R. J., 26, 201
*Math Curse* (Scieszka), 201
Mathematics, 1, 53, 67–68, 103, 137, 157, 159
*Memoir Writing* (Uhlig), 111
Metacognition, 5, 45–55, 224
Middle school, 16, 33, 46–47, 50, 62, 97, 102,
    173–175, 187
Milne, A.A., 187
Morphology and Etymology strategy, 5, 29, 70,
    85–88, 147–148, 225
*The Mother Tongue: English and How It Got That
    Way* (Bryson), 70, 88
Movies. *See* Filmmaking
Music, 91, 126
Mythology, 205–206

National Urban Alliance, 24
New knowledge, 45, 49. *See also* Metacognition
Nonfiction, 12–13, 111
Notebook, 10–11, 25–27
Notetaking, 28
Nouns, 71, 72–75, 83, 88–89
*Number the Stars* (Lowry), 173–174
Nursery rhymes, 39–41, 184–186

Ogle, D., 46
Opinion. *See* Point of view
Organization, 2, 26, 93, 100
*Our Marvelous English Tongue—The Life and Times
    of the English Language*( Claiborne), 75–76

Paragraph development, 64
Parts of speech, 81, 83, 87. *See also* specific parts
    of speech
Peer review, 214–215
Perkins, D., 45
Perrault, C., 176–177
Personal essays, 130, 132–134. *See also*
    Autobiography
Personal identity, 31–32, 119, 149–150. *See also*
    Autobiography
Personal thesaurus, 25
Personifications and Interactions strategy,
    6, 195–198, 205, 207, 230
Persuasive essays, 131, 134–135
*The Phantom Tollbooth* (Juster), 187, 188, 195
*The Pigman* (Zindel), 182
Pinker, S., 57, 72
Plaintiff v. defendant, 177–181

Planning wheel, 3–5
*Playmaking* (Sklar), 166
Poetry, 14
Point of view:
    opinion, 132, 135, 215. *See also* Persuasive
        essay
    persona, 177, 182, 195–196, 201
Poor children, 24
Premise statement, 165–166
Premises, Premises strategy, 6, 164, 173, 229.
    *See also* Filmmaking
Prepositions, 71
Primary grades, 100–101, 196, 217
Process, 10, 210
Profiles, 93–100, 124–126, 147, 166–167, 179, 226
Profiles and Frames strategy, 5, 93, 226

Quotable Quotes strategy, 6, 183–193, 230

Reading aloud, 38, 214
Reasons, Causes, Results strategy, 6, 136, 228
Resources, 16, 19
Revising, 21, 209–212
Robinson, A., 46
Role-playing, 196–197, 206
Rubrics, 216–218

Schemata, 26. *See also* Organization
Science, 53, 222–230.
Scieszka, J., 200
Scott, J. A., 23–24
Scriptwriting, 169–170
Sentences:
    expanded, 81–82
    improvement of, 36, 212, 215, 219
    in an essay, 132
    starting, 50–51, 139
    topic, 103, 116
    variety of, 108
Set design, 171
*Shooting for Excellence* (Mahiri), 205
Sklar, D. J., 166
Social studies, 36, 49, 53, 63, 137, 157
Sports, 99–100
*Standards for the English Language Arts*
    (National Council of Teachers of English
    & International Reading Association), 72
*The Story of English* (McCrum), 88
Strategies. *See* Writing Strategies
Storyboards, 169–170
Summarizing, 41–42

*The Tale of Peter Rabbit* (Potter)/
    Potter, B., 164, 166, 168–170
Taxonomies:
    across the curriculum, 33–34
    building, 23–25, 30–33
    overview of, 3–5

use of, 26, 29–30
    *See also* specific taxonomy subjects
Teacher feedback, 209, 215–218
Teaching grammar. *See* Grammar
Teaching writing. *See* Writing instruction
Templates:
    Defining Format, 58, 60–61, 224
    organizing, 48, 100
    morphology, 85, 148
    profile, 94, 179, 203
    *See also* Frames
Terms, 30, 58–59, 62-63, 142–144. *See also*
    Vocabulary
*The Uses of Enchantment*
    (Bettelheim), 174–175
Theme, 216
Thesaurus, personal, 25
Thesis, 216
Threes, 131–132
*Through the Looking Glass* (Carroll), 69
Tomlinson, C. A., 43
Tools, 15–16
Topics, 17–18
Transitions, 132, 212–213
Types of writing. *See* Genres

*The Ugly Duckling* (Andersen), 199–200
Uhlig, E., 111

VanTassel-Baska, J., 9
Venn diagrams, 66–67
Verbs, 41–42, 71, 75–77, 84, 86–89
Viewpoint, 215. *See* Point of view
Vocabulary, 23–25, 29, 35, 41, 44, 52. *See also*
    Keywords strategy
Voice, 195–196, 216

*The Way Mothers Are* (Schlein), 187
Weaver, C., 72
Web sites. *See* Computer links
*What Smart Students Know* (Robinson), 46
Where in the World strategy, 6, 142, 147, 157.
    *See also* Geography
Who's Who strategy, 6, 111, 157, 227. *See also*
    Biographies
Winnie the Pooh, 187
Word processor, 21. *See also* Computers
Words. *See* Etymology, Keywords, Vocabulary
World languages, 160–162
*Write for Mathematics* (Rothstein), 1
Writing:
    across the curriculum. *See* Writing across the
        curriculum
    computers and, 15, 21, 211
    evaluation of, 216–218
    genres of, 12–14, 130–132, 137
    improvement of, 211-212, 219.
        *See also* Editing

instruction of. *See* Teaching writing
   to a Martian, 57, 58
Writing across the curriculum, 2, 3, 9, 36, 53, 137,
   157, 221–223. *See also* specific subjects
Writing instruction, 2–4, 10–11, 70, 142.
   *See also* Writing strategies
Writing notebook, 10–11, 25–27
Writing process, 10, 210
Writing strategies:
   Composing With Keywords,
      5, 35–44, 223
   Defining Format, 5, 57–60, 63–68, 83–84,
      146–147, 224
   integration of, 221–223
   Metacognition, 5, 45–55, 224
   Morphology and Etymology, 5, 29,
      70, 85–88, 147–148, 225

overview of, 3–6
Personifications and Interactions,
   6, 195–198, 205, 207, 230
Premises, Premises, 6,
   164, 173, 229
Profiles and Frames, 5, 93, 226
Quotable Quotes, 6, 183–193, 230
Reasons, Causes, Results, 6, 136, 228
Where in the World, 6,
   142, 147, 157, 228
Who's Who, 6, 111, 157, 227
Writing to a Martian, 57–58
Writing tools, 15–16
Writing topics, 17–18, 154

Zindel, P., 182
Zinsser, W., 17

**CORWIN PRESS**

The Corwin Press logo—a raven striding across an open book—represents the union of courage and learning. Corwin Press is committed to improving education for all learners by publishing books and other professional development resources for those serving the field of PreK–12 education. By providing practical, hands-on materials, Corwin Press continues to carry out the promise of its motto: **"Helping Educators Do Their Work Better."**